Communications
in Computer and Information Science 2075

Rationale

The CCIS series is devoted to the publication of proceedings of computer science conferences. Its aim is to efficiently disseminate original research results in informatics in printed and electronic form. While the focus is on publication of peer-reviewed full papers presenting mature work, inclusion of reviewed short papers reporting on work in progress is welcome, too. Besides globally relevant meetings with internationally representative program committees guaranteeing a strict peer-reviewing and paper selection process, conferences run by societies or of high regional or national relevance are also considered for publication.

Topics

The topical scope of CCIS spans the entire spectrum of informatics ranging from foundational topics in the theory of computing to information and communications science and technology and a broad variety of interdisciplinary application fields.

Information for Volume Editors and Authors

Publication in CCIS is free of charge. No royalties are paid, however, we offer registered conference participants temporary free access to the online version of the conference proceedings on SpringerLink (http://link.springer.com) by means of an http referrer from the conference website and/or a number of complimentary printed copies, as specified in the official acceptance email of the event.

CCIS proceedings can be published in time for distribution at conferences or as post-proceedings, and delivered in the form of printed books and/or electronically as USBs and/or e-content licenses for accessing proceedings at SpringerLink. Furthermore, CCIS proceedings are included in the CCIS electronic book series hosted in the SpringerLink digital library at http://link.springer.com/bookseries/7899. Conferences publishing in CCIS are allowed to use Online Conference Service (OCS) for managing the whole proceedings lifecycle (from submission and reviewing to preparing for publication) free of charge.

Publication process

The language of publication is exclusively English. Authors publishing in CCIS have to sign the Springer CCIS copyright transfer form, however, they are free to use their material published in CCIS for substantially changed, more elaborate subsequent publications elsewhere. For the preparation of the camera-ready papers/files, authors have to strictly adhere to the Springer CCIS Authors' Instructions and are strongly encouraged to use the CCIS LaTeX style files or templates.

Abstracting/Indexing

CCIS is abstracted/indexed in DBLP, Google Scholar, EI-Compendex, Mathematical Reviews, SCImago, Scopus. CCIS volumes are also submitted for the inclusion in ISI Proceedings.

How to start

To start the evaluation of your proposal for inclusion in the CCIS series, please send an e-mail to ccis@springer.com.

Chao-Yang Lee · Chun-Li Lin ·
Hsuan-Ting Chang
Editors

Technologies and Applications of Artificial Intelligence

28th International Conference, TAAI 2023
Yunlin, Taiwan, December 1–2, 2023
Proceedings, Part II

Springer

Editors
Chao-Yang Lee (iD)
National Yunlin University of Science
and Technology
Douliou, Taiwan

Chun-Li Lin (iD)
National Yunlin University of Science
and Technology
Douliou, Taiwan

Hsuan-Ting Chang (iD)
National Yunlin University of Science
and Technology
Douliou, Taiwan

ISSN 1865-0929 ISSN 1865-0937 (electronic)
Communications in Computer and Information Science
ISBN 978-981-97-1713-2 ISBN 978-981-97-1714-9 (eBook)
https://doi.org/10.1007/978-981-97-1714-9

This Springer imprint is published by the registered company Springer Nature Singapore Pte Ltd.
The registered company address is: 152 Beach Road, #21-01/04 Gateway East, Singapore 189721, Singapore

Paper in this product is recyclable.

Preface

The Artificial Intelligence Society of the Republic of China aims to promote research, development, application, and exchange in the field of artificial intelligence and related areas. Since its establishment in 1995, over 20 years of dedicated effort has brought together numerous AI technology research and development talents from universities, research institutions, and industry in Taiwan. To facilitate the exchange of academic and practical experiences in artificial intelligence, the society has been organizing the International Conference on Artificial Intelligence annually since 1995, and since 1999 it has also been hosting an additional AI Forum each year. These events provide a platform for experts and scholars from domestic and international universities, research units, and industry to exchange AI technologies and application results. Participants in the past have included researchers and students from Taiwan, as well as experts and scholars from other countries such as mainland China, Japan, Thailand, India, Russia, Malaysia, USA, Singapore, Vietnam, Norway, and more. Over the past two decades, with the contributions and efforts of many, it has become the most important AI conference and academic exchange venue in Taiwan.

The International Conference on Technologies and Applications of Artificial Intelligence (TAAI) is committed to the technological development of artificial intelligence. With the efforts of many pioneers, it has become Taiwan's most important international AI academic conference, offering an annual event for experts and scholars in related fields from home and abroad to showcase research achievements and exchange research insights and experiences. This year's event, the 28th edition, was cohosted by the Artificial Intelligence Society of the Republic of China and the National Yunlin University of Science and Technology. In addition to calling for papers on related technologies for presentation, the conference also invited well-known experts and scholars from home and abroad for keynote speeches to discuss the current important trends in the field of artificial intelligence. A special feature of the event is the annual bilateral exchange with the Japanese Society for Artificial Intelligence (JSAI), with many members of JSAI attending the event. Additionally, the conference plans activities such as the AI CUP E.Sun Bank Artificial Intelligence Challenge, Young Woman Rising Star in AI, and High School Sessions, inviting Japanese scholars, industry experts, and young students to participate in the AI event. This conference received a total of 193 submissions, each of which was reviewed by three reviewers in a single-blind process, and finally 47 papers were accepted for publication.

December 2023   Prof. Chuan-Yu Chang

Organization

Organizing Committee

Honorary Chair

Neng-Shu Yang · · · · · · · · · · · · · · National Yunlin University of Science and Technology, Taiwan

General Chairs

Chuan-Yu Chang · · · · · · · · · · · · · National Yunlin University of Science and Technology, Taiwan

Chuan-Kang Ting · · · · · · · · · · · · National Tsing Hua University, Taiwan

Program Chairs

Chien-Chou Lin · · · · · · · · · · · · · National Yunlin University of Science and Technology, Taiwan

Hung-Yu Kao · · · · · · · · · · · · · · National Cheng Kung University, Taiwan

Tzong-Han Tsai · · · · · · · · · · · · · National Central University, Taiwan

Publication Chairs

Hsuan-Ting Chang · · · · · · · · · · · National Yunlin University of Science and Technology, Taiwan

Chao-Yang Lee · · · · · · · · · · · · · National Yunlin University of Science and Technology, Taiwan

Chun-Li Lin · · · · · · · · · · · · · · · National Yunlin University of Science and Technology, Taiwan

Sponsorship Chair

Shih-Yu Chen · · · · · · · · · · · · · · National Yunlin University of Science and Technology, Taiwan

Special Session Chairs

Yi-Lung Lin   National Yunlin University of Science and
                               Technology, Taiwan
Dun-Wei Cheng   National Yunlin University of Science and
                               Technology, Taiwan

Public Relations Chairs

Chian C. Ho   National Yunlin University of Science and
                               Technology, Taiwan
Szu-Hong Wang   National Yunlin University of Science and
                               Technology, Taiwan

Publicity Chairs

Jen-Chun Lin   Academia Sinica, Taiwan
Jun-Cheng Chen   Academia Sinica, Taiwan

AI Competition Chair

Tzong-Han Tsai   National Central University, Taiwan

Game Tournament Chair

Shi-Jim Yen   National Dong Hwa University, Taiwan

Young Woman Star Session Chair

Min-Chun Hu   National Tsing Hua University, Taiwan

High School Chair

Jen-Wei Huang   National Cheng-Kung University, Taiwan

Advisory Committee

He Zheng Xin   National Taiwan University of Science and
                               Technology, Taiwan
Von-Wun Soo   National Tsing Hua University, Taiwan
Yau-Hwang Kuo   National Cheng-Kung University, Taiwan

Wen-Lian Hsu	Asia University, Taiwan
Hsiang Jieh	National Taiwan University, Taiwan
S. M. Chen	National Taiwan University of Science and Technology, Taiwan
Chun-Nan Hsu	Academia Sinica, Taiwan
Vincent S. Tseng	National Yang Ming Chiao Tung University, Taiwan
Yung-jen Hsu	National Taiwan University, Taiwan
I-Chen Wu	National Yang Ming Chiao Tung University, Taiwan
Hui-Huang Hsu	Tamkang University, Taiwan
Chia-Hui Chang	National Central University, Taiwan
Hung-Yu Kao	National Cheng-Kung University, Taiwan
Chuan-Kang Ting	National Tsing Hua University, Taiwan

Program Committee

Albert Bakhtizin	Central Economics and Mathematics Institute of Russian Academy of Sciences, Russia
Aldy Gunawan	Singapore Management University, Singapore
Andrea Salfinger	Johannes Kepler University Linz, Austria
Anthony Y. H. Liao	Asia University, Taiwan
Ayush Singhal	University of Minnesota, USA
Been-Chian Chien	National University of Tainan, Taiwan
Bi-Ru Dai	National Taiwan University of Science and Technology, Taiwan
Bor-Shen Lin	National Taiwan University of Science and Technology, Taiwan
Cameron Browne	Queensland University of Technology, Australia
Chang-Shing Lee	Engineer Ambitiously-NI, USA
Chang-Tien Lu	Virginia Polytechnic Institute and State University, USA
Chao-Chun Chen	National Cheng Kung University, Taiwan
Che Nan Kuo	CTBA Business School, Taiwan
Cheng-Fa Tsai	National Ping Tung University of Science and Technology, Taiwan
Cheng-Te Li	National Cheng Kung University, Taiwan
Cheng-Hsuan Li	National Taichung University of Education, Taiwan
Chen-Sen Ouyang	I-Shou University, Taiwan
Cheng-Zen Yang	Yuan Ze University, Taiwan
Chenn-Jung Huang	National Dong Hwa University, Taiwan

Chia-Hung Yeh	National Sun Yat-Sen University, Taiwan
Chia-Hui Chang	National Central University, Taiwan
Chien-Chou Lin	National Yunlin University of Science and Technology, Taiwan
Chien-Feng Huang	National University of Kaohsiung, Taiwan
Chih-Chieh Hung	National Chung Hsing University, Taiwan
Chih-Chin Lai	National University of Kaohsiung, Taiwan
Chih-Hua Tai	National Taipei University, Taiwan
Ching-Hu Lu	National Taiwan University of Science and Technology, Taiwan
Chih-Hung Wu	National University of Kaohsiung, Taiwan
Chih-Ya Shen	National Tsing Hua University, Taiwan
Chuan-Kang Ting	National Chung Cheng University, Taiwan
Chu-Hsuan Hsueh	National Yang Ming Chiao Tung University, Taiwan
Chung-Kuang Chou	National Taiwan University, Taiwan
Chung-Ming Ou	Kainan University, Taiwan
Chun-Hao Chen	National Taipei University of Technology, Taiwan
Chun Tsai	National Chung Hsing University, Taiwan
Chun-Chi Lai	National Yunlin University of Science and Technology, Taiwan
Chung-Hong Lee	National Kaohsiung University of Applied Sciences, Taiwan
Chung-Nan Lee	National Sun Yat-Sen University, Taiwan
Chun-Wei Lin (Jerry Lin)	Western Norway University of Applied Sciences, Norway
Chun-Wei Tsai	National Chung Hsing University, Taiwan
Churn-Jung Liau	Academia Sinica, USA
Dan Goldberg	Texas A&M University, USA
David L. Sallach	Argonne National Laboratory and the University of Chicago, USA
Daw-Tung Lin	National Taipei University, Taiwan
De-Nian Yang	Academia Sinica, Taiwan
Eri Sato-Shimokawara	Tokyo Metropolitan University, Japan
Frank S. C. Tseng	National Kaohsiung First University of Science and Technology, Taiwan
Fred Morstatter	University of Southern California, USA
Fu-Shiung Hsieh	Chaoyang University of Technology, Taiwan
Gene P. K. Wu	Hong Kong Polytechnic University, China
Grace Lin	Institute for Information Industry, Taiwan
Giuseppe D'Aniello	University of Salerno Fisciano, Italy
Guan-Ling Lee	National Dong Hua University, Taiwan
Hao-Chuan Wang	National Tsing Hua University, Taiwan

Hiroki Shibata	Tokyo Metropolitan University, Japan
Hiroshi Kawakami	Kyoto University, Japan
Hong-Han Shuai	National Yang Ming Chiao Tung University, Taiwan
Hong-Jie Dai	National Kaohsiung University of Science and Technology, Taiwan
Hsiao-Ping Tsai	National Chung Hsing University, Taiwan
Hsien-Chou Liao	Chaoyang University of Technology, Taiwan
Hsin-Chang Yang	National University of Kaohsiung, Taiwan
Hsin-Hung Chou	Chang Jung Christian University, Taiwan
Hsin-Min Wang	Academia Sinica, Taiwan
Hsiu-Min Chuang	National Defense University, Taiwan
Hsin-Te Wu	National Penghu University of Science and Technology, Taiwan
Hsuan-Tien Lin	National Taiwan University, Taiwan
Hsueh-Ting Chu	Asia University, Taiwan
Hsun-Ping Hsieh	National Cheng Kung University, Taiwan
Hsu-Yung Cheng	National Central University, Taiwan
H. T. Chu	Asia University, Taiwan
Huei-Fang Yang	National Sun Yat-Sen University, Taiwan
Hui-Ju Hung	The Pennsylvania State University, USA
Hung-Yi Lee	National Taiwan University, Taiwan
Hung-Yu Kao	National Cheng Kung University, Taiwan
I-Chen Wu	National Yang Ming Chiao Tung University, Taiwan
I-Fang Chung	National Yang-Ming University, Taiwan
I-Hsien Ting	National University of Kaohsiung, Taiwan
I-Shyan Hwang	Yuan Ze University, Taiwan
Jason Jung	Chung-Ang University, Korea
Jenn-Long Liu	I-Shou University, Taiwan
Jenq-Haur Wang	National Taipei University of Technology, Taiwan
Jen-Tzung Chien	National Yang Ming Chiao Tung University, Taiwan
Jen-Wei Huang	National Cheng Kung University, Taiwan
Jialin Liu	Lawrence Berkeley National Lab, USA
Jian-Sing Li	National University of Tainan, Taiwan
Jiann-Shu Lee	National University of Tainan, Taiwan
Jiun-Long Huang	National Yang Ming Chiao Tung University, Taiwan
Jose Luis Ambite	University of Southern California, USA
Jr-Chang Chen	National Taiwan University, Taiwan
Ju-Chin Chen	National Kaohsiung University of Science and Technology, Taiwan

Judy C. R. Tseng	Chung-Hua University, Taiwan
Jung-Kuei Yang	National Dong Hwa University, Taiwan
Kawuu W. Lin	National Kaohsiung University of Science and Technology, Taiwan
Kazunori Mizuno	Takushoku University, Japan
Keh-Yih Su	Academia Sinica, Taiwan
Keng-Pei Lin	National Sun Yat-sen University, Taiwan
Klaus Brinker	University of Applied Sciences Hamm-Lippstadt, Germany
Ko-Wei Huang	National Kaohsiung University of Science and Technology, Taiwan
Koong Lin	National University of Tainan, Taiwan
Kun-Ta Chuang	National Cheng Kung University, Taiwan
Kuo-Hsien Hsia	Far East University, Taiwan
Leilei Shi	Bank of China International (China), China
Li-Chen Cheng	National Taipei University of Technology, Taiwan
Lieu-Hen Chen	National Chi Nan University, Taiwan
Ling-Jyh Chen	Academia Sinica, Taiwan
Li-Wei Ko	National Yang Ming Chiao Tung University, Taiwan
Lung-Pin Chen	Tunghai University, Taiwan
Mark H. M. Winands	Maastricht University, Netherlands
Martin Michalowski	University of Minnesota, Twin Cities, USA
Marie-Liesse Cauwet	TAO, Inria Saclay-CNRS-LRI, University Paris Sud, France
Masakazu Muramatsu	The University of Electro-Communications, Tokyo, Japan
Matteo Gaeta	University of Salerno Fisciano, Italy
Mayank Kejriwal	University of Southern California, USA
Min-Chun Hu	National Tsing Hua University, Taiwan
Min Sun	National Tsing Hua University, Taiwan
Ming-Feng Tsai	National Chengchi University, Taiwan
Ming-Shun Tsai	Taiwan AI Academy, Taiwan
Min-Yuh Day	Tamkang University, Taiwan
Mitsunori Matsushita	Kansai University, Japan
Mi-Yen Yeh	Academia Sinica, Taiwan
Mong-Fong Horng	National Kaohsiung University of Applied Sciences, Taiwan
Mu-Chun Su	National Central University, Taiwan
Mu-En Wu	National Taipei University of Technology, Taiwan
Naohiro Matsumura	Osaka University, Japan
Po-Hsun Cheng	National Kaohsiung Normal University, Taiwan
Po-Ruey Lei	ROC Naval Academy, Taiwan

Po-Yuan Chen	Jinwen University of Science and Technology, Taiwan
Ray-Bing Chen	National Cheng Kung University, Taiwan
Rong-Ming Chen	National University of Tainan, Taiwan
Rung-Ching Chen	Chaoyang University of Technology, Taiwan
Sai-Keung Wong	National Yang Ming Chiao Tung University, Taiwan
Shan-Hung Wu	National Tsing Hua University, Taiwan
Sheng-Mao Chang	National Cheng Kung University, Taiwan
Shie-Jue Lee	National Sun Yat-sen University, Taiwan
Shih-Cheng Horng	Chaoyang University of Technology, Taiwan
Shih-Hung Wu	Chaoyang University of Technology, Taiwan
Shi-Jim Yen	National Dong Hwa University, Taiwan
Shing-Tai Pan	National University of Kaohsiung, Taiwan
Shirley Ho	National Chengchi University, Taiwan
Show-Jane Yen	Ming Chuan University, Taiwan
Shou-De Lin	National Taiwan University, Taiwan
Shun-Chin Hsu	Chang-Jung Christian University, Taiwan
Shunichi Hattori	Central Research Institute of Electric Power Industry (CRIEPI), Japan
Spencer Polk	Carleton University, Canada
Tao-Hsing Chang	National Kaohsiung University of Science and Technology, Taiwan
Thibaut Lust	UPMC-LIP6, France
Ting Han Wei	University of Alberta, Canada
Tsaipei Wang	National Yang Ming Chiao Tung University, Taiwan
Tsan-Sheng Hsu	Academia Sinica, Taiwan
Tsung-Che Chiang	National Taiwan Normal University, Taiwan
Tsung-Ting Kuo	University of California San Diego, USA
Tuan-Fang Fan	National Penghu University of Science and Technology, Taiwan
Tung-Kuan Liu	National Kaohsiung University of Science and Technology, Taiwan
Tzong-Han Tsai	National Central University, Taiwan
Tzong-Yi Lee	Chinese University of Hong Kong, Shenzhen, China
Tzu-Hsien Yang	National Cheng Kung University, Taiwan
Tzung-Pei Hong	National University of Kaohsiung, Taiwan
Waskitho Wibisono	ITS Indonesia, Indonesia
Wei-Guang Teng	National Cheng- Kung University, Taiwan
Wei-Min Liu	National Chung Cheng University, Taiwan
Wei-Shinn Ku	Auburn University, USA

Wei-Ta Chu	National Chung Cheng University, Taiwan
Wen-Chih Peng	National Yang Ming Chiao Tung University, Taiwan
Wen-Chung Shih	Asia University, Taiwan
Wen-Huang Cheng	National Yang Ming Chiao Tung University, Taiwan
Wen-Hung Liao	National Chengchi University, Taiwan
Wen-Yang Lin	National University of Kaohsiung, Taiwan
Wing-Kwong Wong	National Yunlin University of Science and Technology, Taiwan
Wu-Chih Hu	National Penghu University of Science and Technology, Taiwan
Vincent S. Tseng	National Yang Ming Chiao Tung University, Taiwan
Yao-Ting Huang	National Chung Cheng University, Taiwan
Yasufumi Takama	Tokyo Metropolitan University, Japan
Yen-Chieh Lien	University of Massachusetts Amherst, USA
Yi-Cheng Chen	National Central University, Taiwan
Yi-Cheng Chen	Tamkang University, Taiwan
Yi-Chung Chen	National Yunlin University of Science and Technology, Taiwan
Yih-Chuan Lin	National Formosa University, Taiwan
Yi-Hsin Ho	Takushoku University, Japan
Yi-Hsuan Yang	Academia Sinica, Taiwan
Yi-Hung Wu	Chung Yuan Christian University, Taiwan
Yi-Jen Su	Shu-Te University, Taiwan
Yi-Leh Wu	National Taiwan University of Science and Technology, Taiwan
Yi-Ling Chen	National Taiwan University of Science and Technology, Taiwan
Yin-Fu Huang	National Yunlin University of Science and Technology, Taiwan
Ying-Ping Chen	National Yang Ming Chiao Tung University, Taiwan
Yi-Ren Yeh	Chinese Culture University, China
Yi-Shin Chen	National Tsing Hua University, Taiwan
Yuan Gao	Northwest University, China
Yu-Chiang Wang (Frank Wang)	National Taiwan University, Taiwan
Yu-Da Lin	Penghu University of Science and Technology, Taiwan
Yue-Shi Lee	Ming Chuan University, Taiwan
Yuh-Ming Cheng	Shu-Te University, Taiwan
Yu-Huei Cheng	Chaoyang University of Technology, Taiwan

Yu-Ling Hsueh	National Chung Cheng University, Taiwan
Yung-Chun Chang	Taipei Medical University, Taiwan
Yung-jen Hsu	National Taiwan University, Taiwan
Yun-Nung Chen	National Taiwan University, Taiwan
Yu-Sheng Chen	National Taiwan University, Taiwan
Yusuke Nojima	Osaka Metropolitan University, Japan
Yu-Ting Wen	National Yang Ming Chiao Tung University, Taiwan

Contents – Part II

Contents – Part I

Autonomous Navigation Development of Solar Panel Cleaning Vehicle

Wen-Chang Cheng[1] and Hung-Chou Hsiao[2(✉)]

[1] Department of Computer Science and Information Engineering, Chaoyang University of Technology, Taichung City, Taiwan
wccheng@cyut.edu.tw

[2] Department of Information Management, Chaoyang University of Technology, Taichung City, Taiwan
s10814902@gm.cyut.edu.tw

Abstract. This study presents an automated navigation system for solar panel cleaning vehicles. Since self-positioning and navigation cannot be achieved on solar panels through self-built mapping, we utilize the vanishing points formed by the perspective transformation of many coplanar parallel lines on the solar panel to accomplish navigation. This is complemented by fuzzy control to align the vehicle with the parallel lines and proceed along the straight lines of the solar panel. When the solar panel cleaning vehicle reaches the boundary, it will turn to the next row's direction to continue cleaning along the straight lines of the solar panel until the cleaning is complete or autonomous navigation is deactivated. Preliminary experimental results show that the average standard deviation of the x-coordinate during straight-line movement is 1.70 pixels, and the average error between the maximum and minimum x-coordinates is approximately 6.33 pixels. After adjusting the speeds of the two-wheel servo motors, calibrating the camera's centre point, and repeating the experiments, the results demonstrate an average standard deviation of 0.43 pixels, and the maximum and minimum errors in the x-coordinate of straight lines have decreased to 2 pixels, achieving practical usability.

Keywords: Canny edge detection · fuzzy control · Hough transform · perspective transform · Raspberry Pi · Vanishing point

1 Introduction

With the rapid development of the solar energy market and the increasing prevalence of solar power plants, the demand for solar panel cleaning vehicles has also increased. Currently, numerous companies are introducing products of solar panel-cleaning vehicles. For instance, domestic companies like Songxiang Co., Ltd. [1] and Lixue Technology Co., Ltd. [2] exist. On the international front, China has manufacturers like Zhenda Co., Ltd. [3], Israel has Ecoppia [4], India has Cleanmax Solar [5], Germany has SunBrush [6], and Switzerland has Swiss solar [7]. Overall, the prospects for developing solar panel cleaning vehicles are up and coming, as they will become an indispensable part of the solar power generation industry and simultaneously accelerate the growth of the solar energy sector.

© The Author(s), under exclusive license to Springer Nature Singapore Pte Ltd. 2024
C.-Y. Lee et al. (Eds.): TAAI 2023, CCIS 2075, pp. 1–13, 2024.
https://doi.org/10.1007/978-981-97-1714-9_1

A solar panel cleaning vehicle is a specialized vehicle designed for cleaning solar panels. Its primary function is to remove pollutants such as dust, dirt, and oil films from the surface of solar panels to enhance their power generation efficiency. Typically, this vehicle is equipped with a high-pressure water gun and a cleaning solution pump. It can spray high-pressure water and cleaning solution onto the solar panels for cleaning purposes. Additionally, it features a stable suspension system ensuring safety and adaptability to various terrains and incline angles, as depicted in Fig. 1.

Fig. 1. Solar panel cleaning vehicle [2]

The autonomous navigation feature of the solar panel cleaning vehicle aims to enable the vehicle to move back and forth in a straight line along the solar panels. This eliminates the inconvenience of manual remote control and achieves automated cleaning functionality, enhancing cleaning efficiency and operational convenience. Figure 2 illustrates the solar panel cleaning vehicle's automatic navigation system schematic diagram.

To address the autonomous navigation function, the first challenge to tackle is the issue of positioning. A positioning system is a system that measures the location of an object in space, encompassing systems such as celestial systems, global systems, regional systems, and more, with wide-ranging applications. From a practical perspective, these can be categorized into Indoor Positioning Systems (IPS) and Outdoor Positioning Systems (OPS) [8]. The most common outdoor positioning system is the Global Positioning System (GPS), developed by the United States government. Its primary advantages include high signal penetration, global coverage of around 98%, high efficiency, and versatile applications. GPS achieves positioning accuracy of approximately 0.3 to 6 m (1 to 20 feet) [9].

Indoor positioning systems are commonly used within buildings, underground spaces, and similar environments. Commonly employed technologies include WiFi, RFID, Inertial Measurement Units (IMUs), Simultaneous Localization and Mapping (SLAM), and more [10]. Solar panels are primarily employed outdoors, so an outdoor

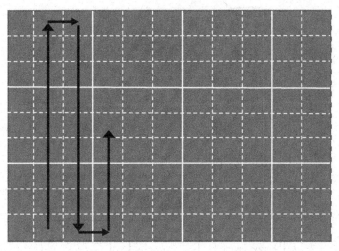

Fig. 2. Schematic diagram of automatic navigation of solar panel cleaning vehicle.

positioning system should be utilized. However, due to current limitations in the accuracy of outdoor positioning systems, they are not yet suitable for positioning solar panel cleaning vehicles. Consequently, a path-tracking navigation mode is adopted.

Due to numerous parallel lines on the solar panels, these coplanar parallel lines converge to a point in the distance when captured by a camera with a horizontal or slightly below horizontal viewing angle. This point is referred to as the vanishing point. When the vehicle's orientation aligns with these parallel lines, the vanishing point lies at the centre of the image. Therefore, vanishing point detection will be employed for this autonomous navigation functionality, coupled with fuzzy control. This combination allows the vehicle to align itself parallel to the lines and proceed along the straight path of the solar panel. Upon reaching the boundary, the solar panel cleaning vehicle will then reverse direction to continue cleaning along the straight path of the solar panel until the cleaning is complete or the autonomous navigation function is disengaged.

2 System Flowchart

Figure 3 depicts the system flowchart. Upon initiating the autonomous navigation function, the distance sensors detect the boundary. If the boundary is not reached, the camera captures images. Vanishing point detection is performed on the input images, and the difference (dx) between the x-coordinate value of the vanishing point's x-coordinate value and the image centre is computed. This difference is then used as input for the fuzzy controller, generating differential wheel speed (dv) for the solar panel cleaning vehicle to achieve autonomous navigation. The autonomous navigation function stops when the boundary is reached, and turning actions are executed based on row parity. For odd-numbered rows, a clockwise 90-° turn, followed by forward movement, and another clockwise 90-° turn are executed. A counterclockwise 90-° turn, forward movement, and another counterclockwise 90-° turn are executed for even-numbered rows. The following sections provide further explanations on vanishing point detection and fuzzy control.

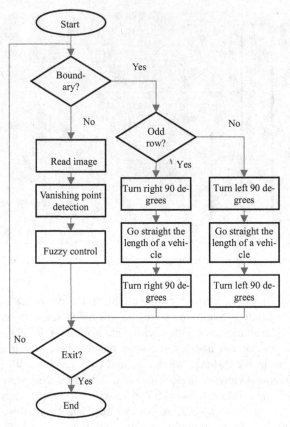

Fig. 3. System flowchart.

3 Vanishing Point Detection

The vanishing point of an image refers to the position where parallel lines on the ground when extended to infinity, converge to a single point as viewed from a camera with a horizontal or slightly below horizontal viewing angle, as indicated by the red dot in Fig. 5(b). In other words, the vanishing point is a visual phenomenon that occurs due to the distance variations when distant objects are projected onto an image. In artistic disciplines like drawing, photography, and filmmaking, the concept of the vanishing point holds great significance. It assists artists and designers in accurately depicting perspective and depth, resulting in more realistic and three-dimensional artworks. Given numerous parallel lines on solar panels, these coplanar parallel lines converge to a point in the distance when captured by a camera with a horizontal or slightly below horizontal viewing angle. When the vehicle's orientation aligns with these parallel lines, the vanishing point appears at the centre of the image. Therefore, for this autonomous navigation functionality, vanishing point detection is utilized to align the vehicle's orientation parallel to the lines and facilitate forward movement along the straight path of the solar panel.

On the other hand, when the camera is positioned in front of the vehicle to capture a horizontal or slightly below horizontal viewing angle, the solar panels are obstructed by the cleaning brush, preventing a clear view. Consequently, the camera is repositioned to the sides of the cleaning vehicle. However, a new issue arises when the cleaning process is active-the mist generated by the brushes can cause the captured images to become blurry. We attempted to adopt a bird's-eye view for the camera to address this challenge. In other words, the camera is positioned looking downward, and protective shields are installed around the camera to mitigate the impact of mist. Nonetheless, this solution introduces another dilemma: when the camera employs a bird's-eye view, the coplanar parallel lines on the solar panels cannot generate a vanishing point, as depicted in Fig. 5(a). To resolve this issue, the captured bird's-eye view images are transformed through transposition to simulate a horizontal or slightly below-horizontal view, as illustrated in Fig. 5(b).

Figure 4 illustrates the process of vanishing point detection. Initially, the input image undergoes Canny edge detection [11], resulting in an edge image, as shown in Fig. 5(c). Subsequently, the Hough line segment detection technique is applied to the edge image [12], resulting in green line segments as depicted in Fig. 5(b). As these segments are coplanar straight lines, the vanishing point's position can be inferred by extrapolating these segments' intersections, indicated by the red dot in Fig. 5(b). The algorithm for calculating the vanishing point's position is as follows:

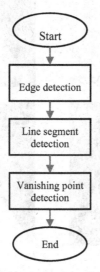

Fig. 4. Vanishing point detection flow chart.

Step 1: Arrange the line segments in descending order by length and retain the top N longest segments.
Step 2: Calculate the intersection point $(x_0, y_0)_i$ of the extended lines for the ith line segment L_i and the $(i + 1)$th line segment L_{i+1}.

Step 3: Compute the perpendicular distance d_k between the extended line L_k of each N line segment and the intersection point $(x_0, y_0)_i$, accumulating these perpendicular distances d_k to obtain $d_{acc}(i)$.

Step 4: Repeat Steps 2 and 3 until i reaches N-1.

Step 5: Identify the minimum $d_{acc}(j)$, then $(x_0, y_0)_j$ corresponds to the final vanishing point.

Figure 5 is an example. Figure 5(a) is a bird's-eye image because it is very close to the solar panel; only part can be seen. Figure 5(b) is the perspective image of Fig. 5(a). Figure 5(c) is the edge image in Fig. 5(b). Due to the lack of information in the perspective image part, it appears black, and redundant edges are generated between the black area and the boundary of the perspective image. In order not to affect the detection of the vanishing point, the redundant edge is removed by using the mask in Fig. 5(d). Finally, Hough line segment detection is performed using the retained edge images, and the result is shown in Fig. 5(b).

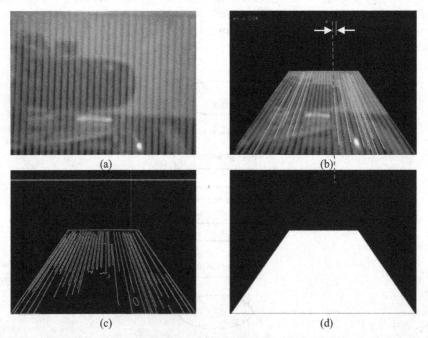

(a)   (b)

(c)   (d)

Fig. 5. An example of vanishing point detection. (a) bird's-eye image. (b) perspective image. (c) edge image. (d) image mask.

4 Fuzzy Csontrol

Fuzzy control is a method for controlling systems [13]. It uses techniques from fuzzy logic and fuzzy inference to transform fuzzy inputs into fuzzy outputs, enabling the control and adjustment of a system. The advantage of fuzzy control is its ability to handle uncertain and fuzzy problems and its strong adaptability and fault tolerance. In practical applications, fuzzy control has been widely used in industrial, robot, traffic, and temperature control fields and has achieved excellent results.

After detecting the vanishing point from the input image, the difference dx (as shown by the white arrow in Fig. 5(b)) is calculated between the x-coordinate of the vanishing point (marked by the red dot in Fig. 5(b)) and the x-coordinate of the image centre (indicated by the red dashed line in Fig. 5(b)). When $dx = 0$, the solar panel cleaning vehicle parallels the lines. If $dx > 0$, it implies that the vehicle needs to adjust towards the right to become parallel with the lines. Conversely, if $dx < 0$, the vehicle requires adjustment to the left for parallel alignment. Therefore, dx is input for the fuzzy controller, generating differential wheel speeds dv for the solar panel cleaning vehicle. These dv values correct the output of the left and right wheels to achieve autonomous navigation. Figure 6 illustrates the conceptual diagram of the fuzzy control system.

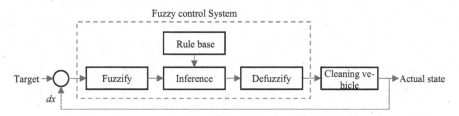

Fig. 6. Schematic diagram of the fuzzy control system.

In this study, we utilized the Scikit-fuzzy package [14]. Figure 7(a) and 7(b) depict the input and output fuzzy sets, each comprising 9. For the input, these are labelled as P1, P2, P3, P4, Ze, N1, N2, N3, and N4. The output fuzzy sets are named B1, B2, B3, B4, Ce, S1, S2, S3, and S4. The rule base for this single-input and single-output fuzzy system is defined as follows:

IF dx is P4 then dv is B4,
IF dx is P3 then dv is B4,
IF dx is P2 then dv is B3,
IF dx is P1 then dv is B2,
IF dx is Ze then dv is Ce,
IF dx is N1 then dv is S2,
IF dx is N2 then dv is S3,
IF dx is N3 then dv is S4,
IF dx is N4 then dv is S4,

Figure 8 illustrates the input and output functions for the fuzzy control system. The horizontal axis represents the input $dx(t)$, and the vertical axis represents the output

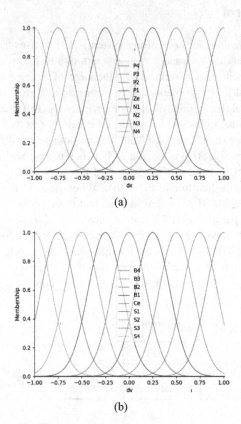

Fig. 7. Fuzzy sets. (a) Input. (b) Output.

$dv(t)$. After obtaining $dv(t)$, a proportional control is applied to the left and right wheels through a proportionality factor. This can be defined as follows:

$$V_R(t + 1) = V - \alpha dv(t),\tag{1}$$

$$V_L(t + 1) = V + \alpha dv(t),\tag{2}$$

where $V_R(t + 1)$ and $V_L(t + 1)$ are the next time $(t + 1)$ output speeds for the right and left wheels, respectively, V is the basic speed output, $dv(t)$ is the output of the fuzzy control system at time t, and α is a proportionality coefficient adjusted according to the actual vehicle speed.

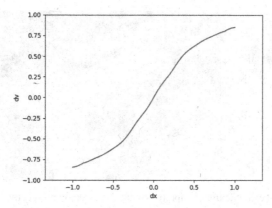

Fig. 8. The functions of the fuzzy control system.

5 Experiments

In the experimental setup, we employed a two-wheeled driven small vehicle to simulate the solar panel cleaning vehicle. The central control unit was based on the Raspberry Pi 400 microcomputer platform, which includes a Raspberry Pi 4 Model B module with 4 GB of memory integrated within a compact keyboard module, as shown in Fig. 9.

To assess the actual path of the detection vehicle, we additionally set up a camera in a third-person perspective to record the vehicle's movement path. Figure 10 displays the view captured by this camera. For convenient position detection of the vehicle, we affixed Aruco markers [15] onto the vehicle. Through marker detection, we obtained the vehicle's position. Furthermore, we transformed the solar panel's image using a top-down perspective, facilitating the evaluation of the vehicle's x-coordinate, as illustrated in Fig. 11.

Fig. 9. Two-wheeled driven vehicle.

Fig. 10. An example image captured by the third-person perspective camera.

Fig. 11. The bird's-eye image of the solar panel in Fig. 10.

Figure 12 illustrates the experimental results of the vehicle moving back and forth in a straight line on the solar panel. Due to reflections or angles, certain Aruco markers couldn't be detected in specific positions, hence their absence in Fig. 12. Despite this limitation, we can still evaluate the results. To understand the x-coordinate variation during straight-line movement, we calculated the standard deviation σ of the vehicle's x-coordinate for each straight-line motion. The standard deviation σ is defined as Eq. (3):

$$\sigma = \sqrt{\frac{\sum(x - \bar{x})^2}{(n - 1)}}, \tag{3}$$

Where n is the number of samples, and $\bar{x}$ is the mean of the sampled values. Table 1 provides the maximum (Max.), minimum (Min.), and mean values of each straight-line x-coordinate, the range of maximum and minimum discrepancies (Max.-Min.), and the standard deviation (STD). The average standard deviation of the x-coordinates for the 8 straight-line motions in Fig. 12 is 1.70 pixels. The maximum and minimum discrepancies in x-coordinates are approximately 6.33 pixels. From Fig. 12, it can be observed that there is a bias in straight-line movement. We adjusted the servo motor zero point and camera center calibration to address this. The results of this repeated experiment are

Table 1. Experimental data in Fig. 12.

Column	Max (x-coord.)	Min (x-coord.)	Max.-Min (pixels)	Mean (x-coord.)	STD (σ)
1	118	112	6	114.93	1.59
2	182	174	8	176.91	1.59
3	275	268	7	271.23	2.12
4	336	330	6	332.27	1.70
5	429	422	7	425.98	1.84
6	491	484	7	486.90	2.10
7	581	573	8	576.64	2.11
8	648	642	6	644.94	1.59
Avg	-	-	**6.33**	-	**1.70**

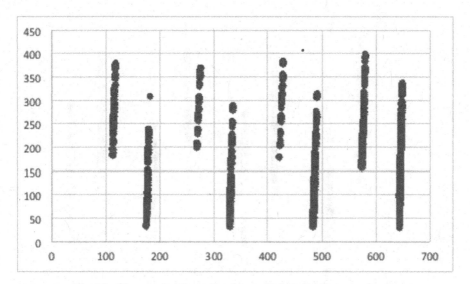

Fig. 12. The actual path results of the vehicle in the first experiment.

shown in Fig. 13. Table 2 shows the average standard deviation is 0.43 pixels, and the maximum and minimum discrepancies in the x-coordinates of straight-line motion are reduced to 1.88 pixels.

Table 2. Experimental data in Fig. 13.

Column	Max (x-coord.)	Min (x-coord.)	Max.-Min (pixels)	Mean (x-coord.)	STD (σ)
1	142	140	2	140.94	0.59
2	205	203	2	203.63	0.50
3	322	320	2	320.22	0.43
4	383	382	1	382.94	0.24
5	501	499	2	500.01	0.23
6	564	562	2	563.12	0.51
7	682	680	2	680.86	0.39
8	745	743	2	743.60	0.52
Avg	–	–	**1.88**	-	**0.43**

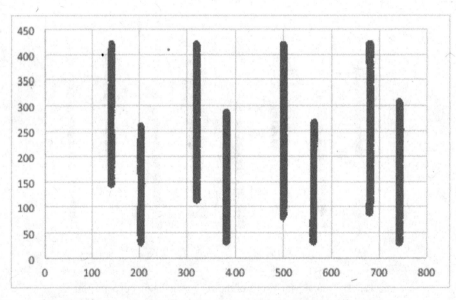

Fig. 13. The actual path results of the vehicle in the second experiment.

6 Conclusion

This study proposed an autonomous navigation feature for solar panel cleaning vehicles. A preliminary implementation was conducted using a three-wheeled, two-wheel-drive vehicle. The vehicle could autonomously navigate in a back-and-forth manner on a single solar panel (video link: https://youtu.be/9q4QUN6UBgE). The best experimental results indicated that the average standard deviation of the x-coordinate during the vehicle's straight-line movement was 0.43 pixels, with maximum and minimum errors below 2 pixels. Due to the limited camera perspective of the vehicle to a small area in front of the vehicle, the navigation relies on local features. As the vehicle's travel range increases, the maximum and minimum errors in the x-coordinate of straight-line movement also increase. Therefore, in the future, we will attempt to incorporate global features to make the system suitable for larger-scale applications.

Acknowledgment. This study is the result of an industry-academia cooperative project between the Department of Computer Science & Information Engineering, Chaoyang University of Technology and Lixue Technology Co., Ltd. (Project No. TJ4-111B518). We would like to thank Lixue Technology Co., Ltd. For their assistance.

References

1. Songxiang co., ltd., Monster robot (2023). https://www.de-tools.com.tw/. Accessed 11 Oct 2023
2. Lixue Technology Co., Ltd., Solar Panel Cleaning Robot (2023). https://www.lixue.com.tw/. Accessed 11 Oct 2023
3. Zhenda Brush (2023). https://www.zhendabrush.com/. Accessed 11 Dec 2023
4. Ecoppia, 2023. https://www.ecoppia.com/. Accessed 11 Oct 2023
5. Cleanmax Solar (2020). https://www.cleanmax.com/. Accessed 11 Oct 2023
6. SunBrush, Sunbrush Mobil Compact Universally Deployable (2023). https://www.sunbrushmobil.com/produkte/sunbrush-mobil-compact. Accessed 11 Oct 2023
7. Swiss solar (2023). https://www.swissenergy-solar.ch/. Accessed 11 Oct 2023
8. Positioning system, Wikipedia. https://en.wikipedia.org/wiki/Positioning_system. Accessed 11 Oct 2023
9. Global Positioning System, Wikipedia. https://en.wikipedia.org/wiki/Global_Positioning_System. Accessed 11 Oct 2023
10. Indoor positioning system, Wikipedia. https://en.wikipedia.org/wiki/Indoor_positioning_system. Accessed 11 Oct 2023
11. Canny detection, OpenCV (2023.) https://docs.opencv.org/4.x/da/d22/tutorial_py_canny.html. Accessed 11 Oct 2023
12. Hough line detection, OpenCV (2023). https://docs.opencv.org/3.4/d9/db0/tutorial_hough_lines.html. Accessed 11 Oct 2023
13. Fuzzy Control, Wikipedia. https://en.wikipedia.org/wiki/Fuzzy_control_system. Accessed 11 Oct 2023
14. SciKit-Fuzzy. https://pythonhosted.org/scikit-fuzzy/overview.html. Accessed 11 Oct 2023
15. Garrido-Jurado, S., Muñoz-Salinas, R., Madrid-Cuevas, F.J., Marín-Jiménez, M.J.: Automatic generation and detection of highly reliable fiducial markers under occlusion. Pattern Recogn.Recogn. **47**, 2280–2292 (2014)

Design and Implementation of Optical Lens Defect Detection and Classification System

Hsien-Huang Wu, Cheng-Yi Lin, and Syuan-Ciao Huang$^{(\boxtimes)}$

National Yunlin University of Science and Technology, Yunlin, Taiwan
{wuhp,m11012047}@yuntech.edu.tw, m11112051@gemail.yuntech.edu.tw

Abstract. The glass lens production process requires cutting, grinding and polishing, it is easy to cause lens defects, and the production quality needs to be maintained through inspection. In the past, people relied on manual methods to detect the defects, but it causes inconsistent quality standards and costs a lot of manpower to carry out this operation. In this paper, we developed a proper image acquisition system and combine deep learning techniques and image processing algorithms to implement stringent inspection criteria based on different inspection specification requirements. Finally, a defect detection and classification system for glass lenses was successfully implemented with a defect recognition accuracy of over 95% by comparison and verification.

Keywords: Computer Vision · Optical Lens · Defect Detection · Deep Learning · Automated Optical Inspection

1 Motivation and Purpose of the Study

Currently, glass lens manufacturers still relied on manual inspection for defects in the production of lenses as shown in Fig. 1., where the surface of the lens was carefully inspected with the naked eye under bright light to observe defects on the surface of the lens. With this method of detecting, the fatigue of the inspectors often leads to missed or false inspections, resulting in lower and inconsistent quality standards. In addition, the inspectors need to perform inspections in a strong light environment for a long time and might cause visual impairments or risks of damage.

In order to improve inspection quality and reduce labor costs, glass lens manufacturers would like to take the advantage of the recent improvements in industrial automation technology to upgrade their industrial structure by introducing automated inspection machines. The AOI machine can effectively reduce production labor costs, avoid occupational injury of eyes and achieve quality requirements to improve production yields and efficiency.

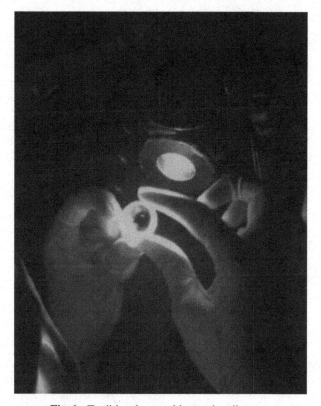

Fig. 1. Traditional manual inspection diagram.

2 Introduction to Basic Theory

2.1 Camera Imaging

In the field of AOI, industrial cameras and lenses are the two most important components. It's not difficult to get a good photo as long as they match up properly [1-3]. However, since this study aims to capture the appearance defects of the glass lens, considering that the glass lens is a curved surface, it is necessary to adjust the position of the imaging components for shooting different part of the object. In addition, because the glass is a transparent object, it is easy to cause light scattering and ghosting. The actual image acquisition structure can be referred to Fig. 2., where angle of lighting and camera are crucial for the defect detection and classification. In the experiments, defects are better imaged when they are close to the light source (Fig. 3). Therefore, this imaging method is finally adopted as the hardware optical structure of the system.

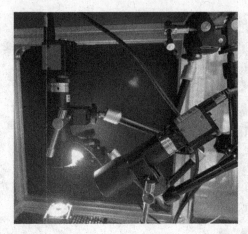

Fig. 2. Image Acquisition Framework.

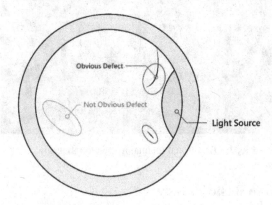

Fig. 3. Lighting setup for the imaging.

2.2 Object Detection

Object detection is the process of labeling and localizing specific objects in a video or image and classifying what kind of objects they are, and is an important technical application in the field of deep learning that has been used in ADAS, autonomous driving, security surveillance, and other fields.

2.3 Image Segmentation

Image Segmentation refers to the process of dividing an image into multiple regions or objects with semantic or specific features, the main goal is to detect and classify image pixels while preserving the original image features, there are many applications such as automatic driving, face recognition, medical imaging, etc.

2.4 Image Processing

Image processing refers to the digital signal processing of image data for the purpose of improving image quality, enhancing image features or extracting data information from images and achieving other specific goals, including image segmentation, compression, and recognition. It is also an important branch of modern computer science, mathematics and engineering. Common image processing algorithms include image filtering, histogram equalization, edge detection, morphology, feature extraction, etc.

3 System Hardware Architecture

This section will introduce the hardware components used in the imaging system.

3.1 Cameras

The DFK 33UX264 industrial camera (Fig. 4(a)), manufactured by The Image Source (TIS) was selected for this study. DFK 33UX264 industrial camera is equipped with global shutter to meet the needs of dynamic shooting. Equipped with USB3.0 transmission technology, the transmission speed is fast and stable. It has a resolution of 5 million pixels, and can support up to 38 FPS (frames per second).

(a)camera   (b)len   (c)light source

Fig. 4. Hardware equipment.

3.2 Lens

A good lens will give a better image, but attention must also be paid to the working distance to accommodate the field of view, as well as the choice of lens magnification to accommodate the full range of FOV. Because of the curvature of the object under inspection, this study required two different surfaces to be photographed using the same hardware setup. Two telecentric lens (Fig. 4(b)) with a lens magnification of 0.5 and a working distance of 65mm was chosen for the system.

3.3 Light Source

The correct light source will make the defects more visible and a good image can be captured so that image preprocessing steps can be avoided. As this study was conducted with a glass lens, the curvature of the lens itself made it easy for the light to penetrate or scatter irregularly. After many tests, a high angle circular white light (Fig. 4(c)) was chosen as the light source for this study.

3.4 Objects to Be Tested

In this study, we collaborated with an industry manufacturer of optical lenses to provide type (Fig. 5) with two concave surfaces. The diameter is 28.5 mm and one side can be called as R1(front) inspection surface and the other side as R2(back) inspection surface (Fig. 6). The characteristic is that the processes of cutting, grinding, and polishing may cause some minor cosmetic defects such as pitting damage, scratches, etc. during the production process. Currently, manual inspection is used, which consumes a lot of labor and cost, so it is necessary to develop a system to automate the inspection process.

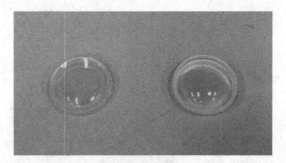

Fig. 5. Glass lens.

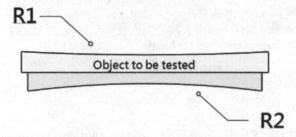

Fig. 6. Optical lens appearance characteristics.

3.5   Defect Analysis

The defects of the optical lenses studied in this paper can be classified into two categories, line defect and point defect, according to different appearance characteristics, as shown in Fig. 7 and Fig. 8.

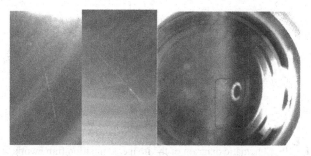

Fig. 7. Lens line Defects.

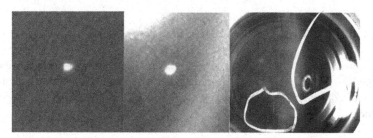

Fig. 8. Lens point Defects.

3.6   Rotating Mechanism of the Object to Be Tested

The imaging method used in this study can effectively capture the defect features, but the working range of its light gathering only covers part of the lens area. If the defect location happens to be within the working range, the features can easy to be seen, but if the defect location is farther away from the light source, the features are less likely to be seen. Therefore, a rotating platform is designed to rotate the lens for complete defect detection and avoid the problem of missing detection.

3.7   Rotating Mechanism of the Object to Be Tested

In this study, in order to obtain the best defect image, in addition to a good lighting method and a specific angle relationship with the light source, it is also very important to adjust the exposure parameters of camera shooting. However, because of the long exposure time of the top image, the image of the periphery of the lens will be overexposed. While detecting the defects of the whole lens by rotating the lens, a side camera is added to complement the defect imaging of the periphery of the lens. Finally, we combine the top camera and the side camera into a dual-camera system as the optical imaging method, as shown in Fig. 9.

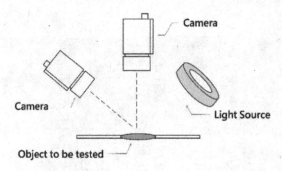

Fig. 9. Schematic diagram of the image acquisition framework.

4   System Software Architecture

Since the defects generated by optical lenses are very small and not easily detected, the system needs to perform more accurate defect analysis to meet the more stringent defect specification requirements. This section will introduce the software system process and architecture.

4.1   System Architecture Flow

The system is designed to avoid the problem of equipment damage, before starting the inspection, the system must be connected to the equipment and other settings before the subsequent inspection operation. When the connection is completed and the inspection is started, the system will identify the optical lens defect, and the result will be divided into OK and NG products for output. If the system identifies the inspection lens as NG, it will keep the defect image for the inspector to carry out the subsequent re-inspection operation, and if the inspection is OK, it will end the single inspection and wait for the next inspection signal. When all tests are completed, the system will also release all connected hardware devices while shutting down the operation.

4.2 Detection Algorithm

The system uses artificial intelligence object detection and image segmentation methods [4–6], combined with traditional image processing algorithms, to develop and design detection algorithms. When the system places the lens object to be detected and starts the detection, the deep learning model of YOLO object detection is first used to detect and classify the possible defects. Then, for more complex background scratch defects and point defects, image segmentation methods and traditional image processing algorithms are used respectively to calculate the size of each defect and filter out defects that are too small to ensure whether the lens meets the corresponding inspection specifications. Finally, the results of the lens sample are output with OK or NG respectively, and the process of the single lens test is finished.

5 Experimental Results

5.1 Hardware Imaging Results

The object to be tested in this paper is a transparent curved object with small size, so it is not easy to capture the defects during the initial evaluation of the acquisition, therefore, it is necessary to adjust the parameters of the camera equipment and conduct various acquisition tests to obtain the best image of the defects with constant parameter settings. Finally, the same camera parameter settings as in Table 1. Were used as the parameter setting results for lens defect imaging.

Since the defects of the optical lens may exist on both side of the lens, the system needs to take images of the defects on the R1(front) and R2(back) sides of the lens separately to avoid the problem of missing inspection. Results of the image taken from the top (or front) and the side of R1(front) surface are shown in Fig. 10. As for the R2(back) surface detection, due to the smaller area of the detection region, one front shot is wide enough to cover the whole R2(back) surface as shown in Fig. 11.

Fig. 10. R1(front) detection surface acquisition results.

Fig. 11. R2(back) detection surface acquisition results.

Table 1. Hardware imaging parameters setting value.

Inspection surface	Photography Method	Exposure time	Gain
R1(front)	Frontal shot	20 ms	15db
	Side shot	20 ms	15db
R2(back)	Frontal shot	20 ms	15db
	Side shot	20 ms	15db

5.2 YOLOv5 Training Results

In the defect detection and classification, YOLOv5 provides five models of different sizes for the user to choose from, and research must be done to find the best model. After many training tests, yolov5s is finally selected as the training and inferring model for our defect detection system. The training categories are divided into two types of defect recognition: point defects and scratch defects. The training samples are divided into a training set of 1000 images and a validation set of 228 images. The image size is 1280 × 1280, the batch size is set to 4, and the epoch is set to 500 times. For detailed parameters, please see Table 2.

The training results for this study are illustrated in Fig. 12. The loss function tends to level off after 100 iterations and slowly converges downward, while Recall and Precision maintain about 80% of the data performance, then the average accuracy of mAP remains between 80% and 90%, with the highest reaching 89%.

In order to further evaluate the model, 100 additional test set images were input for model inference, as shown in Fig. 13. The image inference results were statistically calculated using Precision, Recall and F1-score introduced in Eqs. (1) to (3), and a quantitative table for model evaluation was prepared, as shown in Table 3

$$\text{Precision} = \frac{TP}{TP + FP} \tag{1}$$

$$\text{Recall} = \frac{TP}{TP + FN} \tag{2}$$

$$F1 - \textbf{score} = \frac{2 \times (\textbf{Precision} \times \textbf{Recall})}{\textbf{Precision} + \textbf{Recall}} \quad (3)$$

Table 2. Table of YOLO Training Parameters.

Training models	YOLOv5s
Total number of categories	Two classes (point and line)
Training	1000 sheets
Validation	223 sheets
Image size	1280*1280
Batch Size	4
Epoch iterations	198/500

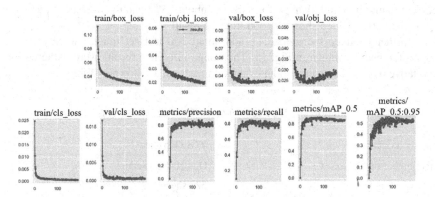

Fig. 12. YOLOv5 Training Results.

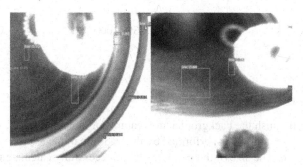

Fig. 13. Results of the frontal shot and side shot inference.

Table 3. Evaluation table for YOLO model.

Categories	Total defects	TP	FP	FN	Precision	Recall	F1-score
line	123	117	0	6	100%	95.1%	97.5%
point	210	208	0	2	100%	99%	99.5%

5.3 Segmentation Training Results

In the image segmentation part, the same YOLOv5s-seg in YOLOv5 is adopted as the training and inference model for our scratch defect feature extraction. The training category is scratch defect class, and the training samples are divided into a training set of 327 images and a validation set of 86 images. The image size is 320 × 320, the batch size is set to 128, and the epoch is set to 1000 times. Please see Table 4. For detailed parameters.

The training results of this study are shown in Fig. 14. Where loss function has a large oscillation at the beginning of the training, but with the increase of the iterations, it tends to gradually decrease and slowly converge. Meanwhile, the data of Recall and Precision maintain a high data performance of about 95%, and the average accuracy of mAP is over 90%, which shows a good training result.

To further evaluate the model, an additional 200 test set images were input for model inference, as shown in Fig. 15. The image inference results were gathered into quantitative data tables using model evaluation metrics, as shown in Table 5.

Table 4. Table of Segmentation Training Parameters.

Training models	YOLOv5s-seg
Total number of categories	One classes(Scratch)
Training	327 sheets
Validation	86 sheets
Image size	320*320
Batch Size	16
Epoch iterations	398/1000

5.4 Results of Defect Image Processing

It is easier to distinguish the background and features of the point defect, so the feature extraction of the point defect is performed by the traditional image processing method, as shown in Fig. 16. The size of the point defect is successfully calculated by using the contour finding method, as shown in Fig. 17., where the diameter was calculated.

In order to verify the practicality of this algorithm, a larger number of point defects were imported for the above image processing steps and compared with the original

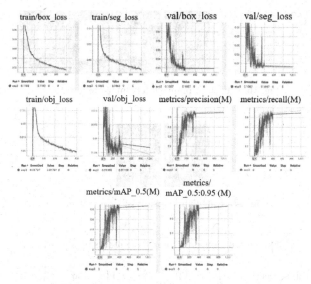

Fig. 14. Segmentation Training Results.

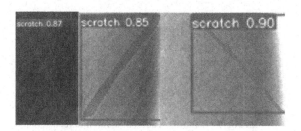

Fig. 15. Result of scratch defects inference.

Table 5. Evaluation table for Segmentation model.

Categories	Total defects	TP	FP	FN	Precision	Recall	F1-score
Scratch	210	200	10	0	95.2%	100%	97.5%

defects, and the results of this experiment were collected quantitatively as shown in Table 6.

After extracting the features by AI method, the same image processing method and simple algorithm are used to calculate the size of the scratch defects, as shown in Fig. 18, for the system to verify the final defects.

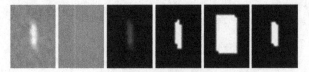

Fig. 16. Result of point defects image processing.

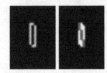

Fig. 17. Calculation results of point defects.

Table 6. Evaluation table for image processing algorithms.

Categories	Total defects	TP	FP	FN	Precision	Recall	F1-score
Point	197	197	0	3	100%	98.5%	99.2%

Fig. 18. Calculation results of scratch defects.

6 Conclusions

The optical lens defect detection and classification system designed in this paper utilizes the characteristics of high-angle annular light and the angular relationship between the defect features to successfully perform preliminary defect image acquisition. Then the YOLO object detection model is used for subsequent defect classification and location of the defect on the images. Size of the scratch and point defects are also calculated to grade the lens. Verified with the ground truth, the detection rate can reach about 95%. In addition, the user interface is developed for both hardware control and software operation, which not only provides the production line inspectors with the ability to conduct real-time inspection operations, but also provides inspectors or engineers with easy access to hardware equipment control and image parameter settings to achieve system ease of maintenance and operability.

Acknowledgement. The authors wish to express their appreciation for the financial support of the National Science Council of Taiwan under project 111-2221-E-224-051-

References

1. Zhang, X., Wang, Q., Liu, J., Liu, Z., Gong, J.: Zipper classification and defect detection based on computer vision. In: 2020 39th Chinese Control Conference (CCC), pp. 6521–6526 (2020)
2. Shang, L., Yang, Q., Wang, J., Li, S., Lei, W.: Detection of rail surface defects based on CNN image recognition and classification. In: 2018 20th International Conference on Advanced Communication Technology (ICACT), pp. 45–51 (2018)
3. Liu, G.: Surface defect detection methods based on deep learning: a brief review. In: 2020 2nd Information Technology and Computer Application (ITCA), pp. 200–203 (2020)
4. Phua, C., Theng, L.B.: Semiconductor wafer surface: automatic defect classification with deep CNN. In: 2020 IEEE Region 10 Conference (TENCON), pp. 714–719 (2020)
5. Ieamsaard, J., Charoensook, S.N., Yammen, S.: Deep learning-based face mask detection using YoloV5. In: 2021 9th International Electrical Engineering Congress (iEECON), pp. 428–431 (2021)
6. Li, B., Fu, M., Li, Q.: Runway crack detection based on YOLOV5. In: 2021 IEEE 3rd International Conference on Civil Aviation Safety and Information Technology (ICCASIT), pp. 1252–1255 (2021)

Video Deblocking Using Multipath Deep Neural Networks·

Ping-Peng Chou[(⊠)] and Jin-Jang Leou

Department of Computer Science and Information Engineering, National Chung Cheng University, Chiayi, Taiwan 621, Republic of China
falcon060425@gmail.com, jjleou@cs.ccu.edu.tw

Abstract. In this study, a video deblocking approach using multipath deep neural networks is proposed. The proposed approach contains temporal fusion subnet, variable-filter-size (VFS) subnet, and enhancement subnet. Video deblocking is performed via early fusion so that temporal correlations between adjacent video frames are employed. Based on the experimental results obtained in this study, in terms of two objective performance metrics and subjective evaluation, the performance of the proposed approach is better than those of four comparison approaches.

Keywords: video deblocking · multipath deep neural network · optical flow computation · temporal fusion subnet · variable-filter-size (VFS) subnet · enhancement subnet

1 Introduction

In video coding, quantization and motion compensation will suffer various video coding artifacts, such as blocking and ringing artifacts [1]. To reduce blocking artifacts, there are two main categories of deblocking approaches: handcrafted feature-based and learning-based. Most traditional video deblocking approaches [2–4] usually use handcrafted video features or filters to reduce blocking artifacts in decompressed video sequences. For learning-based video deblocking approaches, various deep neural networks and techniques [5–15] are developed to perform video deblocking so that the quality of decompressed video sequences can be improved. In this study, a video deblocking approach using multipath deep neural networks is proposed.

This paper is organized as follows. The proposed approach is described in Sect. 2. Experimental results are presented in Sect. 3, followed by concluding remarks.

2 Proposed Approach

2.1 System Architecture

In this study, as shown in Fig. 1, the proposed video deblocking approach using multipath deep neural networks contains temporal fusion subnet, variable-filter-size (VFS) subnet, and enhancement subnet. Video deblocking is performed via early fusion so that temporal

© The Author(s), under exclusive license to Springer Nature Singapore Pte Ltd. 2024
C.-Y. Lee et al. (Eds.): TAAI 2023, CCIS 2075, pp. 28–39, 2024.
https://doi.org/10.1007/978-981-97-1714-9_3

correlations between adjacent video frames are employed. To reduce video decoding artifacts, in this study, optical flow computations, VFS convolutions, skip connections, and two activation functions, namely, rectified linear unit (*ReLU*) and parametric rectified linear unit (*PReLU*), are also employed.

To perform video processing tasks, three strategies may be employed, i.e., in a frame-by-frame manner, via early fusion, and via slow fusion [16, 17]. For the first strategy, video deblocking is performed in a frame-by-frame manner. Because temporal correlations between adjacent video frames are not employed, this strategy may suffer unexpected artifacts. For video deblocking via early fusion, as an illustrated example shown in Fig. 2, the t-th deblocking frame is obtained by processing three consecutive video frames (i.e., $I_{t-1}(x, y), I_t(x, y), I_{t+1}(x, y)$). Temporal correlations between adjacent video frames are employed so that unexpected artifacts will be reduced. For video deblocking via slow fusion, consecutive video frames are segmented into some partially overlapping groups, which are fed into the subsequent layers to generate the deblocking frames. Although the performance of the third strategy is slightly better than that of the second strategy, the third strategy is computationally expensive. In this study, the second strategy is employed.

The input decompressed video frames and the corresponding deblocking video frames are denoted as $I_t(x, y) = \left(I_{R,t}(x, y), I_{G,t}(x, y), I_{B,t}(x, y)\right)$ and $O_t(x, y) = \left(O_{R,t}(x, y), O_{G,t}(x, y), O_{B,t}(x, y)\right)$, respectively, where $0 \leq I_{R,t}(x, y), I_{G,t}(x, y), I_{B,t}(x, y), O_{R,t}(x, y), O_{G,t}(x, y), O_{B,t}(x, y) \leq 255, 1 \leq x \leq W,$ $1 \leq y \leq H, 1 \leq t \leq N$, W and H denote the resolution of video frames, and N denotes the total number of video frames. In this study, to speed up the training process, each input decompressed video frame will be decomposed into non-overlapping sub-frames 128×128 in size, which are fed into the proposed multipath deep neural network.

2.2 Temporal Fusion Subnet

Temporal fusion subnet containing motion compensation module and temporal fusion module is used to estimate and compensate the temporal features extracted from adjacent video frames. The spatial transformer motion compensation (STMC) approach for video superresolution proposed in [18] can be used to estimate the optical flows between adjacent video frames. For two consecutive video frames, $I_t(x, y)$ and $I_{t+1}(x, y)$, and optical flow estimation function θ_{t+1}, the corresponding optical flow can be represented as $\Delta_{t+1} = \left(\Delta_{t+1}^x, \Delta_{t+1}^y; \theta_{t+1}\right)$. Then, compensated video frame $I_{t+1}\prime(x, y)$ can be expressed as:

$$I_{t+1}\prime(x, y) = \mathcal{L}\{I_{t+1}\left(x + \Delta_{t+1}^x, y + \Delta_{t+1}^y\right)\}, \tag{1}$$

where $\mathcal{L}$ denotes the bilinear interpolation operator.

In the proposed motion compensation module, the coarse-to-fine ($\times 4$ and $\times 2$) optical flow modules with two optical flow estimation functions, θ_{t+1}^c and θ_{t+1}^f, are used to handle large-scale motions, whereas the proposed still scene flow module with optical flow estimation function θ_{t+1}^s (without down-sampling) is used to treat still scenes in each video sequence. Three types of optical flows are defined as

$$\Delta_{t+1}^c(x, y) = \left(\Delta_{t+1}^x, \Delta_{t+1}^y; \theta_{t+1}^c\right), \tag{2}$$

$$\Delta_{t+1}^f(x, y) = \left(\Delta_{t+1}^x, \Delta_{t+1}^y; \theta_{t+1}^f\right), \tag{3}$$

$$\Delta_{t+1}^s(x, y) = \left(\Delta_{t+1}^x, \Delta_{t+1}^y; \theta_{t+1}^s\right), \tag{4}$$

where $\Delta_{t+1}^c(x, y)$, $\Delta_{t+1}^f(x, y)$, and $\Delta_{t+1}^s(x, y)$ denote the coarse, fine, and still scene optical flows, respectively. As shown in Fig. 3, the proposed coarse optical flow module, fine optical flow module, and still scene flow module are sequentially performed to obtain three corresponding compensated video frames $I_{t+1}^c(x, y)$, $I_{t+1}^f(x, y)$, and $I_{t+1}\prime(x, y)$, respectively. As shown in Fig. 1, the second motion compensation module for $I_t(x, y)$ and $I_{t-1}(x, y)$ will perform similar computations.

As shown in Fig. 4, input frame $I_t(x, y)$ and two compensated frames $I_{t-1}\prime(x, y)$ and $I_{t+1}\prime(x, y)$ are together fed into the proposed temporal fusion module to merge temporal information in a hierarchical manner and generate the temporal feature map $d_t^{temp}(x, y)$.

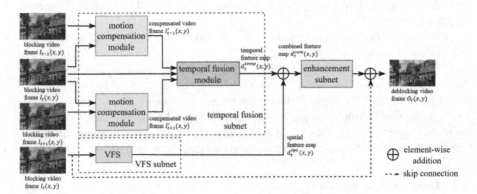

Fig. 1. Framework of the proposed approach.

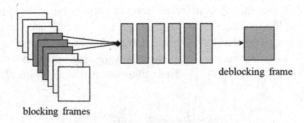

Fig. 2. Video deblocking via early fusion.

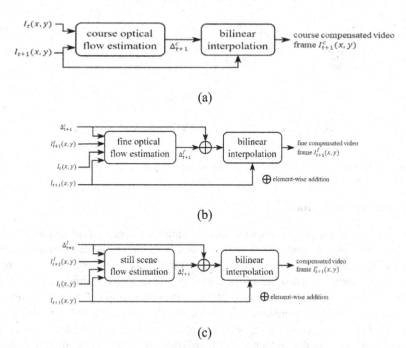

(a)

(b)

(c)

Fig. 3. The proposed coarse optical flow module (a), fine optical flow module (b), and still scene flow module (c).

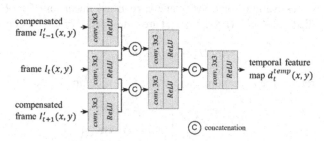

Fig. 4. The proposed temporal fusion module.

2.3 Variable-Filter-Size (VFS) Subnet

A variable-filter-size network containing several VFS convolution (*conv*) blocks [19] can be employed to extract precise features. In the proposed VFS subnet, as shown in Fig. 5, variable-sized filters are used to extract multiscale spatial information in the *t*-th video frame $I_t(x, y)$ and generate the *t*-th spatial feature map $d_t^{spa}(x, y)$. Then, these multiscale spatial features $d_t^{spa}(x, y)$ generated by the proposed VFS subnet and temporal features $d_t^{temp}(x, y)$ generated by the proposed temporal fusion subnet are combined by element-wise addition $\oplus$ as

$$d_t^{com}(x, y) = d_t^{spa}(x, y) \oplus d_t^{temp}(x, y), \tag{5}$$

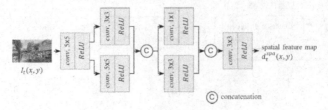

Fig. 5. The proposed VFS subnet.

which will be fed into the proposed enhancement subnet.

2.4 Enhancement Subnet

As shown in Fig. 6, the proposed enhancement subnet, containing three residual blocks, 3×3 *conv* with *ReLU*, and 3×3 *conv*, utilizes both the spatial and temporal detail features to generate the final deblocking video frame $O_t(x, y)$. As shown in Fig. 6(b), each slice operator in each residual block is used to split extracted features into two parts. Part 1 $h \times w \times 16$ in size will concatenate with the processing results of the previous stage, whereas part 2 (the remaining part) is fed into the subsequent layer. Additionally, as shown in Fig. 1, skip connections, standard operators in deep neural frameworks, are employed in the proposed approach to avoid gradient exploding and gradient vanishing.

2.5 Activation Functions, Loss Functions, and Optimizer

In this study, two activation functions, namely, rectified linear unit (*ReLU*) [20] and parametric rectified linear unit (*PReLU*) [21] are employed. $ReLU(\cdot)$ is computed by

$$ReLU(z) = \max(0, z), \tag{6}$$

where $\max(\cdot, \cdot)$ returns the maximum value. $PReLU(\cdot)$ is computed by

$$PReLU(z) = \begin{cases} z, & \text{if } z \geq 0, \\ az, & \text{otherwise,} \end{cases} \tag{7}$$

where a denotes the slope parameter.

In this study, two MSE (mean squared error) loss functions are computed as

$$L_{t-1}^{ME} = \frac{1}{H \cdot W \cdot 3} \sum_{y=1}^{H} \sum_{x=1}^{W} \sum_{k \in \{R,G,B\}} (I_{k,t-1}{}'(x, y) - I_{k,t}(x, y))^2, \tag{8}$$

$$L_{t+1}^{ME} = \frac{1}{H \cdot W \cdot 3} \sum_{y=1}^{H} \sum_{x=1}^{W} \sum_{k \in \{R,G,B\}} (I_{k,t+1}{}'(x, y) - I_{k,t}(x, y))^2 \tag{9}$$

The MSE loss function L_t^{Net} concerning the t-th deblocking video frame $O_t(x, y)$ and the corresponding ground truth $GT_t(x, y)$ is similarly defined. The total loss function for the approach is computed as

$$L_{total} = \alpha\left(L_{t-1}^{ME} + L_{t+1}^{ME}\right) + \beta \cdot L_t^{Net}, \tag{10}$$

where α and β denote two weighting factors (empirically set to 0.01 and 1, respectively). In this study, Adam optimizer [22] is employed for training, which is computed as

$$\tau_m = \gamma_1 \cdot \tau_{m-1} + (1 - \gamma_1)g_m, \tag{11}$$

$$\varphi_m = \gamma_2 \cdot \varphi_{m-1} + (1 - \gamma_2)g_m^2, \tag{12}$$

where τ_m and φ_m denote the exponential moving averages of gradient and squared gradient, respectively, m denotes the number of training iterations, γ_1 and γ_2 denote two hyperparameters (empirically set to 0.9 and 0.999, respectively), and g_m denotes the gradient. Bias corrections for τ_m and φ_m are computed as

$$\hat{\tau}_m = \tau_m/(1 - \gamma_1), \tag{13}$$

$$\hat{\varphi}_m = \varphi_m/(1 - \gamma_2), \tag{14}$$

Adam's weight parameter p_m is updated by

$$p_m = p_{m-1} - \frac{l \cdot \hat{\tau}_m}{\sqrt{\hat{\varphi}_m} + \varepsilon}, \tag{15}$$

where l denotes learning rate and ε is a small positive constant for avoiding ambiguity (empirically set to 1×10^{-8}).

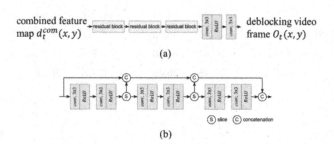

Fig. 6. The proposed enhancement subnet (a) and residual block (b).

3 Experimental Results

In this study, the proposed approach is implemented on Microsoft Windows 10 platform with AMD Ryzen 7 3700X 8-core processor 3.60 GHz (CPU), Nvidia GeForce RTX 2080Ti (GPU), 64 GB main memory (RAM), python v.3.6.13, tensorflow v.1.13.2, CUDA v.10.0, and cuDNN v.7.4.2. The training and test sequences are encoded and decoded by HEVC reference software HM-16.24 in all intra (AI), low-delay (LD), and random access (RA) configurations with quantization parameters (QPs) being 44, 48, and 51. In this study, Vimeo dataset [10] and REDS dataset [23] are used, which consists of 100 video sequences with 448×720 resolution and 200 video sequences with 720×1080 resolution, respectively. The learning rate starts from 0.0001 and decays a power of 10 every 10 epochs. Batch size and the number of epochs are set to 8 and 30, respectively. An input shape containing three consecutive video frames is $128 \times 128 \times 9$ in size.

To evaluate the performance of the proposed video deblocking approach, two performance metrics, namely, peak signal-to-noise ratio (PSNR) and structural similarity index (SSIM) [24], are employed. To evaluate the performance of the proposed video deblocking approach, four comparison approaches, HM16 baseline, SDTS [12], VRCNN-BN [5], and MCSB [9] are employed. In terms of average PSNR (dB) and SSIM, performance comparisons of four comparison approaches and the proposed approach on two datasets are shown in Tables 1, 2, 3, 4, 5 and 6. For subjective video quality evaluation, some final deblocking results of four comparison approaches and the proposed approach on two datasets are shown in Figs. 7, 8 and 9.

Table 1. In terms of average PSNR (dB) and SSIM, performance comparisons of four comparison approaches and the proposed approach in all intra (AI) configuration on Vimeo dataset [10].

Approaches	QP = 44		QP = 48		QP = 51	
	PSNR (dB)	SSIM	PSNR (dB)	SSIM	PSNR (dB)	SSIM
HM16 baseline	36.48	0.739	35.53	0.720	34.84	0.696
SDTS [12]	36.61	0.740	36.38	0.718	36.14	0.692
VRCNN-BN [5]	36.63	0.739	36.40	**0.728**	36.15	**0.697**
MCSB [9]	36.64	0.742	36.20	0.721	36.08	0.693
Proposed	**36.67**	**0.745**	**36.45**	0.724	**36.18**	0.696

Table 2. In terms of average PSNR (dB) and SSIM, performance comparisons of four comparison approaches and the proposed approach in low-delay (LD) configuration on Vimeo dataset [10].

Approaches	QP = 44		QP = 48		QP = 51	
	PSNR (dB)	SSIM	PSNR (dB)	SSIM	PSNR (dB)	SSIM
HM16 baseline	35.33	0.713	35.84	0.696	35.59	0.699
SDTS [12]	36.33	0.710	36.10	0.700	36.19	0.709
VRCNN-BN [5]	36.35	0.717	36.17	**0.712**	36.15	0.710
MCSB [9]	36.33	0.710	36.19	0.700	36.11	**0.712**
Proposed	**36.38**	**0.721**	**36.22**	0.709	**36.21**	0.709

Table 3. In terms of average PSNR (dB) and SSIM, performance comparisons of four comparison approaches and the proposed approach in random access (RA) configuration on Vimeo dataset [10].

Approaches	QP = 44		QP = 48		QP = 51	
	PSNR (dB)	SSIM	PSNR (dB)	SSIM	PSNR (dB)	SSIM
HM16 baseline	36.21	0.703	35.63	0.682	35.40	0.677
SDTS [12]	36.35	0.713	**36.22**	0.695	36.12	0.685
VRCNN-BN [5]	36.21	0.704	36.07	0.685	35.98	0.675
MCSB [9]	36.33	0.713	36.15	0.695	36.01	0.671
Proposed	**36.39**	**0.717**	36.21	**0.702**	**36.15**	**0.691**

Table 4. In terms of average PSNR (dB) and SSIM, performance comparisons of four comparison approaches and the proposed approach in all intra (AI) configuration on REDS Dataset [23].

Approaches	QP = 44		QP = 48		QP = 51	
	PSNR (dB)	SSIM	PSNR (dB)	SSIM	PSNR (dB)	SSIM
HM16 baseline	35.53	0.677	34.78	0.582	34.25	0.515
SDTS [12]	35.95	0.692	35.18	0.603	34.53	0.525
VRCNN-BN [5]	36.13	0.693	35.26	**0.607**	34.60	0.538
MCSB [9]	36.00	0.689	35.20	0.601	34.41	0.523
Proposed	**36.28**	**0.707**	**35.41**	0.605	**34.68**	**0.546**

Table 5. In terms of average PSNR (dB) and SSIM, performance comparisons of four comparison approaches and the proposed approach in low-delay (LD) configuration on REDS Dataset [23].

Approaches	QP = 44		QP = 48		QP = 51	
	PSNR (dB)	SSIM	PSNR (dB)	SSIM	PSNR (dB)	SSIM
HM16 baseline	34.97	0.615	34.47	0.540	34.33	0.522
SDTS [12]	35.28	0.614	34.76	0.547	34.54	0.527
VRCNN-BN [5]	35.41	0.628	34.84	0.556	34.63	0.537
MCSB [9]	35.20	0.621	34.73	0.544	34.43	0.524
Proposed	**35.49**	**0.630**	**34.95**	**0.559**	**34.68**	**0.550**

Table 6. In terms of average PSNR (dB) and SSIM, performance comparisons of four comparison approaches and the proposed approach in random access (RA) configuration on REDS dataset [23].

Approaches	QP = 44		QP = 48		QP = 51	
	PSNR (dB)	SSIM	PSNR (dB)	SSIM	PSNR (dB)	SSIM
HM16 baseline	35.38	0.680	34.99	0.601	34.56	0.558
SDTS [12]	35.87	0.692	35.37	0.625	34.91	0.573
VRCNN-BN [5]	35.94	0.696	35.37	**0.631**	35.00	**0.585**
MCSB [9]	35.52	0.690	35.33	0.626	34.62	0.565
Proposed	**36.09**	**0.703**	**35.44**	0.621	**35.10**	0.583

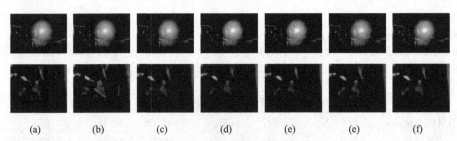

| (a) | (b) | (c) | (d) | (e) | (e) | (f) |

Fig. 7. Experimental results in all intra (AI) configuration with QP = 44 on Vimeo dataset [10]: (a) blocking video frame, (b) ground truth, (c)-(g) deblocking video frames by HM-16 baseline, SDTS [12], VRCNN-BN [5], MCSB [9], and the proposed approach, respectively. Bottom row shows the corresponding detail parts of top row.

Fig. 8. Experimental results in low-delay (LD) configuration with QP = 48 on Vimeo dataset [10]: (a) blocking video frame, (b) ground truth, (c)-(f) deblocking video frames by HM-16 baseline, SDTS [12], VRCNN-BN [5], MCSB [9], and the proposed approach, respectively. Bottom row shows the corresponding detail parts of top row.

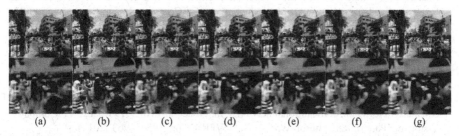

Fig. 9. Experimental results in random access (RA) configuration with QP = 51 on REDS dataset [23]: (a) blocking video frame, (b) ground truth, (c)-(f) deblocking video frames by HM-16 baseline, SDTS [12], VRCNN-BN [5], MCSB [9], and the proposed approach, respectively. Bottom row shows the corresponding detail parts of top row.

4   Concluding Remarks

In this study, a video deblocking approach using multipath deep neural networks is proposed. The proposed approach contains temporal fusion subnet, variable-filter-size (VFS) subnet, and enhancement subnet. Video deblocking is performed via early fusion so that temporal correlations between adjacent video frames are employed. Based on the experimental results obtained in this study, in terms of two objective performance metrics, average PSNR(dB) and SSIM, and subjective evaluation, the performance of the proposed approach is better than those of four comparison approaches.

Acknowledgements. This work was supported in part by National Science and Technology Council, Taiwan, Republic of China under grants MOST 111-2221-E-194-021 and NSTC 112-2221-E-194-030.

References

1. High efficiency video coding, Recommendation ITU-T H.265, November 2019
2. Hashimoto, K., Gohshi, S.: Novel deblocking method for cropped video. In: Proceedings of 2019 International Symposium on Intelligent Signal Processing and Communication Systems (ISPACS), pp. 1–2 (2019)

3. Bougacha, O., Ben Ayed, M. A., Masmoudi, N.: Prefiltering effect on HEVC intra prediction module. In: Proceedings of 2019 16th international Multi-Conference on Systems, Signals & Devices (SSD), pp. 7–11 (2019)
4. Andersson, K., Misra, K., Ikeda, M., Rusanovskyy, D., Iwamura, S.: Deblocking filtering in VVC. In: Proceedings of 2021 Picture Coding Symposium (PCS), pp. 1–5 (2021)
5. Zhao, H., He, M., Teng, G., Shang, X., Wang, G., Feng, Y.: A CNN-based post-processing algorithm for video coding efficiency improvement. IEEE Access **8**, 920–929 (2020)
6. Zhang, Y., Shen, T., Ji, X., Zhang, Y., Xiong, R., Dai, Q.: Residual highway convolutional neural networks for in-loop filtering in HEVC. IEEE Trans. Image Process. **27**(8), 3827–3841 (2018)
7. Qi, Z., Jung, C., Xie, B.: Subband adaptive image deblocking using wavelet based convolutional neural networks. IEEE Access **9**, 62593–62601 (2021)
8. Zhang, Y., Chandler, D. M., Mou, X.: Multi-domain residual encoder–decoder networks for generalized compression artifact reduction. J. Vis. Commun. Image Representation **83**, 103425–103437 (2022)
9. Shi, Z., Mettes, P., Maji, S., Snoek, C.G.M.: On measuring and controlling the spectral bias of the deep image prior. Int. J. of Comput. Vis. **130**, 885–908 (2022)
10. Lu, G., Zhang, X., Ouyang, W., Xu, D., Chen, L., Gao, Z.: Deep non-local Kalman network for video compression artifact reduction. IEEE Trans. Image Process. **29**, 1725–1737 (2020)
11. Wang, X., Chan, K.C., Yu, K., Dong, C., Change Loy, C.: EDVR: video restoration with enhanced deformable convolutional networks. In: Proceedings of 2019 IEEE/CVF Computer Vision and Pattern Recognition Workshops (CVPRW), pp. 1954–1963 (2019)
12. Meng, X., Deng, X., Zhu, S., Zeng, B.: Enhancing quality for VVC compressed videos by jointly exploiting spatial details and temporal structure. In: Proceedings of 2019 IEEE International Conference on Image Processing (ICIP), pp. 1193–1197 (2019)
13. Huang, Z., Sun, J., Guo, X., Shang, M.: One-for-all: an efficient variable convolution neural network for in-loop filter of VVC. IEEE Trans. Circ. Syst. Video Technol. **32**(4), 2342–2355 (2022)
14. Norkin, A.: Generalized deblocking filter for AVM. In: Proceedings of 2022 Picture Coding Symposium (PCS), pp. 355–359 (2022)
15. Li, S., Huang, L., Xiong, X., Xu, D., Zhu, X., Fan, Y.: An area-efficient deblocking filter architecture for multi-standard video codec. In: Proceedings of 2022 IEEE 4th International Conference on Circuits and Systems (ICCS), pp. 149–154 (2022)
16. Tran, D., Bourdev, L., Fergus, R., Torresani, L., Paluri, M.: Learning spatiotemporal features with 3D convolutional networks. arXiv:1412.0767 (2014)
17. Karpathy, A., Toderici, G., Shetty, S., Leung, T., Sukthankar, R., Fei-Fei, L.: Large-scale video classification with convolutional neural networks. In: Proceedings of 2014 IEEE/CVF Conference on Computer Vision and Pattern Recognition (CVPR), pp. 1725–1732 (2014)
18. Caballero, J., Ledig, C., Aitken, A., Acosta, A., Totz, J., Wang, Z., Shi, W.: Real-time video super-resolution with spatio-temporal networks and motion compensation. In: Proceedings of 2017 IEEE/CVF Conf. on Computer Vision and Pattern Recognition (CVPR), pp. 4778–4787 (2017)
19. Dai, Y., Liu, D., Wu, F.: A convolutional neural network approach for post-processing in HEVC intra coding. arXiv:1608.06690 (2016)
20. Nair, V., Hinton, G. E.: Rectified linear units improve restricted boltzmann machines. In: Proceedings of the 27th International Conference on Machine Learning, pp. 807–814 (2010)
21. He, K., Zhang, X., Ren, S., Sun, J.: Delving deep into rectifiers: surpassing human-level performance on imagenet classification. arXiv:1502.01852 (2015)
22. Kingma, D. P., Ba, J. L.: Adam: an approach for stochastic optimization. In: Proceedings of 2015 International Conference on Learning Representations, pp. 1–15 (2015)

23. Nah, S., Baik, S., Hong, S., Moon, G., Son, S., Timofte, R., Lee, K. M.: NTIRE 2019 challenge on video deblurring and super-resolution: dataset and study. In: Proceedings of 2019 IEEE/CVF Computer Vision and Pattern Recognition Workshops (CVPRW), pp. 1996–2005 (2019)
24. Martens, J.B., Meesters, L.: Image dissimilarity. IEEE Trans. Sig. Process. **70**(3), 155–176 (1998)

A Mixture-of-Experts (MoE) Framework for Pose-Invariant Face Recognition via Local Landmark-Centered Feature Extraction

Paulo E. Linares Otoya⬤ and Shinfeng D. Lin[✉]⬤

Department of Computer Science and Information Engineering, National Dong Hwa University,
Hualien, Taiwan, ROC
{811221003,david}@gms.ndhu.edu.tw

Abstract. Most real-world applications in video surveillance and biometric authentication rely on robust face recognition systems capable of dealing with multiple variations of pose, illumination, and expression within the processed images. In this article, we are proposing a Mixture-of-Experts (MoE) framework together with local feature extraction (SIFT) centered around facial landmarks to address pose-invariant face recognition. For this purpose, the framework performs facial landmark detection with a twofold objective. First, head pose classification is conducted by processing a set of landmark locations detected in a face image to spot the visible landmarks. Second, these visible landmark locations are regarded as keypoints, and SIFT descriptors are extracted from them. These descriptors are utilized as inputs to the base learners comprising a MoE system, which is trained to compute the similarity between the subject identity it was trained for, and the unknown identity of the subject from the input image. This similarity is employed later to perform face recognition. We propose two models to be used independently as base learners. The first one is GMM, whereas the second one is a novel GMM-based model (Mahalannobis Similarity) introduced in this work. A performance comparable with state-of-the-art methods is obtained on images with pose angles between ±90° on the CMU-PIE, and Multi-PIE databases.

Keywords: Mixture-of-experts · ensemble learning · face recognition · local feature descriptor · facial landmarks

1 Introduction

Face recognition is a computer vision technique that involves comparing an unknown input face image against a database of known faces in order to identify or verify the individual's identity [1, 2]. The variability in head pose constitutes a significant challenge for accurate face recognition in uncontrolled environments, due to the drastic change in facial appearance caused by the 3D geometry of the head, as well as the self-occlusion of key facial features [3]. In recent years, several computer vision techniques have been developed to address the difficulty of performing pose-invariant face recognition (PIFR). One of these techniques is facial landmark detection. This technique aims to

C.-Y. Lee et al. (Eds.): TAAI 2023, CCIS 2075, pp. 40–52, 2024.
https://doi.org/10.1007/978-981-97-1714-9_4

detect a set of fiducial facial key points (e.g. corners of eyes, mouth borders, nose tip) on a face image [2, 4] to perform further operations on their locations, or on the image regions surrounding them. Indeed, several state-of-the-art works on PIFR performed facial landmark detection as a previous step to get a high recognition rate [3, 5, 6].

Another technique is Head Pose Estimation (HPE). HPE is the problem of computing the three orientation angles of a human face on a digital image. It has been considered a crucial task in computer vision due to its potential use on applications such as human behavior analysis, driving safety, surveillance and VR systems [7]. After performing HPE, it is possible to transform a pose-view face to a frontal-view image (face normalization) [2, 5]. Indeed, several state-of-the-art works achieved good results on PIFR by conjointly utilizing facial landmark detection, head pose estimation, and face frontalization [3, 5, 8]. Face normalization (alignment) is considered as a critical pre-processing step in various contemporary studies on PIFR. Some approaches aim to generate a frontal face image from the input image (entirely or partially) [3]. It has been observed that these methods often encounter a decline in face recognition performance when dealing with images exhibiting extreme pose orientations. In order to address this issue, an adaptive alignment strategy that dynamically learns the appropriate alignment template tailored to the specific head pose is proposed in [9]. This adaptive approach avoids the limitation of rigidly aligning all face images to a frontal orientation, thereby enhancing the overall PIFR performance.

Most of the mentioned PIFR methods adopt a holistic approach (a face image is cropped and processed as a whole) leveraging the power of deep CNNs (DCNN) [10–12]. This approach comprises three well-defined components. The first one involves the design of a DCNN capable of extracting a discriminative (invariant) face embedding, which can be used later for face verification or identification. During the training of these DCNNs, a loss function (e.g. contrastive loss, triplet loss) must be defined such that the inter-class similarity is minimized while maximizing the intra-class similarity. FaceNet [10], ResNet-100, and ResNet-50 are some examples of these DCNNs. The second component entails the design of a loss function specifically tailored to achieve a high accuracy on face recognition. Some renowned works on this component include CosFace [11], and ArcFace [12]. The last component involves the manner face embeddings are employed to perform face recognition (e.g. classification, feature matching). The methods adopting a holistic approach have shown remarkable results in recent years. However, the use of DCNNs implies that a face image is cropped and resized to a small image. By doing this, important face information, present in a face image with a regular size (say 1280×720 pixels), is lost [13]. In contrast, alternative approaches have been explored where feature descriptors extracted from facial landmarks (local approach) are utilized for PIFR [13–16], showing promising results in pose-invariant face recognition.

In this paper, we propose a Mixture-of-experts (MoE) framework to address pose-invariant face recognition. In this approach, facial landmarks are considered as keypoints, and face recognition is carried out as follows. First, head pose classification (HPC) is carried out by processing the facial landmark locations, and employing a SVC model to predict the head pose from a well-defined set of available pose classes. By knowing the pose class, it is possible to select non-occluded facial landmarks for further processing. Second, feature extraction is performed over the selected landmarks by employing

SIFT description algorithm. Third, the SIFT descriptor of each landmark is input to its corresponding base learner within a MoE model. Fourth, the outputs of all the base learners, comprising the MoE model (one model per subject), are processed to compute the degree of similarity between the input face image and the images used to train a MoE system. The base learners' training is performed for each subject in the face database. This process involves obtaining SIFT feature descriptors from regions surrounding a specific landmark in a gallery image, and using these descriptors as the model's training data. We select GMM, and a novel model, called Mahalanobis Similarity, as the base learner models. Finally, face recognition is performed by gathering the MoE systems' outputs from all the subjects, and choosing the one with the highest degree of similarity. In order to validate the face recognition method proposed in this work, CMU-PIE and Multi-PIE are adopted as the benchmark datasets. The experimental results obtained with the proposed approach are compared with several state-of-the-art works, and its superiority is evidenced in face images with poses within the yaw angle range of $\pm 90°$.

As above mentioned, conversely to using a holistic approach (like the current trend on using DCNNs for learning a robust face embedding), the method presented in this work addresses PIFR from a local approach. The main benefit of adopting this view point is that rich facial information around selected landmarks are extracted from the face image in its original size. This is not the case when employing a holistic approach, where a face image is resized to a predefined size, thus losing relevant local information. On the other hand, a higher level of robustness against pose variation may be attained by training a model (base learner) to be an expert in performing face recognition with features extracted exclusively from a specific landmark, and mixing the outputs from all the trained models comprising a MoE system. Indeed, this is a well-known technique to promote diversity in ensemble systems like MoE.

2 Proposed Method

2.1 Head Pose Classification

Head pose classification (HPC) is an implementation of Head Pose Estimation (HPE) but at a coarse level. At this level, the goal is to identify a head pose from a finite set of N_p orientations. To address HPC, the number of pose classes N_p, and the head pose representation of a face image $\mathcal{R}\left(I_j\right)$ must be defined first. The model employed to perform HPC must be capable of predicting the pose class $\rho_j' \in \{1, 2, \ldots, N_p\}$ given $\mathcal{R}$ (I_j), in such a manner that the expression $\sum_j \left[\rho_j' = \rho_j\right]$ reaches its maximum possible value. Where $\rho_j \in \{1, 2, \ldots, N_p\}$ is the real pose label for the jth face image, and I_j is the face image [17, 18]. The term head pose descriptor is employed to denote head pose representation in this work. The head pose descriptor is a vector containing information about the geometrical relations between a set of facial features (e.g. eyes, eyebrows, lip) within a face image. A facial landmark detection model [4] with a 68-landmark scheme (Fig. 1a) is adopted in this study, where $L_m = 12$ facial landmarks from the mouth (depicted in red on Fig. 1b) are taken into account. We propose a head pose description method which processes the 2D spatial locations of a set of facial landmarks and returns a vector called the Face Angle Vector (FAV). This descriptor was introduced in our previous works [13, 16] with an outstanding positive impact on the face recognition results. The FAV contains the angles between the mouth landmarks and the eye centers (Fig. 1b). The angles between the mouth landmarks and the left eye center $c_{le} \in \mathbb{N}^2$ are contained in the vector $\theta_L \in \mathbb{R}^{L_m}$. While $\theta_R \in \mathbb{R}^{L_m}$ contains the angles between the mouth landmarks and the right eye center $c_{re} \in \mathbb{N}^2$. The FAV $\Omega \in \mathbb{R}^{2L_m}$ is defined in (1). We use a Linear Support Vector Classifier (Linear SVC) as the pose classification model, as it was done in [13], and regard $N_p = 5$ classes. This model receives a face image's FAV and returns its pose class as it is described above.

$$\Omega[k_s] = \begin{cases} \theta_L[k_s] & \text{if } k_s < L_m \\ \theta_R[k_s - L_m] & \text{otherwise} \end{cases}; k_s \in \{0, 1, \dots, 2L_m - 1\} \qquad (1)$$

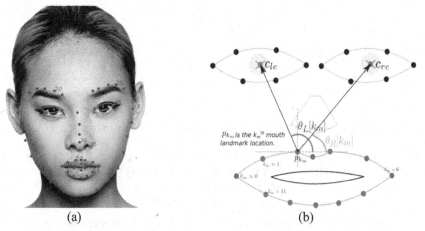

(a)   (b)

Fig. 1. Graphical representation of using facial landmark locations during FAV computation: (a) The 68-Facial landmark scheme employed in this work; (b) The angles entailing the FAV.

2.2 Facial Landmark-Centered Local Feature Extraction

The procedure carried out for describing the facial information surrounding a specific landmark on a face image is defined as Facial landmark description. This procedure is based on the description of a generic point (i.e. a pixel comprising its intensity and location) on a digital image. In this work SIFT is employed as the local descriptor. However, we do not employ the SIFT keypoint detector. Instead, a facial landmark location is considered as a keypoint and the SIFT description algorithm is computed from this keypoint. The output is considered as the facial landmark descriptor $f_{SIFT} \in \mathbb{N}^{128}$. Even though a 68-landmark detection model is employed in this work, only 24 out of the total 68 landmarks are regarded for feature extraction (landmarks from the eyes and mouth).

2.3 Mixture-of-Experts (MoE) Framework for Pose-Invariant Face Recognition

In ensemble systems, multiple weak classifiers (base learners) are created and combined to improve the classification performance [19]. A typical ensemble system consists of three components. The first component comprises a group of base learners, whose classification outputs can be discrete or continuous. A base learner receives input data and produces a classification decision. The second component is the training method, responsible for training the base learners using approaches like Bagging, Boosting, or AdaBoost [19, 20]. Finally, the combination rule determines how the base learners' outputs are processed to obtain the ensemble support value used at the end for classification.

$$D_j = \frac{1}{|\mathcal{K}|} \sum_{k \in \mathcal{K}} d_{j,k} \tag{2}$$

s.t. $\mathcal{K}$ is the set of landmarks selected by BLS block for face recognition.

$$\delta_{\text{GMM}}\left(\vec{f_k}\right) = \ln p\left(\vec{f_k} | \lambda^*\right) \tag{3}$$

$$\delta_{\text{MS}}\left(\vec{f_k}\right) = \left[1 + \ln\left(1 + \min_c\left(\left(\vec{f_k} - \vec{\mu}_c\right)^\top \Sigma_c^{-1}\left(\vec{f_k} - \vec{\mu}_c\right)\right)\right)\right]^{-1} \tag{4}$$

$$J_E = \arg\max_{j \in \mathcal{J}} D_j \tag{5}$$

s.t. $\mathcal{J}$ is the set of subjects' ID included in the face database.

In this study, we employ a Mixture-of-experts (MoE) approach (Fig. 2) where each base learner $\beta_{j,k}$ specializes in face recognition by processing feature descriptor vectors obtained from the kth facial landmark (see landmark scheme in Fig. 1a) of the jth subject in a face database. Each base learner is associated with a specific facial landmark. By processing the input feature descriptor $\vec{f_k}$, $\beta_{j,k}$ outputs a decision support value $\delta_{j,k} \in \mathbb{R}$, indicating its confidence in the recognition task.

A face recognition MoE system consists of multiple base learners trained specifically for the jth person in a face database. The output D_j of this model, called the ensemble support of the ensemble support of the jth ensemble, represents the probability that the landmark descriptors from an input face image match those of the person the ensemble system was trained for. The ensemble support D_j is computed using the mean rule [19, 20], as defined in (2). Two different models are proposed as base learners in the current work. The first model is Gaussian Mixture Model (GMM), and it is trained as follows. First, the descriptors are extracted from the points around the kth landmark location $p_k \in \mathbb{N}^2$ within a radius r, and arranged into a matrix denoted as the descriptor matrix $\mathbf{X}$ (see Fig. 3a). The descriptors contained in the matrix $\mathbf{X}$ are clustered with the GMM model (i.e. the GMM model is trained), as illustrated in Fig. 3b. After training a base learner with GMM, its decision support metric $\delta_{GMM} \in (-\infty, 0]$, , defined in (3), becomes the log-likelihood that the landmark descriptor vector $\vec{f_k}$, extracted from the kth landmark within an input face image, corresponds to the subject for which the GMM model is specifically trained. In this context, λ^* entails the GMM model's parameters, including weights, covariance matrices, and mean vectors, obtained after fitting the GMM model with $\mathbf{X}$. The second model is called Mahalanobis Similarity

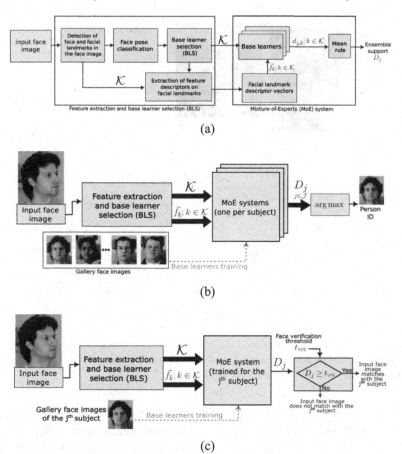

Fig. 2. Proposed MoE framework for PIFR: (a) Workflow of the proposed framework for a single subject; (b) Utilization of the MoE framework for 1:N face identification; (c) Utilization of the MoE framework for 1:1 face verification.

(MS). It employs the Bayesian variant of GMM to cluster the set of feature descriptors in $\mathbf{X}$. After clustering, the mean vectors $\vec{\mu}_c$ and covariance matrices $\mathbf{\Sigma}_c$ (defining the gaussian components) are stored in the MS model (see Fig. 3c). Then $\vec{\mu}_c$, $\mathbf{\Sigma}_c$ are utilized to compute its decision support $\delta_{MS} \in (0, 1]$, , defined in (4). The above-mentioned models are used independently to build the MoE systems, and their face recognition results are gathered for further comparison.

PIFR is performed as follows. First, the face and facial landmarks are detected in the input image. Then, the head pose class is determined by computing the face image's FAV, and feeding it to the proposed HPC model. Next, the Base Learner Selection (BLS) block selects a set of landmarks K, based on the head pose class (Fig. 4), whose corresponding base learners are later exclusively used by a MoE system to compute its decision support. The utilization of HPC in conjunction with the BLS block is justified by the fact that some landmarks might not be visible in face images depicting certain head pose classes.

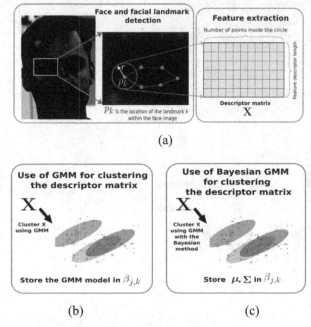

(a)

(b)   (c)

Fig. 3. Graphical representation of the base learner training process: (a) Descriptor matrix X computation; (b) GMM model training; (c) MS model training. A circle in blue indicates the surrounding points of the landmark k within a radius r.

Feature descriptors are then extracted from the image using the selected facial landmark locations as keypoints. These descriptors are input to their corresponding base learners, and their outputs are combined to compute the ensemble support value. For the case of 1:N face identification, the entire procedure shown in Fig. 2a is applied to all MoE systems trained for all the subjects J in the face database. Then, the person's identity J_E, defined in (5), is determined by selecting the ensemble system with the highest ensemble support value, as depicted in Fig. 2b. On the other hand, only the MoE system

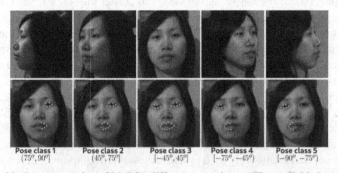

Fig. 4. Graphical representation of BLS for different pose classes. The available base learners are depicted as green circles for each pose class.

corresponding to the subject whose identity we want verify is employed to perform 1:1 face verification, as shown in Fig. 2c. For face verification, the computed D_j is compared with a face verification threshold t_{ver} to know whether the input face matches with the subject j or not. This threshold value is obtained by defining a desired False Acceptance Rate (FAR) value, as detailed in [13].

3 Experimental Results

3.1 Implementation Details

The effectiveness of the proposed pose-invariant face recognition method is tested on images with ambient illumination, neutral expression and yaw angle variation (from $-90°$ to $+90°$) of the CMU-PIE [21], and Multi-PIE [22] (session 1) databases. The frontal image ($0°$), and profile images ($\pm 90°$) are employed as the gallery images during the base learner training procedure. To test the proposed method on CMU-PIE, 612 images are considered (68 subjects, 9 images per subject). On the other hand, 3237 images are employed for testing on Multi-PIE (249 subjects, 13 images per subject). The proposed method is implemented in Python 3 language on an Arch Linux PC with an Intel®Core i5-10500 CPU and 8.00 GB of RAM. Face detection in this work utilizes the Google MediaPipe model, while the implementation of [4] is utilized for facial landmark detection.

Table 1. Performance for face verification and identification on the CMU-PIE, and Multi-PIE databases

Database	Base learner	1:1 Verification TAR@FAR FAR			1:N Identification		
		10^{-3}	10^{-2}	10^{-1}	Rank-1	Rank-5	Rank-10
CMU-PIE	GMM	0.717	0.857	0.933	0.995	0.998	1.00
	MS	0.859	0.937	0.986	1.00	1.00	1.00
Multi-PIE	GMM	0.488	0.615	0.792	0.713	0.819	0.859
	MS	0.646	0.786	0.910	0.962	0.988	0.991

3.2 Performance Evaluation

As mentioned above, a head pose classification method, with $N_p = 5$ possible pose classes, is developed. A total of 13 images from 40 subjects of the Multi-PIE database are used during the training stage (16% of the images from Multi-PIE employed in this work). The performance of this classifier is assessed according to its multiclass confusion matrix. Its overall accuracy is 0.988, while the average of its F-1 scores is 0.986. Several current works on face recognition using the CMU-PIE, and MultiPIE databases evidence their experimental results in terms of the face recognition rate (also known as Rank-1 accuracy). We conduct additional experiments on face verification and identification.

The TAR@FAR metric is used to measure the performance on face verification, while the Rank-N accuracy is employed for face identification [1].

The results of these experiments are summarized in Table 1, evidencing the superiority of using the Mahalanobis Similarity (MS) model, proposed in this work, over GMM as the base learner model. To better visualize the advantage of using MS for face recognition over GMM, their Cumulative Matching Characteristic (CMC) curves are shown in Fig. 5 for both databases. As can be seen in Fig. 5a, GMM shows to achieve good results in a small-scale face database (less than 100 subjects) like CMU-PIE. However, Fig. 5b put in evidence that the performance of using GMM in large-scale databases like Multi-PIE (more than 200 subject) are rather poor, whereas MS shows a satisfactory performance.

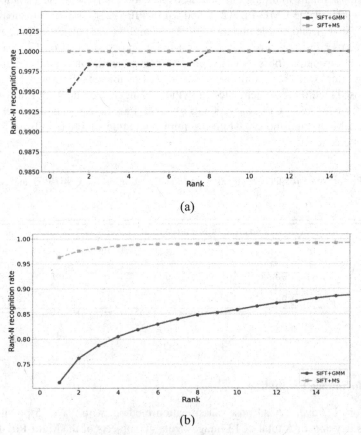

(a)

(b)

Fig. 5. Cumulative Matching Characteristic (CMC) curves of the proposed methods: (a) On CMU-PIE database; (b) On Multi-PIE database.

Additionally, a detailed performance comparison with other state-of-the-art (SOTA) methods on the CMU-PIE, and Multi-PIE databases are shown in Table 2 and Table 3 respectively. As can be seen, a recognition rate of 100% is obtained for every yaw pose angle considered in the CMU-PIE database, by using MS with SIFT. Thus, several state-of-the-art works on CMU-PIE are outperformed. The results of using GMM as the base learner model yields a slightly inferior performance on the CMU-PIE database. Indeed, the Rank-1 accuracy results obtained in CMU-PIE with both GMM and MS are quite similar for every pose angle (see Fig. 6a). In the case of Multi-PIE, there is a significant accuracy drop on the images with angles ±60°, ±75° (see Fig. 6b). This phenomenon, is attributed to head pose misclassifications (e.g. the proposed head pose classification model considers a pose 3 image as a pose 2 image, utilizing less base learners for performing PIFR), and the fact that ±90° images are included in the set of

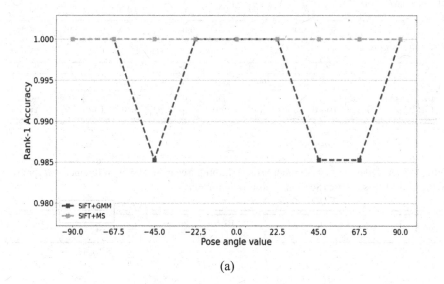

(a)

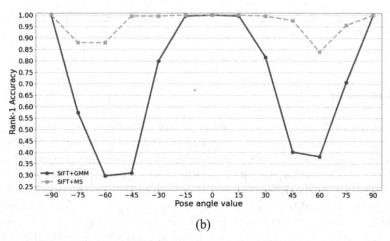

(b)

Fig. 6. Rank-1 accuracy obtained with the proposed methods for different pose values: (a) On CMU-PIE database; (b) On Multi-PIE database.

gallery images. However, as shown in Table 3, the performance of the proposed method surpasses other state-of-the-art works on Multi-PIE for any pose angle, when MS is employed as the base learner model.

Table 2. Detailed performance comparison of the proposed method with SOTA methods for PIFR on the CMU-PIE database

Method	Recognition rate(%)									
	-90°	-67.5^o	-45°	-22.5^o	0°	22.5^o	45°	67.5^o	90°	Overall
Face frontalization + Facial features [23]	-	-	95.60	100.0	100.0	100.0	100.0	-	-	99.3
FLM+PFER-GEM [24]	88.70	100.0	100.0	100.0	100.0	100.0	100.0	98.38	91.90	98.24
Face frontalization + LGBP [5]	-	-	91.2	98.5	100.0	100.0	98.5	-	-	97.05
PBPR-MtFL [3]	100.0	100.0	100.0	100.0	100.0	100.0	100.0	100.0	98.53	99.84
Divide-and-rule + LBP-Huffman [25][†]	-	-	100.0	100.0	100.0	100.0	100.0	-	-	100.0
MoE GMM + SIFT	100.0	100.0	98.53	100.0	100.0	100.0	98.53	98.53	100.0	99.51
MoE MS + SIFT	**100.0**	**100.0**	**100.0**	**100.0**	**100.0**	**100.0**	**100.0**	**100.0**	**100.0**	**100.0**

Table 3. Detailed performance comparison of the proposed method with SOTA methods for PIFR on the Multi-PIE database (Session 1, pose variation only)

Method	Recognition rate(%)													
	-90°	-75°	-60°	-45°	-30°	-15°	0°	15°	30°	45°	60°	75°	90°	Overall
SFC-GAN [26]	-	-	-	-	-	-	98.7	97.7	96.3	91.0	85.8	78.4	62.4	-
Stacked OPR [27]	-	-	-	86.0	95.0	96.7	98.2	97.3	96.7	90.7	-	-	-	94.4
MoE GMM+ SIFT	100	57.4	29.7	30.9	79.9	99.6	100	99.6	81.5	40.2	38.2	70.7	100	71.3
MoE MS + SIFT	**100**	**88.0**	**88.0**	**99.6**	**99.6**	**100**	**100**	**100**	**99.6**	**97.6**	**83.9**	**95.6**	**100**	**96.3**

4 Conclusion

The presented work addressed the problem of face recognition under pose variations (pose-invariant face recognition) by combining the ability of local feature descriptors in representing facial information at specific face regions (facial landmarks), and the power of Mixture-of-Experts (MoE) systems in combining several weak classifiers (base learners) to achieve a high recognition accuracy. In order to perform face recognition, an input face image is processed to detect its facial landmark locations. Then, these landmark locations are processed to compute its Face Angle Vector. This vector is further used to classify the face image according to its pose by employing the proposed Head Pose Classification technique. According to its pose class, facial landmarks are selected and feature extraction is performed on them. The feature vectors are input to their corresponding base learners, and the ensemble decision is computed from the base learners' outputs. Finally, the face identity is computed by choosing the MoE system whose ensemble decision support is the highest. We tested our face recognition framework on the CMU-PIE, and Multi-PIE databases (verification and identification). The results showed that the use of MS as base learner achieved a face recognition rate of 100% on any head pose of CMU-PIE. While a recognition rate higher than 90% is obtained on most of the poses on Multi-PIE, surpassing the results of other state-of-the-art works. On the other hand, the results obtained with GMM on Multi-PIE showed a poor performance, indicating that GMM might not be a suitable base learner model to be used in large scale face databases (Multi-PIE is much larger than CMU-PIE). Finally, it is worth mentioning that, even though the proposed MoE framework has demonstrated a remarkable performance on the mentioned face databases, it requires 3 gallery images per person to achieve a high recognition rate. Furthermore, only images with yaw pose variation were employed in this work. Thus, the presented framework can be further improved in future works to reduce the gallery size to 1 image per person, and attain a good performance under any type of variation in the head pose angles (yaw, pitch, roll).

References

1. Cheng, Z., Zhu, X., Gong, S.: Surveillance face recognition challenge. arXiv (2018)
2. Taskiran, M., Kahraman, N., Erdem, C.E.: Face recognition: past, present and future (a review). Digital Signal Processing **106** (2020)
3. Ding, C., Xu, C., Tao, D.: Multi-task pose-invariant face recognition. IEEE Trans. Image Process. **24**(3), 980–993 (2015)
4. Bulat, A., Tzimiropoulos, G.: How far are we from solving the 2d & 3d face alignment problem? (and a dataset of 230,000 3d facial landmarks). In: International Conference on Computer Vision (2017)
5. Petpairote, C., Madarasmi, S., Chamnongthai, K.: 2d pose-invariant face recognition using single frontal-view face database. Wireless Pers. Commun. **118**(3), 2015–2031 (2021)
6. Sarsenov, A., Latuta, K.: Face recognition based on facial landmarks. In: 2017 IEEE 11th International Conference on Application of Information and Communication Technologies (AICT), pp. 1–5 (2017)
7. Khan, K., Khan, R.U., Leonardi, R., Migliorati, P., Benini, S.: Head pose estimation: a survey of the last ten years. Signal Processing: Image Communication **99** (2021)
8. Bisogni, C., Nappi, M., Pero, C., Ricciardi, S.: PIFS scheme for head pose estimation aimed at faster face recognition. IEEE Trans. Biometr. Behav. Identity Sci. **4**(2), 173–184 (2022)
9. An, Z., Deng, W., Hu, J., Zhong, Y., Zhao, Y.: Apa: Adaptive pose alignment for pose-invariant face recognition. IEEE Access **7**, 14653–14670 (2019)
10. Schroff, F., Kalenichenko, D., Philbin, J.: Facenet: a unified embedding for face recognition and clustering. In: 2015 IEEE Conference on Computer Vision and Pattern Recognition (CVPR), pp. 815–823 (2015)
11. Wang, H., et al.: Cosface: Large margin cosine loss for deep face recognition. In: 2018 IEEE/CVF Conference on Computer Vision and Pattern Recognition, pp. 5265–5274 (2018)
12. Deng, J., Guo, J., Yang, J., Xue, N., Kotsia, I., Zafeiriou, S.: Arcface: Additive angular margin loss for deep face recognition. IEEE Trans. Pattern Anal. Mach. Intell. **44**(10), 5962–5979 (2022)
13. Lin, S.D., Linares Otoya, P.E.: Pose-invariant face recognition via facial landmark based ensemble learning. IEEE Access **11**, 44221–44233 (2023)

14. Feng, Y., An, X., Li, S.: Research on face recognition based on ensemble learning. In: 2018 37th Chinese Control Conference (CCC), pp. 9078–9082 (2018)
15. Zhang, Z., Wang, L., Zhu, Q., Chen, S.K., Chen, Y.: Pose-invariant face recognition using facial landmarks and weber local descriptor. Knowl. Based Syst. **84**, 78–88 (2015)
16. Lin, S.D., Linares, P.: Large pose detection and facial landmark description for pose-invariant face recognition. In: 2022 IEEE 5th International Conference on Knowledge Innovation and Invention (ICKII), pp. 143–148 (2022)
17. Guo, G., Fu, Y., Dyer, C.R., Huang, T.S.: Head pose estimation: classification or regression? In: 2008 19th International Conference on Pattern Recognition, pp. 1–4 (2008)
18. Kim, S.Y., Spurlock, S., Souvenir, R.: Head pose estimation using learned discretization. In: 2017 IEEE International Conference on Image Processing (ICIP), pp. 2687–2691 (2017)
19. Polikar, R.: Ensemble based systems in decision making. IEEE Circuits Syst. Mag. **6**, 21–45 (2006)
20. Kuncheva, L.I.: Combining Pattern Classifiers: Methods and Algorithms, 2nd edn., chap. 3. Wiley (2014)
21. Sim, T., Baker, S., Bsat, M.: The cmu pose, illumination, and expression database. IEEE Trans. Pattern Anal. Mach. Intell. **25**(12), 1615–1618 (2003)
22. Gross, R., Matthews, I., Cohn, J., Kanade, T., Baker, S.: Multi-pie. In: 2008 8th IEEE International Conference on Automatic Face & Gesture Recognition, pp. 1–8 (2008)
23. Mostafa, E.A., Farag, A.A.: Dynamic weighting of facial features for automatic pose-invariant face recognition. In: 2012 Ninth Conference on Computer and Robot Vision, pp. 411–416 (2012)
24. Moeini, A., Moeini, H.: Real-world and rapid face recognition toward pose and expression variations via feature library matrix. IEEE Trans. Inf. Forensics Secur. **10**(5), 969–984 (2015)
25. Zhou, L.F., Du, Y.W., Li, W.S., Mi, J.X., Luan, X.: Pose-robust face recognition with huffman-lbp enhanced by divide-and-rule strategy. Pattern Recogn. **78**, 43–55 (2018)
26. Lin, H., Ma, H., Gong, W., Wang, C.: Non-frontal face recognition method with a side-face-correction generative adversarial networks. In: 2022 3rd International Conference on Computer Vision, Image and Deep Learning & International Conference on Computer Engineering and Applications (CVIDL & ICCEA), pp. 563–567 (2022)
27. Tai, Y., Yang, J., Zhang, Y., Luo, L., Qian, J., Chen, Y.: Face recognition with pose variations and misalignment via orthogonal procrustes regression. IEEE Trans. Image Process. **25**(6), 2673–2683 (2016)

Context Enhanced Recurrent Neural Network for Session-Aware Recommendation

Sue-Chen Hsueh[1], Min-Shan Shih[2], and Ming-Yen Lin[2(✉)]

[1] Department of Information Management, Chaoyang University of Technology, Taichung, Taiwan
[2] Department of Information Engineering and Computer Science, Feng Chia University, Taichung, Taiwan
linmy@mail.fcu.edu.tw

Abstract. Recommender systems, which suggest items that users might find most interesting based on their previous web-clicks or purchased items, have a wide range of applications. While recent methods employing recurrent neural networks, such as session-based, session-aware, and context-aware recommendations, have achieved impressive results, there remains potential for further enhancements. In this study, we introduce a two-layered Gated Recurrent Unit (GRU) architecture augmented with context through the integration of an Attention Mechanism, termed CAII (Context-Aware II). CAII employs Context-Aware Modeling and Attentive Session Modeling to predict the items users are most likely to be interested in. The performance of CAII is assessed using the Amazon EC dataset, which includes context information like prices and images. Evaluated based on Recall and Mean Reciprocal Rank (MRR), CAII not only surpasses traditional methods such as Most-Popular and Item-k-Nearest Neighbor (Item-kNN), but also outperforms established models like GRU4Rec and Multi-View Recurrent Neural Network (MVRNN). Compared to the advanced recommendation method Weighted II-RNN, CAII shows an improvement of 0.6% for Recall@20 and 1.19% for MRR@20. Interestingly, the highest Recall was observed when CAII was enhanced solely with price context. However, when both price and image contexts were incorporated, CAII achieved the best MRR. These results demonstrate the efficacy of CAII in enhancing recommender systems.

Keywords: Session-aware Recommendation · Recurrent Neural Network · Context-aware Recommendation · Attention Mechanism

1 Introduction

With technological advancements, the volume of information has expanded exponentially. In this age of information proliferation, vast amounts of data can be collected and analyzed from users' website browsing histories. In recent years, popular website categories have included e-commerce, service platforms, music video streaming, and news sites. Presenting users with an overwhelming amount of unfiltered product information can deter their attention and hinder desired outcomes. However, the integration of Recommender Systems with data analysis technology offers a solution.

© The Author(s), under exclusive license to Springer Nature Singapore Pte Ltd. 2024
C.-Y. Lee et al. (Eds.): TAAI 2023, CCIS 2075, pp. 53–67, 2024.
https://doi.org/10.1007/978-981-97-1714-9_5

Traditional recommendation systems typically rely on user preferences, item ratings, or implicit feedback obtained from item clicks. For instance, the Item-K-Nearest Neighbor (Item-kNN) [8] primarily considers users' most recent clicks. This approach can mistakenly predict products that users clicked out of curiosity or by accident, leading to inaccurate recommendations. Moreover, Collaborative Filtering (CF) [17] does not account for the sequence of user clicks or the relationships between clicked products. For example, after purchasing an iPhone, users often buy complementary items like cases and protective stickers, but CF systems fail to recognize these patterns. Capturing correlations and sequences in user click patterns can enhance recommendation accuracy.

Machine learning has seen numerous successes in areas like image recognition, voice recognition, and language processing. Combining machine learning with Recurrent Neural Networks (RNN) has shown potential in enhancing traditional recommendation methods, making it a focal point in recommendation system research. To address the limitations of traditional systems, RNNs have been incorporated into session-based recommendations [5], analyzing users' current session click records to make subsequent recommendations. The pioneering application by B. Hidasi et al. [5], which integrated RNNs with session-based recommendation systems, demonstrated a significant improvement of 15% to 30% over the Item-kNN [8], underscoring the benefits of neural network-based methods.

While neural-based methods have shown promise in session-based recommendation systems, they predominantly focus on the most recent interactive session, neglecting prior sessions. This oversight results in the loss of valuable historical data at the onset of a new session. To address this, Session-aware Recommendations were introduced [6, 12], enabling analysis of all past and present sessions. This approach mitigates the issue of limited historical data. However, it often overlooks the context of current item interactions. For instance, during shopping, users might consider factors like item appearance or price. By referencing content information and aligning it with users' long-term preferences, recommendation quality can be enhanced.

Given that recommendation systems often lack user profiles, extracting valuable insights from existing click data has emerged as a new research direction. The Context-aware recommendation approach was proposed [9], focusing on content information and item features. This method aids recommendations by analyzing items with similar features, such as detailed descriptions or images. However, Context-aware Recommendations do not consider the sequence of user clicks, making it challenging to discern users' short-term or long-term interests, potentially leading to inaccurate suggestions.

Recommendation systems typically use long-term historical click records for suggestions. However, if a user's click history is extensive, the model might neglect older data, focusing only on recent interactions. If crucial information from earlier records is overlooked, the system's recommendations may fall short. To address these challenges, the Attention mechanism [19] was introduced. By analyzing users' extensive click histories, the system can make predictions based on the status of all clicked items. The Attention mechanism adjusts focus across items, calculating each item's relevance to the most recent click. After assigning weights to each item, it produces optimized recommendations.

This research introduces a two-layered Gated Recurrent Unit (GRU) recommendation system. The first GRU layer captures the current session's hidden state as a session representation. Concurrently, item-provided context information is processed by the Attention mechanism to obtain a second session representation, emphasizing crucial items. These two representations are weighted and integrated, then passed to the second GRU layer for intensive training. This enriched training session then feeds into the first GRU layer, aiming to enhance subsequent session information. This iterative process seeks to address initial session prediction challenges and product feature considerations, ultimately refining item scoring.

Experimental analysis using Amazon's e-commerce dataset was conducted to test and compare the proposed method against other recommendation system models. The results indicate that the proposed approach delivers superior recommendation performance.

2   Related Work

Traditional recommendation systems leverage a user's browsing history to construct a detailed user profile, reflecting their preferences. Historically, these systems primarily recommended popular items. Over time, they evolved to recommend based on similarities between items or sessions.

Several prevalent similarity-based recommendation methods exist, including Collaborative Filtering (CF) [8, 17], Matrix Factorization (MF) [10, 11], Markov Chain (MC) [4, 18, 20], and Factorizing Personalized Markov Chains (FPMC) [15]. Among these, the simplest approach is the Most-Popular (POP) method. POP bases its recommendations on the aggregate number of clicks from all users, typically suggesting the most-clicked products to users.

The pioneering recommendation system that utilized the neural network approach is GRU4Rec [5]. B. Hidasi, A. Karatzoglou, and two other researchers introduced this method in 2016, marking the first application of RNN to session-based recommendation systems. Given the chronological nature of session data, it was modeled using RNN. Experimental results demonstrated that RNN outperformed traditional recommendation systems, solidifying RNN's role in recommendation methodologies.

In 2017, B. Hidasi and colleagues introduced a novel ranking loss function to enhance RNN's performance [7]. The results indicated that the Mean Reciprocal Rank and Recall@20 metrics improved by 35% compared to GRU4Rec and even surpassed traditional collaborative filtering methods by 53%. Thus, this new ranking loss function significantly boosts the recommendation efficacy of RNN. Aiming to enable RNN to more effectively utilize item feature information, B. Hidasi and colleagues introduced a novel training framework and strategy alongside RNN, termed Parallel RNN (P-RNN) [6]. This model was informed by user-click behavior patterns and the item's feature information. B. Hidasi and his team also introduced the Hierarchical RNN (H-RNN) [13], designed to integrate the current session with prior training sessions. Experimental results indicated that the Hierarchical RNN significantly outperformed standalone RNN methods.

Also in 2017, M. Ruocco and associates proposed the Inter-Intra RNN (II-RNN) model, further divided into II-RNN-LHS and II-RNN-AP [16]. While II-RNN-LHS captures the temporal characteristics of a session, II-RNN-AP focuses on averaging session features, iterating them to ensure that past session click behaviors influence future click predictions. However, this model primarily analyzes a single session state, neglecting both temporal and average characteristics of the current session.

P. Y. Chen [2] then enhanced the model initially developed by M. Ruocco et al. [16], resulting in the Weighted II-RNN [2]. Unlike the original II-RNN [16], this improved model evaluates both the average and temporal characteristics of a session. These two features are then integrated into a new session feature representation, each assigned different weights, prior to making recommendations. Experimental results demonstrated that a holistic analysis of item features yields superior performance compared to evaluating individual characteristics.

In 2016, Q. Liu, S. Wu, and their team introduced the CA-RNN (Context-aware Recurrent Neural Network) [9]. Contextual information, in this context, pertains to data present when users interact with an item. This includes external factors like time and weather, as well as internal factors such as the item icon and its description. Over the years, it has been established that such contextual information can significantly influence models. Consequently, adapting model operations to harness this rich contextual data became the primary objective of their study.

In 2019, L. Rakkappan and V. Rajan suggested a model that concurrently captures both a user's sequential interactions and their context interactions for recommendation systems [14]. Their Context-Aware Sequential Recommendation for Stacked Recurrent Neural Networks is designed to simultaneously account for dynamic context interactions and temporal patterns.

By 2020, Q. Cui, S. Wu, and colleagues presented the MV-RNN (A Multi-View Recurrent Neural Network for Sequential Recommendation) [3]. Their research highlighted improvements in addressing the cold start problem. They demonstrated that leveraging additional information as features can enhance recommendation efficiency, especially when more current data is available.

In 2020, W. Yuan, H. Wang, and their team introduced the RNN-based ACA-GRU (Attention-based Context-Aware sequential recommendation) approach [19]. This method integrates various types of contextual information and incorporates an Attention mechanism specifically tailored for sequence recommendations. Given that each item's contribution to predictions can vary due to time-dependent factors, this approach bases its predictions on the relationships between adjacent items and the evolution of the sequence. By minimizing or even disregarding the impact of outliers, the ACA-GRU enhances the efficacy of the recommendation system.

From the literature reviewed, it's evident that the session-aware recommendation captures a user's long-term interests. Concurrently, by considering both the similarity and sequence between items, more accurate recommendation results are achieved. The attention mechanism plays a pivotal role in discerning the significance of each item to the user, thereby enhancing the model's efficiency.

Given the findings from existing recommendation method research, experimental results indicate potential enhancements when applying the current research framework to e-commerce applications. Consequently, this study introduces a framework that integrates Context-aware recommendation with the attention mechanism, aiming to substantially boost the recommendation performance for e-commerce datasets.

3 The Proposed Method

3.1 Problem Definition

This section provides definitions and interpretations of symbols used in this study. Within the recommendation system:

- $U = \{H_1, H_2, \ldots, H_n\}$ represents the set of all users, totaling n users.
- Each user u possesses a historical click record $H = \{S_1, S_2, \ldots, S_t\}$ of length $|S_t|$. This interactive session is based on the user's click time t.
- Each session S_t consists of $|i_v^t|$ items, represented as $S_t = \{i_1^t, i_2^t, \ldots, i_v^t\}$, where i_v^t denotes the v-th item clicked in session S_t at time t. Within the model, the embedding representation for each i_v^t is denoted as $R_{i_v^t}$.
- The set of all items, comprising $|i_m|$ distinct items, is given by $I = \{i_1, i_2, \ldots, i_m\}$.
- The corresponding price set for all items, containing $|p_m|$ unique prices, is represented as $P = \{p_1, p_2, \ldots, p_m\}$.
- The image set for all items, with $|im_m|$ distinct images, is expressed as $IM = \{im_1, im_2, \ldots, im_m\}$.

While recommendation systems can be applied across various domains, such as news articles on news websites or songs on music platforms, this research primarily focuses on products within e-commerce platforms. Henceforth, clicks within a session will be referred to as 'items'.

The primary objective of the recommendation model is to train on and predict based on a user's most recent interactions. The model takes into account all click sessions to forecast the next item i_{v+1}^t a user might click. The aim is to achieve high prediction accuracy for i_{v+1}^t.

3.2 Architecture

The framework of this study is depicted in Fig. 1. The primary structure is segmented into three components: Context-Aware Modeling, Attentive Session Modeling, and Prediction. The session S_t from a user's website browsing history H serves as the model input. The Context-Aware Modeling aims to train the user's last hidden state of the session R_t and predict the subsequent click.

The Attentive Session Modeling's objective is to incorporate contextual information into the attention mechanism model, thereby capturing pivotal information. Initially, the weighted session representation is computed as W_{ATT} and W_{LHS}, yielding a comprehensive representation of the current session ($\{r_1, r_2, \ldots, r_t\}$). Subsequently, this representation is passed to GRU_2 for performance-enhancing training, after which it is relayed back to the Context-Aware Modeling to predict the next session's clicks. Ultimately, the Prediction component calculates scores for all items, sorting them to produce the recommended item lists.

Notably, the output prediction score from the Attentive Session Modeling is faster than that of the Context-Aware Modeling. This speed advantage compensates for the general limitation in session-based recommendations, where recommendations might not be readily available at the session's onset.

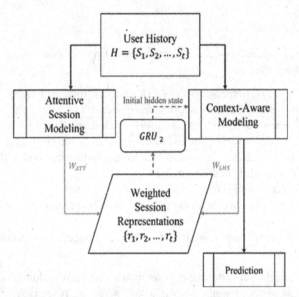

Fig. 1. Framework of the proposed CAII (Context-Aware II) method

3.3 Context-Aware Modeling

The Context-Aware Modeling is illustrated in Fig. 2. Initially, the "User Session" session $S_t = \{i_1^t, i_2^t, \ldots, i_v^t\}$ is taken as input. The first click, i_1^t, undergoes Embedding to yield its embedded representation $R_{i_1^t}$. This Embedding process employs the Item2Vec method [1]. Subsequently, the representation is fed into GRU_1 to determine the current hidden state corresponding to the i_v^t click. This process continues iteratively until the final hidden state associated with the i_v^t click is discerned. The primary objective here is to capture the temporal characteristics of the session and to extract the session's final hidden state, R_t.

The Context-Aware Modeling then forwards R_t to the Attentive Session Modeling. Here, it undergoes a weighting calculation with the Attentive Session characteristics ATT_t, producing a comprehensive session representation r_t. This representation is then input into GRU_2 within the Attentive Session Modeling for the initial hidden state computation.

Upon completion of the Attentive Session Modeling operations, the initial hidden state set $(\{r_{t-(m-1)}, r_{t-(m-2)}, \ldots, r_{t-1}, r_t\})$ is relayed back to the Context-Aware Modeling. This set serves as a reference for past preferences for the upcoming session. Ultimately, GRU_1 within the Context-Aware Modeling incorporates a dropout mechanism for training and predicting the current session's clicks.

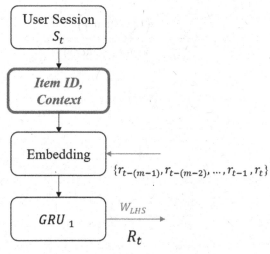

Fig. 2. Context-Aware Modeling

3.4 Attentive Session Modeling

The Attentive Session Modeling is depicted in Fig. 3. The input focuses solely on the contextual information of the item. Initially, the "User Session" session S_t is taken as input. After processing through the attention mechanism, the ATTentive session characteristics ATT_t are derived. The Attention mechanism is described by Formula (2). By considering the weight distribution of each item relative to the final target item, irrelevant information is suppressed or all clicked items are analyzed, thereby reducing potential model inaccuracies.

Subsequently, the results are passed through Embedding and the Weighted Session Representations for computation. The Attentive Session characteristics and the session's last hidden state are proportionally combined with W_{ATT} and W_{LHS}, as shown in Formula (1) $r_t = R_t * W_{LHS} + ATT_t * W_{ATT}$. By adjusting the proportions of the session's last hidden state W_{LHS} and the Attentive Session characteristics W_{ATT}, a comprehensive session representation r_t is derived. This representation encapsulates both the temporal nature of the user's session clicks and the attention characteristics during the clicking process.

The composite sessions $\{r_{t-(m-1)}, r_{t-(m-2)}, \ldots, r_{t-1}, r_t\}$ serve as inputs to GRU_2 within the Attentive Session Modeling. Assuming the latest session is r_t and m designates the temporal point indicating how many sessions to consider, if the current time point is t = 6 and m = 3, then the inputs are ($\{r_3, r_4, r_5\}$).

The primary objective of GRU_2 within the Attentive Session Modeling is to bolster efficiency. It ultimately produces the Initial hidden state, which is then relayed back to the Context-Aware Modeling for further modeling and click list L prediction. Re-initializing the hidden state ensures that previous operation results introduce no interference.

$$r_t = R_t * W_{LHS} + ATT_t * W_{ATT} \tag{1}$$

$$\alpha_{item} = \frac{exp\left(f\left(\hat{h}_t, \text{item}\right)\right)}{\sum_{l=1}^{|S_2|-1} exp\left(f\left(\hat{h}_t, \text{item}\right)\right)} \tag{2}$$

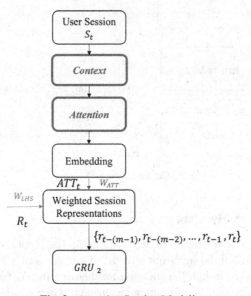

Fig. 3. Attentive Session Modeling

Fig. 4. Prediction

3.5 Prediction

Prediction results for each click item in the current session are derived from the Context-Aware Modeling. These results are then mapped back to the original item dimension using a Feedforward mechanism. The Item Score produces a score for each item, which is subsequently used for ranking and generating predictions.

The method employed for selecting and ranking recommended items involves identifying the top k items based on their scores (Score Ranking) within the current session. These items are then ranked according to the predefined k value in the evaluation method. The outcome of this ranking process yields the Recommendation Item List L tailored for the user, as illustrated in Fig. 4.

3.6   Three Types of Enhanced CAII Models

The first model, termed CAII-Price (CAII-P), focuses exclusively on analyzing the item ID and its associated price within the contextual information. Within the Attentive Session Modeling, the output characteristics of the Attention mechanism are denoted as $PATT_t$, and the associated weight multiplier is labeled W_{PATT}. The weighted session is formulated using Formula (3) as $r_t = R_t * W_{LHS} + PATT_t * W_{PATT}$, as illustrated in Fig. 5. The subsequent modeling process aligns with the overarching operations of CAII.

The second model, termed CAII-Image (CAII-I), focuses on analyzing the item ID and its associated images within the contextual information. Within the Attentive Session Modeling, the output characteristics of the Attention mechanism are denoted as $IMATT_t$, and the associated weight multiplier is labeled W_{IMATT}. The weighted session is formulated using Formula (4) as $r_t = R_t * W_{LHS} + IMATT_t * W_{IMATT}$, as illustrated in Fig. 6.

It's worth noting that the Context-Aware Modeling does not incorporate contextual information. This exclusion is due to the fact that image information is missing in 99% of the overall data. Incorporating images into the temporal characteristics would compromise overall accuracy, leading to the decision to omit contextual information from the Context-Aware Modeling.

The third model is termed CAII-PriceImage (CAII-PI). It analyzes the item ID, with the contextual information encompassing both price and image. The weighted session is formulated using Formula (5) as $r_t = R_t * W_{LHS} + PATT_t * W_{PATT} + IMATT_t * W_{IMATT}$, as depicted in Fig. 7.

$$r_t = R_t * W_{LHS} + PATT_t * W_{PATT} \tag{3}$$

$$r_t = R_t * W_{LHS} + IMATT_t * W_{IMATT} \tag{4}$$

$$r_t = R_t * W_{LHS} + PATT_t * W_{PATT} + IMATT_t * W_{IMATT} \tag{5}$$

Similar to CAII-I, the CAII-PI's Context-Aware Modeling does not incorporate image information. Consequently, within the Context-Aware Modeling, only the price is considered as the contextual information.

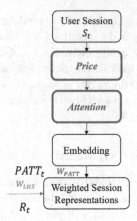

Fig. 5. Attentive Session Modeling in CAII-P

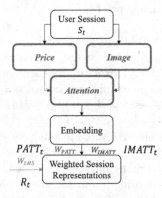

Fig. 6. Attentive Session Modeling in CAII-I

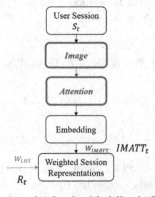

Fig. 7. Attentive Session Modeling in CAII-PI

4 Experimental Results

4.1 Dataset and Platform

The experiments utilize a test dataset from Amazon, spanning from 2012 to 2014 [21]. This dataset encompasses timestamps of user clicks on items, shopping basket details, and adheres to a data threshold of 5 cores. Ultimately, it comprises 402,093 customers, 140,116 distinct items, and 770,290 sessions. Given that the finest granularity of time provided in the Amazon dataset is in days, all clicks within the experiment are consolidated into a single session.

The experimental setup operates on a Windows 10 64-bit platform. The machine learning components, specifically the neural network aspects, are implemented using Python 3.6.12 in conjunction with TensorFlow. The system is powered by an AMD Ryzen 5 2400G processor clocked at 3.6 GHz, complemented by 56 GB of RAM. For graphical processing, it employs an NVIDIA GeForce RTX 2080 Ti TURBO GPU, equipped with 11 GB of VRAM.

4.2 Data Preprocessing

The Amazon dataset is multifaceted. Initially, a new format is created that ranks orders, encompassing user purchase sequences, purchased items, item prices, and item images. Subsequently, entries corresponding to individual users and sessions are removed. Specifically, sessions where a user clicked on an item only once are deleted, as are data entries with fewer than three items in a user's browsing session. The session length is standardized to a multiple of 20. Following this, missing values and supplementary values for item prices and images are addressed.

For the pricing component, items with significant price disparities have their prices averaged to determine a singular price. If an item lacks price information, the average price of all items is calculated, using 49 as the numerator and the frequency of user purchases for that item as the denominator. The resulting quotient serves as the supplementary value for the product price. All prices are then normalized.

Image preprocessing involves applying a Gaussian blur to each image, followed by dimensionality reduction using Principal Component Analysis (PCA). For missing image data, three distinct methods are employed based on session context and other factors:

1. Replace the missing image with the preceding item's image.
2. If the missing image corresponds to the first clicked product, use the subsequent item's image as a replacement.
3. If an entire session lacks image data, randomly select an item's image from the current session as a placeholder.

The preprocessed dataset then comprises 9,733 customers, 46,958 distinct items, and 735,048 sessions. After the aforementioned preprocessing steps, the Amazon dataset is partitioned such that the initial 80% serves as the training set, with the remaining 20% designated as the test set.

4.3 Evaluation Metrics and Parameter Settings

In this study, the evaluation metrics employed are Recall and Mean Reciprocal Rank (MRR). For both metrics, a higher score indicates superior recommendation results. Evaluation is conducted using k values of 5, 10, and 20.

The model parameters are set as follows:

- Dropout rate for the GRU: 0.8
- Learning rate: 0.001
- Maximum session length: 20
- Number of GRU layers in the overall system architecture: 1
- Window size in GRU_1: 16 x 20
- Window size in GRU_2: 16 x 1
- Weights W_{LHS} and W_{PATT} in CAII-P: 0.8 and 0.2, respectively
- Weights W_{LHS} and W_{IMATT} in CAII-I: 0.9 and 0.1, respectively
- Weights W_{LHS}, W_{PATT}, and W_{IMATT} in CAII-PI: 0.7, 0.2, and 0.1, respectively
- Batch Size: 16
- Number of prior reference sessions: 14
- Number of hidden layers: 300
- Epochs: 20

4.4 Baseline Models for Comparisons

The subsequent analysis compares various recommendation methods. The optimal model parameter settings for each method, as proposed in their respective papers, are applied to the dataset used in this study to obtain final recommendation results. The baseline methods compared are:

1. Most Popular (POP): This is one of the simplest traditional recommendation methods. It recommends the most popular items on e-commerce platforms.
2. Item-k-Nearest Neighbor (Item-kNN) [8]: This method defines similarity as the cosine similarity between session vectors. It recommends k items that bear the most resemblance to the actual items.
3. GRU4Rec [5]: This was the pioneering model to incorporate RNN into the recommendation system. Besides considering the temporality of clicks, it also serves as a foundational method for comparison.
4. Weighted II-RNN [2]: This method takes into account both the user's final session characteristics and average characteristics. Its architecture is similar, making it apt for comparison.
5. MV-RNN [3]: This method factors in the contextual information present when a user clicks. Apart from its similarity to the dataset of this research, it also considers comparable contextual information for evaluation.

The comparative results are presented in Table 1. Notably, the Weighted II-RNN emerges as the superior evaluation method among the baselines. This prominence might be attributed to its comprehensive analysis of user interests spanning from past to present, setting it apart from other methods in the comparison.

However, when juxtaposing the Weighted II-RNN with the CAII-P model proposed in this study, the latter demonstrates superior performance in both Recall and MRR metrics. This underscores the significance of incorporating contextual information in the model. Utilizing the Attention mechanism to sift through relevant information and assist the model proves to be invaluable. Effectively balancing the two weights to derive a new representation for recommendations is pivotal. With respect to CAII-P, the optimal values for W_{LHS} and W_{PATT} are 0.8 and 0.2, respectively, when considering Recall. Conversely, for MRR, the most significant results are observed when W_{LHS} and W_{PATT} are set to 0.7 and 0.3, respectively.

Table 1. Comparisons with Baseline Models.

Methods	Recall			MRR		
	@5	@10	@20	@5	@10	@20
Most-Popular	0.0041	0.0075	0.0151	0.0022	0.0025	0.0031
Item-kNN	0.2172	0.2239	0.2261	0.1796	0.1804	0.1806
GRU4Rec	0.0816	0.0816	0.0818	0.0737	0.0737	0.0737
Weighted II-RNN	0.2298	0.2332	0.2358	0.21	0.2105	0.2107
MV-RNN	-	-	0.0224	-	-	0.0115
CAII-P	0.2306	0.2346	0.2373	0.2106	0.2111	0.2113

Table 2. Comparisons with Recent Models.

Methods	Recall			MRR		
	@5	@10	@20	@5	@10	@20
Most-Popular	0.0041	0.0075	0.0151	0.0022	0.0025	0.0031
Item-kNN	0.2172	0.2239	0.2261	0.1796	0.1804	0.1806
GRU4Rec	0.0816	0.0816	0.0818	0.0737	0.0737	0.0737
Weighted II-RNN	0.2298	0.2332	0.2358	0.21	0.2105	0.2107
MV-RNN	-	-	0.0224	-	-	0.0115
CAII-P	0.2306	0.2346	0.2373	0.2106	0.2111	0.2113

4.5 Recent Models for Comparisons

In the subsequent analysis, the outcomes derived from various contextual information characteristics were juxtaposed against recommendation system methodologies and feature techniques, as delineated in Table 2.

The methodologies evaluated in this study encompassed II-RNN, CAII-P, CAII-I, and CAII-PI. Observations from the experimental data revealed that CAII-P exhibited superior performance in terms of Recall. Conversely, upon the integration of imagery into CAII-PI, the MRR metric surpassed all other methods.

Consequently, based on the MRR evaluation criterion, it can be inferred that for recommendation systems aiming to precisely predict user click-through item rankings, the efficacy of the CAII-PI model stands out as a commendable recommendation approach.

5 Conclusions

This study introduces a recommendation methodology that synergistically integrates context-aware and session-aware approaches. The model incorporates two distinct contextual information types as input, aiming to ascertain the extent to which such information augments the model and enhances the precision of the recommendation system. An Attention mechanism is embedded within the model, enabling it to discern pivotal items within the current session. This mechanism channels attention towards these salient items, thereby refining the model's recommendation outcomes.

Empirical results corroborate that when prioritizing the accuracy of Recall, the CAII-P model is optimal, whereas for emphasizing the precision of MRR, the CAII-PI model is preferable. Evidently, the recommendation system architecture proposed in this study exhibits superior accuracy in generating user lists compared to preceding recommendation systems.

Acknowledgements. The authors thank the reviewers for the valuable comments. This study was support in part by Feng Chia University under grant 22H00310, and National Science and Technology Council under grant MOST109-2221-E-035-064.

References

1. Barkan, O., Koenigstein, N.: ITEM2VEC: neural item embedding for collaborative filtering. In: 2016 IEEE 26th International Workshop on Machine Learning for Signal Processing (MLSP), pp. 1–6. IEEE (2016)
2. Chen, P.Y.: Session-aware recommendation using hierarchical recurrent network. Master thesis, Feng Chia University, Taiwan (2019)
3. Cui, Q., Wu, S., Liu, Q., Zhong, W., Wang, L.: MV-RNN: a multi-view recurrent neural network for sequential recommendation. IEEE Trans. Knowl. Data Eng. 32(2), 317–331 (2020)
4. Gu, W., Dong, S., Zeng, Z.: Increasing recommended effectiveness with markov chains and purchase intervals. Neural Comput. Appl. 25(5), 1153–1162 (2014)
5. Hidasi, B., Karatzoglou, A., Baltrunas, L., Tikk, D.: Session-based recommendations with recurrent neural networks. arXiv:1511.06939 (2016)
6. Hidasi, B., Quadrana, M., Karatzoglou, A., Tikk, D.: Parallel recurrent neural network architectures for feature-rich session-based recommendations. In: Proceedings of the 10th ACM Conference on Recommender Systems, pp. 241–248. ACM, New York (2016)

7. Hidasi, B., Karatzoglou, A.: Recurrent neural networks with top-k gains for session-based recommendations. In: Proceedings of the 27th ACM International Conference on Information and Knowledge Management, pp. 843–852. ACM, New York (2018)

8. Linden, G., Smith, B., York, J.: Amazon.com recommendations: item-to-item collaborative filtering. IEEE Internet Comput. **7**(1), 76–80 (2003)

9. Liu, Q., Wu, S., Wang, D., Li, Z., Wang, L.: Context-aware sequential recommendations. In: Proceedings of the 16th IEEE International Conference on Data Mining (ICDM), pp. 1053–1058. IEEE (2016)

10. Luo, X., Zhou, M., Li, S., Shang, M.: An inherently nonnegative latent factor model for high-dimensional and sparse matrices from industrial applications. IEEE Trans. Industr. Inf. **14**(5), 2011–2022 (2018)

11. Luo, X., et al.: Incorporation of efficient second-order solvers into latent factor models for accurate prediction of missing QoS data. IEEE Trans. Cybernet. **48**(4), 1216–1228 (2018)

12. Phuong, T.M., Thanh, T.C., Bach, N.X.: Neural session-aware recommendation. IEEE Access **7**, 86884–86896 (2019)

13. Quadrana, M., Karatzoglou, A., Hidasi, B., Cremonesi, P.: Personalizing session-based recommendations with hierarchical recurrent neural networks. In: Proceedings of the Eleventh ACM Conference on Recommender Systems, pp. 130–137. ACM, New York (2017)

14. Rakkappan, L., Rajan, V.: Context-aware sequential recommendations with stacked recurrent neural networks. In: Proceedings of the 28th International Conference on World Wide Web, pp. 3172–3178. ACM, New York (2019)

15. Rendle, S., Freudenthaler, C., Schmidt-Thieme, L.: Factorizing personalized Markov chains for next-basket recommendation. In: Proceedings of the 19th International Conference on World Wide Web, pp. 811–820. ACM, New York (2010)

16. Ruocco, M., Skrede, O.S.L., Langseth, H.: Inter-session modeling for session-based recommendation. arXiv:1706.07506 (2017)

17. Sarwar, B., Karypis, G., Konstan, J., Riedl, J.: Item-based collaborative filtering recommendation algorithms. In: Proceedings of the 10th International Conference on World Wide Web, pp. 285–295. ACM, New York (2001)

18. Shani, G., Heckerman, D., Brafman, R.I.: An MDP-based recommender system. J. Mach. Learn. Res. **6**(43), 1265–1295 (2005)

19. Yuan, W., Wang, H., Yu, X., Liu, N., Li, Z.: Attention-based context-aware sequential recommendation model. Inf. Sci. **510**, 122–134 (2020)

20. Zimdars, A., Chickering, D.M., Meek, C.: Using temporal data for making recommendations. arXiv:1301.2320 (2013)

21. Amazon Dataset. http://jmcauley.ucsd.edu/data/amazon. Accessed 02 Aug 2021

From 5-Stars to Real Insight: Geospatial Detection of Campaigned Reviews with Google Maps and Mobility Data

Ying-Zhe Hung, Ming-Hung Wang[✉], and Pao-Ann Hsiung

Department of Computer Science and Information Engineering, National Chung Cheng University, Chiayi, Taiwan
tonymhwang@gmail.com

Abstract. In recent years, online review platforms have become increasingly popular, and many consumers rely on these platforms to search for restaurants before dining. However, some restaurants start long-term or short-term campaigns to boost their ratings and attract more customers to dine there. This behavior affects consumer decision-making and seriously undermines the fairness of the consumption market. Most existing research has primarily focused on the direction of reviews. In this study, we take the restaurant's perspective and propose a method to detect whether restaurants host campaigns. We introduce a series of features based on the overall restaurant information. To enhance the performance of our detection, we employ five different models and conduct a comprehensive evaluation. The experimental results from Google review data suggest that our method performs well in identifying restaurant campaigns.

Keywords: Fake reviews · Restaurant campaign recognition · Google Maps · Machine learning · Deep learning

1 Introduction

With the rapid development of online review platforms, an increasing number of consumers rely on reviews from these platforms as a basis for their purchasing decisions. Furthermore, as this trend continues to grow, more consumers are willing to share their genuine consumption experiences online by posting reviews and sharing their insights. However, whether online reviews are authentic and whether the store influences them has become a concerning issue. Among them, fake restaurant reviews are one of the issues that everyone is concerned about. Positive fake reviews can help restaurants establish a favorable reputation and attract more customers, while negative fake reviews may tarnish their image in the eyes of consumers. Therefore, many restaurants will use incentives to allow consumers to leave fake reviews to improve the restaurant's reputation. This behavior causes subsequent consumers who want to dine to make wrong decisions and go to poor-quality restaurants, creating a negative dining experience.

Google Maps is one of the globally influential review platforms where many stores provide their business information and geographical locations. Consumers voluntarily contribute all the reviews and opinions posted on this platform, primarily based on their real-life experiences. Consequently, these reviews hold significant reference value.

In prior research [1–3], much focus was placed on identifying fake reviews and proposing various detection methods. However, in this study, our primary focus is on the restaurant. We introduce a system to determine whether restaurants use campaign methods to attract consumers to leave fake reviews, affecting the authenticity of reviews on the platform. We utilize both Google reviews and device trajectory datasets to devise a set of features for classification models. We employ five popular models to assess the classification performance. Our results indicate that the features we propose and extract enable the model to achieve good classification results. Furthermore, our method also performs well in analyzing whether restaurants host campaigns every month.

The main contributions of our research are as follows:

1) We have a device trajectory dataset besides the Google reviews dataset and utilize various data from trajectories to enhance classification performance.
2) We introduce a set of features, including information-based, trajectory-based, and review-based features, comprising 17 distinct features to aid in identifying restaurant campaigns.
3) We demonstrate the practicality of our method by exploring the temporal aspects of restaurant campaigns.

This paper is structured as follows. In Sect. 2, we introduce a review of related research on fake review identification. In Sect. 3, we present the dataset, labeling standards, feature extraction processes, and classification models. In Sect. 4, we detail the experimental procedures and evaluation results. Finally, in Sect. 5, we summarize our research and propose directions for future work.

2   Related Work

In the first study on fake review detection in 2008, Jindal and Liu [4]. They identified three types of fake reviews: untruthful opinions, reviews on brands only, and non-reviews. They crawled data from Amazon.com and confirmed the existence of the proposed three types of fake reviews by detecting duplicate reviews and manual labeling. Since then, this issue has attracted more and more attention. Most existing research mainly focuses on identifying fake reviews based on textual and behavioral features.

2.1   Textual-Based Features

Much research has identified fake reviews by analyzing the content of reviews. Ott et al. [5] studied based on AMT data and pointed out significant differences in the word distributions between fake and non-fake reviews. Alsubari et al. [6] analyzed the dataset developed by Ott et al. [5] using sentiment word analysis, language style analysis, and N-gram features [7]. Wang et al. [8] detected fake reviews on Mobile01.com by analyzing the sentiment of the reviews. They found that most fake reviews were positive, while genuine reviews tended to be neutral. Tufail et al. [9] explored the impact of COVID-19 on reviews on Yelp and TripAdvisor platforms by analyzing factors such as review length, the number of verbs and nouns, and keyword counts. Martens and Maalej [10] analyzed fake reviews on app stores and found that fake reviews tend to be longer and use fewer negative words.

2.2 Behavioral-Based Features

In addition to textual features, the behavior of reviewers also plays an essential role in identifying fake reviews. Many researchers have found that using behavioral features improves fake review detection [11–13]. Wu et al. [14] analyzed temporal patterns of users' review behavior to identify fake reviews on Yelp. Liu et al. [15] analyzed the behavior patterns of mobile phone reviewers on Amazon.com and pointed out that spam reviewers tend to post many reviews quickly and typically use anonymous profiles. Wang et al. [16] analyzed Yelp reviews and found that spammers focus on reviewing a single restaurant and have shorter time intervals between their reviews.

Based on our literature analysis, previous research on fake reviews has primarily focused on analyzing review text and reviewer behavior. However, there needs to be more exploration of reviewer geographic locations and their movement trajectories. Therefore, in this study, we introduced device mobility trajectories and approached the issue of fake reviews from a different perspective. We developed a restaurant campaign detection system by analyzing restaurants' geographical location and trajectory data in combination with restaurant information and review content. This system enables consumers to identify better which restaurant reviews are reliable.

3   Proposed Methodology

In this section, we present the approach for detecting restaurant campaigns, which is shown in Fig. 1. First, we will describe our datasets and the labeling process. We then extract features from these datasets. Finally, we use classification models to obtain results.

3.1   Data Collection and Processing

We obtained two datasets through collaboration with Vpon: the Google restaurant reviews dataset (GRR-Dataset) and the device trajectory dataset (DT-Dataset) from June 28, 2022, to June 26, 2023, a one-year-old observation. Table 1 displays detailed information about our dataset.

The GRR-Dataset. The dataset includes the most popular restaurants in Taipei City from Google Maps and the reviews from these restaurants, which are public and accessible to every user. To better analyze the content of the reviews, we filtered for restaurants with more than 100 reviews. In the end, we obtained 69 restaurants and 55,064 reviews.

The DT-Dataset. We obtained device trajectory data through advertising placement. First, we selected device IDs that had passed by at least one restaurant during our observation period. We then selected devices that appeared with at least one trajectory data every hour. Finally, we choose the top 1,500 device IDs with the highest frequency of appearance. As a result, the DT-Dataset consists of 1,500 devices and 8,262,763 trajectory data. The device ID in this dataset has been de-identified.

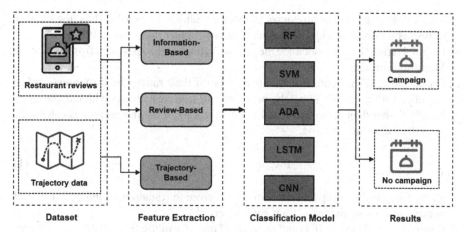

Fig. 1. Overview of restaurant campaign recognition.

Table 1. Datasets details.

Item	Information	Item	Information
(a) GRR-Dataset		(b) DT-Dataset	
# Reviews	55,064	# Trajectories	8,262,763
# Restaurants	69	# Devices	1,500
# Five-star ratings	41,705	# Android devices	507
# One-star ratings	1,933	# iOS devices	993
Avg. Star ratings	4.4	# Districts	12

3.2   Class Labeling

To obtain a list of restaurants that have campaigns, we used keywords such as "review (評論)," "check-in (打卡)," and "free (送)" to find the reviews in the GRR-Dataset and acquire restaurants which reviews have these keywords. We then manually verified whether these restaurants had a campaign. Finally, we found 20 restaurants.

3.3   Feature Extraction for Restaurant Campaign Recognition

In this article, we classify the features into three categories: information-based, trajectories-based, and review-based. We elaborate on the detailed description of the features within each category.

Information-Based Features. The restaurant's basic information in our dataset contains many details. This information includes many features to help us recognize whether the restaurant has campaigns.

a) Number of reviews (F1): This feature calculates the total number of reviews received by the restaurant during our observation period. Restaurants hosting campaigns may attract consumers to leave reviews to receive additional rewards. Thus, the number of restaurant reviews with campaigns is usually higher than those without.

b) Original rating (F2): We obtained the original rating for the restaurant from its Google Maps information.

c) Period rating (F3): Some restaurants may boost their ratings by campaigns during our observation period. Thus, the period rating from restaurants with campaigns is usually higher than those without. The period rating of the restaurant r is calculated as in the following equation:

$$PR_r = \frac{1}{R_r} \sum_{i=1}^{R_r} CR_{r,i} \tag{1}$$

where $CR_{r,i}$ is the rating that consumer i has given to restaurant r, and R_r is the total number of reviews that restaurant r has received.

d) Ratio of five-star rating (F4) and the ratio of one-star rating (F5): These two features are introduced to measure the proportion of five-star and one-star ratings in the total number of reviews for the restaurant. Some restaurants may host campaigns that reward five-star reviews to boost their rating. Thus, these two features could be beneficial in determining whether the restaurant has campaigns.

Trajectory-Based Features

a) Number of trajectories within 30 (F6), 40 (F7), and 50 (F8) meters of the restaurant: This feature calculates the number of trajectories that appeared near the restaurant during our observation period. We use the Haversine formula to calculate the distance between the device and the restaurant. Then, we set the distance thresholds at 30, 40, and 50 m. The distance d is calculated as in the following equation:

$$a = \sin^2\left(\frac{\Delta\varphi}{2}\right) + \cos(\varphi_1)\cos(\varphi_2)\sin^2\left(\frac{\Delta\lambda}{2}\right) \tag{2}$$

$$d = 2(er)\sin^{-1}\left(\sqrt{a}\right) \tag{3}$$

where φ_1 is the device latitude, φ_2 is the restaurant latitude, $\Delta\varphi$ is the difference of latitude and $\Delta\lambda$ is the difference of longitude between two locations, and er is the earth radius.

b) Number of devices within 30 (F9), 40 (F10), and 50 (F11) meters of the restaurant: We calculate the number of devices that appeared near the restaurant using the dataset filtered by F6 to F8.

c) Average dwell time within 30 (F12), 40 (F13), and 50 (F14) meters of the restaurant: This feature calculates the average dwell time of devices appearing near the restaurant. Some restaurants are located near school dormitories or residential areas, leading to unusually long dwell times for specific devices. Thus, we select the dwell time between 10 and 210 min as a reasonable range. The average dwell time is calculated as in the following equation:

$$ADT = \text{median}\{DT_v | v = 1, 2, \ldots, D_v\} \tag{4}$$

where DT_v is the device v dwell time at the restaurant and D_v is the number of devices near the restaurant.

d) Number of trajectories during business hours (F15): This feature calculates the number of trajectories that appeared at the restaurant during business hours. Some restaurants use campaigns to attract a large number of consumers for dining, which may lead to a significant increase in the number of trajectories during business hours.

Review-Based Features

a) Average review length (F16): This feature calculates the average length of consumer reviews when rating the restaurant. When restaurants host campaigns, consumers often leave shorter reviews to receive rewards quickly. Thus, the average review length from restaurants with campaigns is usually shorter than those without. The average review length is calculated as in the following equation:

$$ARL = \frac{1}{R_r} \sum_{i=1}^{R_r} CRL_{r,i} \tag{5}$$

where $CRL_{r,i}$ is the length of restaurant r review given by consumer i.

b) Sentiment ratio (F17): This feature calculates the sentiment ratio of restaurant reviews. We use the Roberta sentiment analysis model [17] to measure the sentiment of the consumer's review. The sentiment score of review w of consumer c is defined in the following equation: devices. Thus, we select the dwell time between 10 and 210 min as a reasonable range. The average dwell time is calculated as in the following equation:

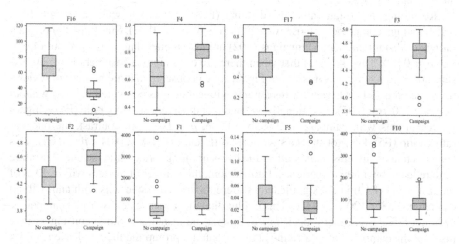

Fig. 2. Box plot of top 8 features.

$$SScore_{c,w} = \begin{cases} -1, & \text{if w.nscr} > \text{w.pscr} \\ 1, & \text{if w.nscr} < \text{w.pscr} \\ 0, & \text{otherwise} \end{cases} \tag{6}$$

where w.nscr and w.pscr are the reviews of the negative and positive scores, respectively. Then, the sentiment ratio of reviews by restaurant r can be defined $SR_r = \frac{1}{R_r} \sum_{i=1}^{R_r} SScore_{c,w}$. The value of the sentiment ratio feature ranges from -1 to 1. The closer the value of the sentiment ratio of a restaurant to -1 or 1, the stronger the negative or positive sentiment of reviews received by this restaurant.

3.4 Feature Analysis

In this section, we employ the ReliefF feature selection method [18] to calculate the ranking of our proposed features. Due to space constraints, we focus on the top 8 features for further investigation. The box plots of selected features are shown in Fig. 2. We conduct statistical analysis on these proposed features using the Welch Two Sample t-test method, at a significance level of 5%, to examine whether a significant difference exists between restaurants with campaigns and those without.

Average review length (F16) can be observed from Fig. 2, where it is evident that restaurants with campaigns have a shorter average review length compared to those without ($35.910 < 69.415$, $p < 0.05$). Additionally, the sentiment ratio of reviews (F17) indicates that restaurants with campaigns have a higher sentiment ratio compared to those without ($0.57 > 0.46$, $p < 0.05$). When restaurants host campaigns, consumers leave shorter, more positive reviews to receive rewards. Conversely, without campaigns, reviews tend to provide more genuine evaluations of the restaurant's ambiance, service quality, and food quality.

Regarding the restaurant's period rating (F03), restaurants with campaigns have higher ratings compared to those without ($4.6 > 4.4$, $p > 0.05$). Similarly, the original ratings of restaurants with campaigns (F02) are also higher than those without ($4.6 > 4.3$, $p < 0.05$). This indicates that when there are campaigns, consumers leave higher-star ratings to receive rewards. From Fig. 2, we can observe that the number of reviews for restaurants (F1) is higher for restaurants with campaigns compared to those without ($1413 > 570$, $p < 0.05$). Additionally, we find that the five-star rating ratio (F4) is higher for restaurants with campaigns ($0.805 > 0.636$, $p < 0.05$). In contrast, the one-star rating ratio (F5) does not show a significant difference ($0.038 < 0.047$, $p > 0.05$). This suggests that campaigns mainly affect the five-star rating ratio, while the one-star rating ratio reflects the dining experience. Furthermore, the number of devices within 40 m of the restaurant (F10) is not significantly different between restaurants with and without campaigns ($88 < 120$, $p > 0.05$). This implies that the presence or absence of campaigns does not affect consumers' decisions to dine at the restaurant. Some consumers may discover the campaign after arriving at the restaurant, prompting them to leave reviews.

3.5 Classification Models

To evaluate our method, we used three machine learning models, including RF [19], Adaboost (ADA) [20], and SVM [21], and two deep learning models, including LSTM [22] and CNN [23]. These five classification models were utilized to calculate classification results.

4 Experience and Result

In this section, we evaluate the performance of the proposed restaurant campaign recognition method. First, we introduce the experimental setup and the metrics for evaluating the models. We then show the performance of these models and analyze the impact of the proposed features on identifying restaurant campaigns. Finally, we analyze the periods during which restaurants have campaigns.

4.1 Experience Setup

K-Fold Cross-Validation. We used 5-fold cross-validation to evaluate the classifier's performance. This method divides the dataset into five equal subsets. In each round, four subsets will be the training set, and the remaining subset will be the validation set. This process is repeated five times, and the results are obtained by averaging the results of these five rounds. In this article, we used a random oversampling technique with different seeds to generate the experimental dataset. The dataset was used for 5-fold cross-validation for training. We repeated this process 50 times. The final results were obtained by calculating the average from these 50 training rounds.

Hyperparameter Tuning. To improve the performance of the classifiers, we employed the Grid search cross-validation (GridsearchCV) method to search for the best hyperparameters for each classifier. We used random oversampling techniques to generate a balanced dataset. Then, we used 5-fold cross-validation and grid search to find the best hyperparameters. This process was repeated ten times. The best hyperparameters for each model were chosen based on the most frequently occurring values among these rounds. The best hyperparameters that were used to train the models are shown in Table 2.

4.2 Evaluation Metrics

In this article, we used popular metrics, including accuracy, precision, recall, F1-score, and AUC, to measure the performance of our proposed restaurant campaign recognition method.

4.3 Model Performance Comparison

In this section, we present the experimental results of the classifier models, as shown in Table 3. RF exhibits the best performance with an accuracy of 0.929 (92.9%), while CNN shows the lowest performance with an accuracy of 0.869 (86.9%). The experimental results show that deep learning models may not necessarily outperform machine learning models in small data classification.

Table 2. The best hyperparameters for classifiers.

Classifier	Hyperparmeter	Candidate parameter	Best value
RF	max_features n_estimators criterion	{sqrt, log2} {25, 50, 100, 200, 300, 400, 500} {gini, entropy}	sqrt 50 gini
SVM	cache_size C kernel degree	{50, 100, 200, 400} {1, 10, 100} {rbf, linear} {1, 2, 3, 4}	50 10 rbf 1
ADA	n_estimators learning_rate	{50, 100, 150, 200, 250, 500} {0.001, 0.01, 0.1, 0.2, 0.3, 0.5, 0.7, 1}	200 0.2
LSTM	batch_size epochs	{32, 64, 128, 256} {50, 100, 150, 200, 250, 500}	64 150
CNN	batch_size epochs	{32, 64, 128, 256} {50, 100, 150, 200, 250, 500}	256 150

Table 3. The performance of different models.

Models	Accuracy	Precision	Recall	F1-Score	AUC
RF	**0.929**	**0.913**	**0.962**	**0.933**	0.976
SVM	0.902	0.885	0.935	0.905	0.970
ADA	0.922	0.910	0.952	0.925	**0.983**
LSTM	0.927	0.910	0.926	0.931	0.926
CNN	0.869	0.847	0.872	0.873	0.872

4.4 Feature Importance Analysis

We analyzed by individually inputting each feature category into the classifier to assess the performance of different feature categories. The results are shown in Fig. 3. Notably, the review-based features outperformed the others, with RF achieving an AUC of 0.976 (97.6%). Information-based features followed while trajectory-based features exhibited the weakest performance. Based on these findings, we conclude that review-based features are the most effective in identifying whether a restaurant hosts campaigns. This implies that features extracted from the reviews' content significantly impact classifier model performance.

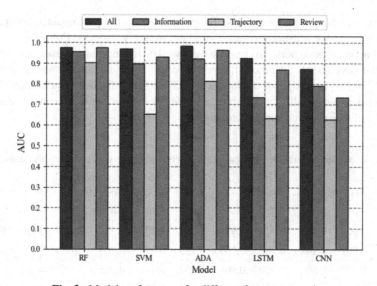

Fig. 3. Model performance for different feature categories.

4.5 Monthly Analysis of Restaurant Campaigns

Our experiments used the entire year to identify whether a restaurant was hosting campaigns. However, restaurant campaigns typically have temporal patterns, with some lasting for just a few days, a few months, or even specific to certain holidays. To explore this problem, we divided the two datasets into 12 equal segments based on months, as illustrated in Fig. 4. Notably, the GRR-dataset consistently contains over 3,500 monthly reviews. In contrast, the DT-dataset consistently boasts over 450,000 trajectories, with peaks reaching as high as 1.1 million during specific periods. This shows the substantial appeal of these restaurants. Using keyword searching, we identified 177 time periods with campaigns and 627 without campaigns. We seek to determine whether we can achieve effective classification results using the same recognition method for these time-based

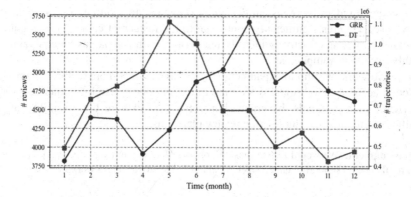

Fig. 4. Restaurant reviews and device trajectories by month.

campaigns and no campaign periods. Table 4 illustrates the performance comparison between our approach using the entire year and monthly datasets. From the table, it's evident that our method performs impressively well on the monthly dataset. In particular, RF performs even better than the entire year datasets, achieving an outstanding accuracy of 0.981 (98.1%) and AUC of 0.998 (99.8%). These classification results illustrate the applicability and reliability of our approach. We believe our approach can be beneficial to the identification of restaurant campaigns.

Table 4. Model performance comparison between the entire year and monthly datasets.

Models	Accuracy		Precision		Recall		F1-Score		AUC	
	All[a]	Mon[b]	All	Mon	All	Mon	All	Mon	All	Mon
RF	0.929	**0.981**	0.913	**0.970**	0.962	**0.993**	0.933	**0.981**	0.976	**0.998**
SVM	0.902	0.905	0.885	0.909	0.935	0.901	0.905	0.905	0.970	0.973
ADA	0.922	0.898	0.910	0.909	0.952	0.884	0.925	0.895	0.983	0.969
LSTM	0.927	0.934	0.910	0.908	0.926	0.934	0.931	0.935	0.926	0.934
CNN	0.869	0.955	0.847	0.935	0.872	0.956	0.873	0.956	0.872	0.956

[a]The entire year's datasets
[b]The monthly datasets

5 Conclusion and Future Work

In this study, we propose an approach to identify restaurant campaigns. We utilize GRR-dataset and DT-dataset, extracting three categories of features: information-based, trajectory-based, and review-based. Feature analysis shows that restaurants with campaigns have higher ratings than those without and tend to have more reviews. In addition, we found that when restaurants have campaigns, consumers often leave shorter and more positive reviews. Experimental results demonstrate the effectiveness of our proposed method in identifying restaurants with campaigns. In addition, we found that the review-based features significantly contribute to the restaurant campaign recognition. Furthermore, we can effectively identify the periods with campaigns by analyzing the monthly restaurant campaigns.

In future work, we aim to expand our datasets and extract more features to improve prediction accuracy. Additionally, we plan to expand our research to other categories of reviews, such as hotels, beverage shops, etc., and explore the feasibility of our identification method on other online review platforms.

Acknowledgment. We would like to thank Vpon Big Data Group (https://www.vpon.com/zh-hant/) for their kind support in data collection and valuable advice to our work.

References

1. Mukherjee, A., Venkataraman, V., Liu, B., Glance, N.: Fake review detection: classification and analysis of real and pseudo reviews. In: UIC-CS-03-2013, Technical report (2013)
2. Sun, C., Du, Q., Tian, G.: Exploiting product related review features for fake review detection. Math. Probl. Eng. **2016**, 1–7 (2016)
3. Kauffmann, E., Peral, J., Gil, D., Ferrández, A., Sellers, R., Mora, H.: A framework for big data analytics in commercial social networks: a case study on sentiment analysis and fake review detection for marketing decision-making. Ind. Mark. Manage. **90**, 523–537 (2020)
4. Jindal, N., Liu, B.: Opinion spam and analysis. In: Proceedings of the 2008 International Conference on Web Search and Data Mining, pp. 219–230 (2008)
5. Ott, M., Choi, Y., Cardie, C., Hancock, J.T.: Finding deceptive opinion spam by any stretch of the imagination. arXiv preprint arXiv:1107.4557 (2011)
6. Alsubari, S.N., et al.: Data analytics for the identification of fake reviews using supervised learning. Comput. Mater. Continua **70**(2), 3189–3204 (2022)
7. Li, Y., Feng, X., Zhang, S.: Detecting fake reviews utilizing semantic and emotion model. In: 2016 3rd International Conference on Information Science and Control Engineering (ICISCE), pp. 317–320. IEEE (2016)
8. Wang, C.C., Day, M.Y., Chen, C.C., Liou, J.W.: Temporal and sentimental analysis of a real case of fake reviews in Taiwan. In: Proceedings of the 2017 IEEE/ACM International Conference on Advances in Social Networks Analysis and Mining, pp. 729–736 (2017)
9. Tufail, H., Ashraf, M.U., Alsubhi, K., Aljahdali, H.M.: The effect of fake reviews on e-commerce during and after Covid-19 pandemic: SKL-based fake reviews detection. IEEE Access **10**, 25555–25564 (2022)
10. Martens, D., Maalej, W.: Towards understanding and detecting fake reviews in app stores. Empir. Softw. Eng. **24**(6), 3316–3355 (2019)
11. Mukherjee, A., Venkataraman, V., Liu, B., Glance, N.: What yelp fake review filter might be doing? In: Proceedings of the International AAAI Conference on Web and Social Media, vol. 7, no. 1, pp. 409–418 (2013)
12. Zhang, D., Zhou, L., Kehoe, J.L., Kilic, I.Y.: What online reviewer behaviors really matter? Effects of verbal and nonverbal behaviors on detection of fake online reviews. J. Manag. Inf. Syst. **33**(2), 456–481 (2016)
13. Barbado, R., Araque, O., Iglesias, C.A.: A framework for fake review detection in online consumer electronics retailers. Inf. Process. Manage. **56**(4), 1234–1244 (2019)
14. Wu, X., Dong, Y., Tao, J., Huang, C., Chawla, N.V.: Reliable fake review detection via modeling temporal and behavioral patterns. In: 2017 IEEE International Conference on Big Data, pp. 494–499. IEEE (2017)
15. Liu, P., Xu, Z., Ai, J., Wang, F.: Identifying indicators of fake reviews based on spammer's behavior features. In: 2017 IEEE International Conference on Software Quality, Reliability and Security Companion (QRS-C), pp. 396–403. IEEE (2017)
16. Wang, X., Zhang, X., Jiang, C., Liu, H.: Identification of fake reviews using semantic and behavioral features. In: 2018 4th International Conference on Information Management (ICIM), pp. 92–97. IEEE (2018)
17. Zhang, J., et al.: Fengshenbang 1.0: Being the foundation of Chinese cognitive intelligence. arXiv preprint arXiv:2209.02970 (2022)
18. Kononenko, I., Šimec, E., Robnik-Šikonja, M.: Overcoming the myopia of inductive learning algorithms with RELIEFF. Appl. Intell. **7**, 39–55 (1997)
19. Breiman, L.: Random forests. Mach. Learn. **45**, 5–32 (2001)
20. Freund, Y., Schapire, R.E.: A decision-theoretic generalization of on-line learning and an application to boosting. J. Comput. Syst. Sci. **55**(1), 119–139 (1997)

21. Cortes, C., Vapnik, V.: Support-vector networks. Mach. Learn. **20**, 273–297 (1995)
22. Graves, A., Graves, A.: Long short-term memory. In: Supervised Sequence Labelling with Recurrent Neural Networks, vol. 385, pp. 37–45. Springer, Heidelberg (2012). https://doi.org/10.1007/978-3-642-24797-2_4
23. LeCun, Y., Bottou, L., Bengio, Y., Haffner, P.: Gradient-based learning applied to document recognition. Proc. IEEE **86**(11), 2278–2324 (1998)

Fruit Weight Predicting by Using Hybrid Learning

Chao-Yang Lee[(⊠)] [iD]

National Yunlin University of Science and Technology, Douliu, Yunlin, Taiwan
Chaoyang@yuntech.edu.tw

Abstract. Modern lifestyle diseases are closely linked to diet, including weight control, healthy eating habits, and physical activity. This is particularly critical for individuals with poor blood sugar metabolism, who need to manage blood sugar-related conditions. A fast and intelligent algorithmic tool for quickly assessing carbohydrate content in food is crucial for effective management. Nutritionists often spend a lot of time on dietary assessments. With the widespread use of smartphones today, previous research has shown that assessing nutrients using a 45-degree plane photography method can introduce significant errors. Therefore, having an accurate tool for analyzing food carbohydrate content can help people understand their daily diet, explore nutritional patterns, and maintain a healthy diet. Food weight estimation is essential for carbohydrate analysis. Our research focuses on inferring food weight in fruits. We use a lightweight convolutional neural network model integrated with fast machine learning techniques, enabling real-time food weight prediction when taking smartphone photos. Through experiments, our model achieved an impressive 99.81% accuracy when tested with images of apples, bananas, and oranges, captured at different sizes, distances, and angles. However, dietary patterns are diverse and complex. Therefore, inferring various nutrients in diverse diets will require further research and development. This study lays the foundation for future exploration in this area.

Keywords: Fruit Weight Predicting · Hybrid Learning · Deep Learning

1 Introduction

In the 2021 report from the Ministry of Health and Welfare, it was revealed that diabetes is a pressing concern in Taiwan, ranking as the fifth leading cause of death [1]. The International Diabetes Federation paints a gloomy picture for the global scenario, predicting a staggering increase in diabetes cases, with an estimated 578 million cases by 2030, poised to rise to a staggering 783 million by 2045 [2, 3]. This alarming trend is largely attributed to unhealthy food consumption patterns, including nutritional imbalances and excessive calorie intake, which contribute to the prevalent issue of obesity. Clearly, there is an urgent and compelling need for significant improvements in lifestyle and dietary habits.

As a response to this escalating health crisis, there has been a noticeable surge in the demand for tools and methods that can aid in dietary tracking and calorie control.

© The Author(s), under exclusive license to Springer Nature Singapore Pte Ltd. 2024
C.-Y. Lee et al. (Eds.): TAAI 2023, CCIS 2075, pp. 81–91, 2024.
https://doi.org/10.1007/978-981-97-1714-9_7

Previous research has highlighted the effectiveness of traditional dietary assessment methods, such as the 24-h dietary recall (24 h), in assisting individuals in examining their dietary behaviors and providing a foundation for targeted interventions to address underlying health concerns. The 24 h process, led by experienced dietitians, typically involves participants recalling all the food items they consumed in the past 24 h and estimating portion sizes through visual observation. However, it is worth noting that the accuracy of portion size estimation in this approach heavily relies on individual subjectivity, introducing the potential for significant biases and inaccuracies. Despite their effectiveness, the conventional dietary assessments conducted by nutritionists are known to be time-consuming and lack real-time feedback mechanisms [4], which can limit their practicality in addressing the modern challenges of dietary health. With the growing prevalence of diabetes and obesity, the need for innovative, efficient, and automated dietary assessment methods becomes increasingly evident. Consequently, there is a burgeoning interest in leveraging advancements in computer vision, artificial intelligence, and image-based technologies to develop tools that not only streamline dietary assessments but also offer real-time insights and support for individuals striving to make healthier dietary choices.

The recent strides in computer vision and artificial intelligence have revolutionized health monitoring, giving rise to a host of innovative applications. Notably, image-based mobile apps have come to the forefront, offering support for dietary records, such as image-based food diaries and real-time feedback through smartphone applications [5]. An image-based approach can significantly alleviate the workload of dietitians when conducting dietary assessments. However, the adoption of image-based dietary assessment methods is more intricate, as it heavily depends on computational algorithms owing to its fully automated nature [6]. Furthermore, due to market demand, various commercial services and products have emerged, indicating significant business opportunities in the field of artificial intelligence for food carbohydrate analysis [7]. In summary, as diabetes and health management continue to gain prominence, image-based dietary assessment methods and smart technologies will continue to provide improved tools for individuals to effectively manage their health and diet.

Numerous studies are currently being conducted in the field of food recognition [8], food ingredient identification [9], Food State Recognition [10], Food Value Estimation [11], and dietary assessment methods [12], which require the calculation of food carbohydrates. To achieve this, food type recognition is a crucial initial step. Tian et al. [13] proposed an image-based recognition algorithm that leverages depth information, extracting gradient information from fruit images and introducing graph-based segmentation algorithms. This approach aids in accurately identifying and locating the target fruits. Yuesheng et al. [14] optimized Google's GoogLeNet model by reducing the number of convolution kernels. GoogLeNet, known for integrating multiple basic modules (referred to as Inception), creates a deep convolutional neural network by stringing these modules together. The authors' optimization resulted in a nearly 48% reduction in GoogLeNet's parameters. Their paper focused on the classification of apples, lemons, oranges, pomegranates, tomatoes, and peppers, achieving an identification accuracy of 96.88%. Jiang et al. [15] developed a deep model-based food recognition and dietary assessment system. They used the Faster R-CNN (Faster Regions with Convolutional

Neural Network) model to classify food into different categories and locate them in the original images. The system then analyzed nutritional components, calculating calories, fat, carbohydrates, and protein content based on the identification results, and generating dietary assessment reports. Turmchokkasam *et al.* [16] proposed a method for estimating food calorie content based on ingredients using nutritional knowledge and heat information. They first identified the food in photos and retrieved ingredient and nutritional knowledge from a database. Using fuzzy logic, they classified all boundaries into components based on their heat patterns and intensity, eventually calculating the total calories. Konstantakopoulos *et al.* develop an automated image-based dietary assessment system with a focus on Mediterranean cuisine. It includes the creation of the MedGRFood image dataset and employs deep learning for food image classification. The study's classification model, based on the EfficientNetB2, achieves high accuracy in classifying Mediterranean food images. Additionally, the research outlines a methodology for estimating food volume through stereo vision techniques, achieving an overall Mean Absolute Percentage Error (MAPE) of 10.5% for 148 different dishes. This comprehensive approach offers promise for enhancing dietary assessment accuracy and promoting healthier eating habits.

The research mentioned earlier underscores the significance of employing image-based techniques for assessing food composition, providing a convenient and efficient method to analyze the nutritional properties of various foods. Despite the advantages of image-based methods, it is worth noting that there remains a limited body of literature exploring the potential of deep learning for food analysis. This is particularly relevant in the context of our rapidly aging global population and the concurrent increase in the prevalence of diabetes. Managing blood glucose levels through appropriate nutrition is paramount for individuals with diabetes. However, accurately assessing the carbohydrate content of foods can be a formidable challenge for the general population, often necessitating significant time and effort for education and awareness. In light of these challenges and the increasing importance of nutritional awareness, this study zeroes in on the pivotal carbohydrate components found in fruits. The study employs cutting-edge deep learning techniques for fruit-type classification, leveraging the power of artificial intelligence to distinguish between different types of fruits effectively. Additionally, the study utilizes regression analysis to infer the carbohydrate content of these fruits, offering a multifaceted approach to tackling the complex issue of carbohydrate assessment in dietary choices. By combining advanced technologies with a focus on a specific food group, this research aims to contribute valuable insights into improving nutritional awareness and making informed dietary decisions, which is increasingly critical in the context of contemporary health challenges and dietary needs.

The aim of this research is to assist in the non-invasive application of artificial intelligence to predict the carbohydrate content in food intake. Typically, nutritionists calculate dietary information based on the quantity of food and then manually search for the nutritional components in traditional tables. This process can be inconvenient and challenging for users to estimate accurately. Consequently, in response to the needs of the general public for health, fitness, and chronic disease control, there has been a proliferation of commercial services and products in the market, presenting significant business opportunities. Therefore, this study focuses on inferring the weight content of fruits. It employs a lightweight convolutional neural network model and integrates machine learning regression analysis for fast computation. This approach allows for real-time prediction of carbohydrate content in fruits through smartphone photography and computation.

2 Fruit Weight Predicting

The Taiwan Food and Drug Administration (TFDA) offers a valuable resource on its website, the Consumer Knowledge Service section, allowing users to access comprehensive information about the nutritional content of various foods available in Taiwan. This service empowers users to select specific foods they wish to inquire about and gain detailed insights into their nutritional components. For instance, let's take American Fuji apples as an example. Users can discover that these apples contain 13.8 g of total carbohydrates per 100 g. To calculate the carbohydrate content accurately, one must subtract the dietary fiber content from the total carbohydrates and then multiply the result by the weight of the food, yielding precise carbohydrate values. This method emphasizes the significance of knowing the weight of the food, which plays a pivotal role in determining the accurate nutritional content.

As a result, this research prioritizes the development of a robust framework for accurately predicting the weight of various fruits. This weight prediction model is of immense importance as it serves as the foundational element for estimating a wide range of nutritional components in foods. Since the primary objective is to develop a mobile application for future use, there is a paramount focus on ensuring that the prediction model is both lightweight and capable of fast computation. The proposed method for predicting carbohydrate content in fruits leverages a lightweight artificial neural network and machine learning regression analysis. This approach has the dual advantage of being efficient and suitable for real-time prediction of fruit weight through smartphone photography and computation. By combining technological innovation with a focus on user-friendly applications, this research aims to provide a practical and accessible solution for individuals seeking to make informed dietary choices based on accurate nutritional data, which is increasingly important in today's health-conscious society.

This study employs a hybrid learning model architecture. It utilizes Yolo as the Encoder for feature extraction and employs a regression model in the Decoder for weight inference. The hybrid learning model architecture, as depicted in Fig. 1, follows a multi-agent artificial intelligence framework. The main objective is to interconnect various small artificial intelligence models with distinct functionalities, combining them into a larger artificial intelligence model. This approach eliminates the need for each small artificial intelligence model to have an excessively deep and complex architecture, while the assembled large architecture artificial intelligence model still achieves high efficiency.

Generally, achieving extremely precise performance requires the use of deep and complex models, which can be challenging to implement on mobile devices. Therefore, this research uniquely adopts a hybrid learning model architecture, combining two low-computational models. This combined model allows for high-speed computation. Initially, the study captures image data through sensors. Subsequently, two artificial intelligence models are linked together:

1. The object recognition model is responsible for fruit feature extraction. It recognizes the fruit category in the image and obtains its positional information within the image.
2. This positioning information, along with estimated distance data, is then transmitted to the hybrid learning-based fruit weight inference model.
3. The primary purpose of the fruit weight inference model is to infer the weight of all fruits in the photo.

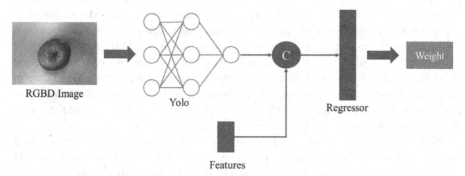

Fig. 1. The hybrid learning model architecture for fruit weight inference.

Fig. 2. The equipment used in this study, from left to right, are an electronic scale, a camera, and a laser ruler.

This study employs a comprehensive approach that involves the estimation of real distances by capturing images with a smartphone and subsequently utilizes a precision weighing scale to acquire the actual weight of various objects, with the collected data being incorporated into both the training and experimental datasets. The hardware setup and equipment used for this research are depicted in Fig. 2, illustrating the seamless integration of technology to address the core objectives of the study. On the left side of Fig. 2, we have an electronic scale that plays a pivotal role in measuring the precise weight of the fruit, ensuring accuracy and reliability in the dataset. In the center, we find the Intel RealSense Depth Camera D435i, a cutting-edge device equipped with advanced depth-sensing capabilities. This camera is instrumental in determining the distance from the camera to the recognized fruit, providing a critical component for the estimation of real distances. Finally, on the right side of the figure, a laser ruler is introduced, serving as a valuable tool to measure the actual distance between the camera and the subject fruit. The combination of these hardware elements facilitates a comprehensive and data-rich approach to address the research objectives effectively, ensuring the highest level of precision and reliability in the experimental process.

The object detection model utilized in this study is based on the Convolutional Neural Network (CNN) architecture known as YOLO (You Only Look Once). YOLO is an efficient real-time object detection model that has the ability to predict multiple object positions and categories in a single pass. This End-to-End algorithm significantly enhances recognition speed, making it capable of real-time detection while maintaining high accuracy. YOLO begins by extracting features from the input image, resulting in a feature map of 13×13 (for a color image, the feature map is 3, and for a grayscale image, it's 1). The input image is divided into a grid of 13×13 cells. During the data collection process for this test, if the center of an object falls within one of these cells, that cell is responsible for making predictions. Each cell predicts a fixed number of bounding boxes containing the confidence that an object is present. The red dots represent potential object centers within the grid cell, and each corresponding bounding box can define the center coordinates, width, height, and candidate score. This allows for accurate prediction of the target's position and the identification of all objects in the image.

Using the object detection model described above, as shown in Fig. 1, this study employs YOLO v4 tiny deep learning model to simultaneously identify various fruit types. Subsequently, the model infers deformation parameters, such as the spherical shape of an apple. It then extracts the length and width of the object in the image. In addition, the Intel RealSense Depth Camera D435i is used to acquire the real-world distance between any point in the image and the camera. Consequently, five feature parameters are collected, which include fruit type, length, width, distance, and deformation parameters. Finally, these five feature parameters are input into a regression analysis model. Regression analysis is employed to explore the relationship between the dependent variable (the target) and the independent variables (the predictors). Hence, it is well-suited for inferring the weight of the fruit. This study utilizes a machine learning-based regression analysis model for rapid carbohydrate estimation.

Finally, regarding the fruit weight model inference, the regressor used in this study is the Extra Tree Regressor method. An Extra Tree is a type of tree-based model that, like a Random Forest, falls under the category of ensemble learning. A Random Forest is a classifier that includes multiple decision trees, and its output class is determined by the mode of the classes output by individual trees. Random Forest is a method of averaging multiple deep decision trees to reduce variance. Decision trees are trained on different portions of a dataset. This comes at the cost of a slight increase in bias and some loss of interpretability but often greatly improves performance in the final model.

Random Forest, with an added randomization step, gives rise to Extremely Randomized Trees, also known as Extra Trees. Like regular Random Forests, they are an ensemble of individual trees, but there are differences. First, each tree is trained using the entire learning sample. Second, top-down splits are random. It does not compute the best split points for each feature (e.g., based on information entropy or Gini impurity) but instead chooses split points randomly. This value is uniformly chosen randomly from the empirical range of the feature. The highest scoring split among all the random split points is chosen as the split point for a node. Similar to regular Random Forests, you can specify the number of features to be chosen for each node.

3 Experiment Results

This study developed two distinct datasets, including a training dataset and an experimental dataset. The training dataset comprises three categories, representing apples, tangerines, and bananas. Each category includes six feature parameters, namely image, weight, length, width, distance, and deformation parameters. There are 10,000 images for each category, resulting in a total of 30,000 images in the training dataset, as shown in Fig. 3.

Apple   Banana   Orange

Fig. 3. The datasets

In this study, the YOLO (You Only Look Once) algorithm plays a central role as the primary model for implementing hybrid learning. It effectively serves to extract crucial feature parameters from a diverse range of fruits, as visualized in Fig. 4. This strategic utilization of the YOLO algorithm is instrumental in capturing the distinctive characteristics and features of fruits, enabling the model to distinguish and classify them accurately. The training phase of the YOLO algorithm was a meticulous and extensive process, involving a total of 6344 iterations, which spanned approximately 4.9 h of computational effort. This rigorous training approach was executed with the utmost precision to ensure that the model could learn comprehensively and effectively. The results of this dedicated training effort are highly promising, as indicated by the remarkably low loss value of 0.0623 achieved. This minimal loss signifies a remarkably high level of recognition accuracy, highlighting the model's exceptional ability to discern and categorize fruits with precision and reliability. The YOLO algorithm's performance in this study underscores its effectiveness as a powerful tool for object detection and classification, particularly when applied to the task of fruit recognition and analysis.

In this study, the YOLO algorithm and Extra Trees regression model are combined to form a hybrid learning approach. Table 1 presents the experimental results of this hybrid learning method. The experiment involved three categories of fruits: apples, tangerines, and bananas. For each category, five fruits of different sizes and the same variety were used, resulting in a total of 15 different fruits. These fruits were photographed from various angles and distances, resulting in a dataset of 9,000 images. Following the same data construction method used for the training dataset, an experimental dataset was created. Different machine learning algorithms were then applied to evaluate their accuracy. Accuracy is calculated as (TP + TN)/(TP + FP + FN + TN), where TP (True Positive) represents correctly predicted positive samples, TN (True Negative) represents correctly predicted negative samples, FP (False Positive) represents incorrectly predicted as positive samples, and FN (False Negative) represents incorrectly predicted as negative samples.

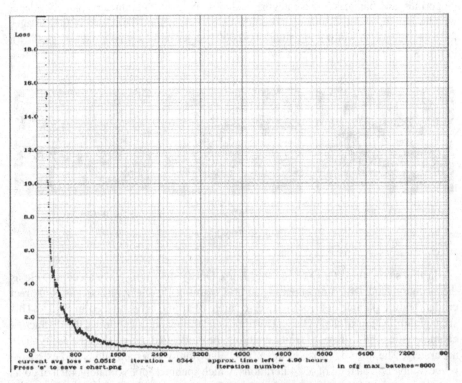

Fig. 4. The loss rate (%) during Yolo v4 training process.

From Table 1, it can be observed that the accuracy of predictions using Yolo + Linear Regression is relatively low. This is because it seeks the curve of least loss through curve fitting, which makes it susceptible to inaccuracies when distances vary. The accuracy of successful predictions is only 0.33479, with an error of 0.129525954. Similarly, the model combining Yolo with Gradient Boosting demonstrates modest performance, achieving an accuracy of only 0.48897 with an error of 0.109159216. In contrast, Yolo + SVM outperforms Linear Regression, achieving an accuracy of 0.56344 and an error of 0.098447573. When Yolo is combined with KNN for regression analysis, the predictions exhibit fluctuations, indicating that KNN can only learn to infer fruit weight from image size. Since this study assumes users will predict sugar content under varying angles and distances, and KNN cannot capture size changes of fruits at different distances, it may not be suitable for fruit weight inference. Its accuracy is 0.66154, with an error of 0.083360725. The integration of Yolo with Bagging Regressor, a machine learning ensemble algorithm, yields an accuracy of 0.95863. However, an analysis of error patterns reveals misjudgments attributed to distance-related factors, resulting in an error of 0.068245687. Random Forest, a well-known algorithm, combined with Yolo as part of a hybrid learning model, improves accuracy, achieving a rate of 0.96548 and an error of 0.064280815. Finally, this study employed the Extra Tree Regressor for experiments, which yielded excellent results. The accuracy reached 0.99815, with an error of 0.038488749. It demonstrated minimal instances of misjudgment in weight estimation, even under different angles and distances. Consequently, based on the experimental results, the proposed method for predicting sugar content in fruits using the Extra Tree Regressor model is highly accurate in estimating fruit weight.

Table 1. Table captions should be placed above the tables.

Methods	Accuracy	Error
Yolo + Linear Regression	0.33479	0.129525954
Yolo + SVM	0.56344	0.098447573
Yolo + KNN	0.66154	0.083360725
Yolo + Gradient Boosting	0.48897	0.109159216
Yolo + Bagging	0.95863	0.068245687
Yolo + Random Forest	0.96548	0.064280815
Yolo + Extra Tree	0.99815	0.038488749

4 Conclusion

The occurrence of modern lifestyle-related diseases is closely linked to diet, particularly for individuals with chronic conditions or those needing blood sugar management. Metabolic syndrome, a set of abnormalities associated with insulin-mediated glucose uptake resistance, increases the risk of developing coronary heart disease. Substituting saturated fats with unsaturated fats in the diet, without increasing protein or carbohydrate intake, may be beneficial for individuals with hypercholesterolemia, metabolic syndrome, or both. Currently, many hospitals employ nutritionists who assess the nutritional content of food through photographs. However, this process is costly, time-consuming, and labor-intensive. Moreover, assessing nutritional content based on a 45-degree photograph often introduces significant human errors, highlighting the limitations of traditional methods for image-based food nutrient analysis. The future trend is moving towards the application of artificial intelligence (AI) as a tool for prediction and monitoring, which can eliminate human errors. AI technology allows for rapid analysis of the sugar content in food, providing more opportunities for individuals to understand their daily dietary habits, establish a timely review of their nutritional status, and adopt healthy eating patterns. According to the Taiwan Food and Drug Administration (FDA) Consumer Knowledge Service website, the calculation of sugar content involves multiplying the total carbohydrates by weight, yielding the sugar content value. Therefore, based on this method of sugar calculation, knowing the weight of the food is sufficient to accurately calculate its sugar content. Consequently, the most critical aspects of this study are inferring the correct "category" of fruit and its "weight," making these key focal points in addressing the problem.

Therefore, the key features of the fruit weight estimation method proposed in this study based on hybrid learning can be summarized in two points: Firstly, the study focuses on inferring the distance of food in photos to estimate its weight. This is accomplished by using parameters such as the area covered by the food in the image and the inferred distance. Machine learning methods are employed to achieve precise food weight estimation. Secondly, the study emphasizes the application of lightweight design for machine learning methods, facilitating broader practical use. As per experimental analysis, the Extra Tree Regressor method achieved an accuracy rate of 99.81%. Thus, the proposed fruit weight estimation method in this study exhibits a combination of speed and accuracy. Given the diverse and complex nature of dietary patterns in the general population, the intelligent analysis of nutrient needs in various diets will require the gradual development of extensive databases, warranting further research into dietary nutrient prediction.

Acknowledgments. This work was financially supported by the "Intelligent Recognition Industry Service Research Center" from The Featured Areas Research Center Program within the framework of the Higher Education Sprout Project by the Ministry of Education (MOE) in Taiwan.

References

1. Department of Statistics Ministry of Health and Welfare Taiwan Homepage. https://www.mohw.gov.tw/cp-16-70314-1.html. Accessed 30 June 2022
2. Cho, N., et al.: IDF diabetes atlas: global estimates of diabetes prevalence for 2017 and projections for 2045. Diabetes Res. Clin. Pract. **138**, 271–281 (2018)
3. Yau, K.-L.A., Chong, Y.-W., Fan, X., Wu, C., Saleem, Y., Lim, P.-C.: Reinforcement learning models and algorithms for diabetes management. IEEE Access **11**, 28391–28415 (2023)

4. Anthimopoulos, M.M., Gianola, L., Scarnato, L., Diem, P., Mougiakakou, S.G.: A food recognition system for diabetic patients based on an optimized bag-of-features model. IEEE J. Biomed. Health Inform. **18**(4), 1261–1271 (2014)

5. Lo, F.P.-W., Sun, Y., Qiu, J., Lo, B.P.L.: Point2Volume: a vision-based dietary assessment approach using view synthesis. IEEE Trans. Industr. Inf. **16**(1), 577–586 (2020)

6. Lo, F.P.-W., Sun, Y., Qiu, J., Lo, B.: Image-based food classification and volume estimation for dietary assessment: a review. IEEE J. Biomed. Health Inform. **24**(7), 1926–1939 (2020)

7. Ciocca, G., Napoletano, P., Schettini, R.: Food recognition: a new dataset, experiments, and results. IEEE J. Biomed. Health Inform. **21**(3), 588–598 (2017)

8. Horiguchi, S., Amano, S., Ogawa, M., Aizawa, K.: Personalized classifier for food image recognition. IEEE Trans. Multimedia **20**(10), 2836–2848 (2018)

9. Chen, J., Zhu, B., Ngo, C.-W., Chua, T.-S., Jiang, Y.-G.: A study of multi-task and region-wise deep learning for food ingredient recognition. IEEE Trans. Image Process. **30**, 1514–1526 (2021)

10. Alahmari, S.S., Salem, T.: Food state recognition using deep learning. IEEE Access **10**, 130048–130057 (2022)

11. Sultana, J., Ahmed, B.M., Masud, M.M., Huq, A.K.O., Ali, M.E., Naznin, M.: A study on food value estimation from images: taxonomies, datasets, and techniques. IEEE Access **11**, 45910–45935 (2023)

12. Chang, L., et al.: A new deep learning-based food recognition system for dietary assessment on an edge computing service infrastructure. IEEE Trans. Serv. Comput. **11**(2), 249–261 (2018)

13. Tian, Y., et al.: Fast recognition and location of target fruit based on depth information. IEEE Access **7**, 170553–170563 (2019)

14. Fu, Y., et al.: Circular fruit and vegetable classification based on optimized GoogLeNet. IEEE Access **9**, 113599–113611 (2021)

15. Jiang, L., Qiu, B., Liu, X., Huang, C., Lin, K.: DeepFood: food image analysis and dietary assessment via deep model. IEEE Access **8**, 47477–47489 (2020)

16. Turmchokkasam, S., Chamnongthai, K.: The design and implementation of an ingredient-based food calorie estimation system using nutrition knowledge and fusion of brightness and heat information. IEEE Access **6**, 46863–46876 (2018)

17. Konstantakopoulos, F.S., Georga, E.I., Fotiadis, D.I.: An automated image-based dietary assessment system for mediterranean foods. IEEE Open J. Eng. Med. Biol. **4**, 45–54 (2023)

Artificial Intelligence for Diagnosis of Pancreatic Cystic Lesions in Confocal Laser Endomicroscopy Using Patch-Based Image Segmentation

Clara Lavita Angelina[1,2] , Tsung-Chun Lee[3,4] , Hsiu-Po Wang[5],
Rungsun Rerknimitr[6], Ming-Lun Han[7], Pradermchai Kongkam[6,8],
and Hsuan-Ting Chang[1,2(✉)]

[1] Graduate School of Engineering Science and Technology, National Yunlin University of Science and Technology, Douliu, Yunlin, Taiwan
htchang@yuntech.edu.tw

[2] Department of Electrical Engineering, National Yunlin University of Science and Technology, Douliu, Yunlin, Taiwan

[3] Division of Gastroenterology and Hepatology, Department of Internal Medicine, Taipei Medical University Shuang Ho Hospital, New Taipei City, Taiwan

[4] Department of Internal Medicine, School of Medicine, College of Medicine, Taipei Medical University, Taipei, Taiwan

[5] Department of Internal Medicine, National Taiwan University Hospital and College of Medicine, National Taiwan University, Taipei, Taiwan

[6] Excellent Center for Gastrointestinal Endoscopy and Division of Gastroenterology, Chulalongkorn University and King Chulalongkorn Memorial Hospital, Bangkok, Thailand

[7] Department of Integrated Diagnostics and Therapeutics, National Taiwan University Hospital, Taipei, Taiwan

[8] Pancreas Research Unit and Division of Hospital and Ambullatory Medicine, Department of Medicine, Faculty of Medicine, Chulalongkorn University, Bangkok, Thailand

Abstract. The early identification of pancreatic cystic lesions plays a vital part in the treatment of patients diagnosed with pancreatic cancer. However, it continues to provide a significant difficulty. This study employs the VGG19 network to construct a deep-learning model aimed at predicting the specific type of pancreatic cyst. The dataset utilized for training consists of 127,332 picture patches derived from five distinct types of pancreatic cystic videos. The training images are preprocessed using Gaussian filtering and an image patch segmentation scheme. Data augmentation is achieved by rotating the circular component in the training images. During the testing phase, a Gaussian filtering approach is applied to the test video as a preprocessing step prior to classification. The image patch segmentation scheme is also employed throughout the testing phase of our study. Our proposed methodology has the capability to autonomously categorize the specific feature type of pancreatic cystic in the test videos, while simultaneously documenting the prediction outcomes on a frame-by-frame basis. The methodology was assessed using 18 test videos, including a total of 11,059 frames. The experimental results demonstrate that the proposed methodology achieves a classification accuracy of up to 83% for different types of pancreatic cysts.

© The Author(s), under exclusive license to Springer Nature Singapore Pte Ltd. 2024
C.-Y. Lee et al. (Eds.): TAAI 2023, CCIS 2075, pp. 92–104, 2024.
https://doi.org/10.1007/978-981-97-1714-9_8

Keywords: VGG19 · Image patch · Pancreatic cystic · Gaussian filtering

1 Introduction

Pancreatic cancer is the 6th deathly cancer in the world for 2020 [1]. Fortunately, if the cancer can be detected in the early stage when surgical removal of the cancer is possible, the survival rate is 20% [2]. Progress in survival among patients with solid pancreatic cancer can be credited to effective modalities of early detection and identification of cancer types [3]. Pancreatic cancer is known for two types cystic, malignant, and begin. The malignant types of pancreatic cancer are Intraductal papillary mucinous neoplasms (IPMN) and Mucinous cystic neoplasms (MCN). The benign types are Neuroendocrine tumor (NET), Serous cystic neoplasm (SCN), and Pseudocyst. All types of pancreatic cystic have different features that can be used to classify one type from another. The malignant type is urgently required to detect because it is highly likely to spread to other body organs and it will be very dangerous for the patient. This type needs to be detected as soon as possible to perform surgery before it becomes too late. However, there is no acceptable screening test that can identify the pancreatic cystic types one from another. Many studies try to describe these differences [4, 5], which become the basic knowledge for generating classification networks.

Confocal Endomicroscopy (CEM) is an emerging technology that allows real-time, non-invasive, in vivo imaging with tissue characterization during conventional endoscopic examination and now used in the evaluation of pancreatic lesions [2]. However, the operation and diagnosis efficiency strongly depend on the experiences of well-trained physicians. Recently, the computer-aided diagnosis based on medical image processing cooperating the deep learning techniques has been intensively developed. By providing a large amount of training dataset, we can efficiently design a deep learning network that can achieve an effective detection of the disease symptoms in the early stage.

Considering Napoleon Bertrand et al.'s research, we establish the signature of each pancreatic cystic type and generate our dataset along with it. To the best of our knowledge, there is no other study on deep learning-based computer-aided diagnosis work for classifying the pancreatic cystic types based on the CEM videos. Therefore, in this paper, we propose a deep learning method to efficiently classify the five types of pancreatic cystic symptoms in the endomicroscopy videos using the VGG19 network. In this study, most of the endomicroscopy videos are collected from Chulalongkorn Memorial Hospital, Thailand. By applying adequate image selection and preprocessing schemes in videos, we can enhance the training image quality such that the accuracy of the classifier can be increased. The experimental results have verified the effectiveness of the proposed deep learning method.

2 Related Work

Recently, computer-aided detection and diagnosis techniques have been applied to pancreatic cancer. Shah et al. proposed a method to detect pancreatic tumors based on computer tomography (CT) images and the accuracy can reach 60% [6]. Vipin Dalal et al. stratify the pancreatic cystic lesions based on radiomics [7]. They classified the pancreatic cancer lesions into two categories: non-neoplastic (Pseudocyst) and neo-plastic (SCN, MCN, IPMN, and SPEN) cystic types. Recently, many researchers have introduced deep learning techniques on medical image segmentation [8–15], due to the ability of self-learning from a large dataset. Hao et al. use U-Net to change the detec-tion technique of a brain tumor from manual to automatic detection [8]. Matthew Lai use Convolution neural network (CNN) in the diagnosis of Alzheimer's disease [9]. Moeskops et al. also use CNN to perform segmentation on MRI images of brain, breast, and cardiac [10]. Wang et al. use P-Net and BIFSeg to do image segmentation of the placenta, brain, lungs, and kidneys of the fetus [11]. Zhang et al. use Res-Net and U-Net to do medical image segmentation with the help of pyramid dilated convolution [12]. Alom et al. use R2U-Net to do medical image segmentation [13] while Oktay et al. use attention U-Net to do pancreas segmentation on CT images [14]. Ahn et al. use the VGG19 as their architecture as a transfer network for processing X-Ray images [15]. In our previous research, Lee et al., used VGG19 to classify the five pancreatic cysts types [16]. We implement region of interest (ROI) based classification using manual and automatic ways. We compare the results from the two ways and find out that the manual ROI is giving the best accuracy. The drawback of manual ROI is that the ROI is chosen from an individual perspective. This means that different people can lead to different outcomes.

From all the research above, cancer detection using computer-aided technology and neural network architecture, especially on behalf of pancreatic cystic, still has been an enormous challenge. One reason is that not all neural network architectures can match to train and process the medical image. Even if the type of cancer is the same, different dataset combinations will need different types of architecture and parameters—the combination of parameters in training the network is also important to increase detection accuracy. For example, the learning rate and batch size are the two important parameters that need to be carefully chosen.

3   Proposed Method

3.1   Neural Network Architecture

In this paper, we utilize the VGG19 deep learning network with 19 convolution and max-pool layers for pancreatic cystic type classification. VGG19 was invented by the Visual Geometry Group in Oxford University [17]. Figure 1 shows the layer composition of VGG19 network architecture, which consists of 16 convolution layers with 3×3 kernel sizes, five max-pooling layers with 2×2 pool sizes, and the last output layer with a Softmax activation function. The reason of using Softmax is its capability of multiclass-class classification.

3.2   Dataset

We collected the dataset which contains 50 and 18 pancreatic endomicroscopy videos for training and test stages, respectively. All the training videos are segmented into

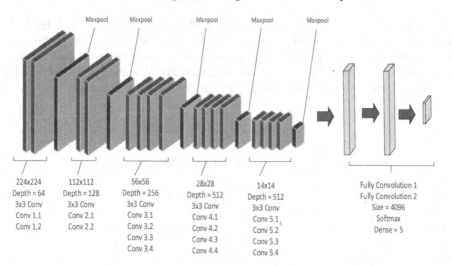

Fig. 1. Architecture of VGG19.

consequential frames. However, not every frame in the training video can be used in the training stage. We discard the frames which are with too much noise or blurred. In order to ensure that we can obtain an effective model, several preprocessing steps are conducted so that the frames with clear features are used as training data. First, all the frames are observed one by one to guarantee that we use the frames with clear features for each type of pancreatic cystic. Then we just take one frame from every four consecutive and similar frames. In addition, we quickly reviewed the original video. If there is a part of the video where the doctors stop moving the endoscopic needle to perform an examination on the pancreas, then we consider that video part as an important one and select all the frames for training. After collecting the frames, we cut the biggest rectangle region out of it and utilized image rotation. We then segment the rotated image into nine corresponding patches with overlapping. Figure 2 shows the way to segment nine patches from one image frame. Note that every patch has overlapping parts with its neighbors.

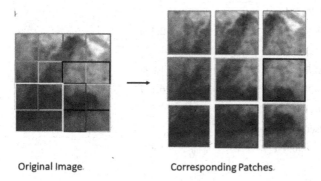

Original Image   Corresponding Patches

Fig. 2. Nine corresponding patches

We use these patches and apply Gaussian filtering especially for NET types. In summary, we select the significant image frames with clear and specific features and also implement the Gaussian filtering on the specific cystic type as our data training. Note that the training and test videos are obtained from Dr. Pradermchai and Refs. [5, 18]. Table 1 shows the number of training images for the five feature types.

Table 1. Training dataset information

Feature type	Training patch number
IPMN	34,236
MCN	10,044
SCN	32,400
NET	15,120
Pseudocyst	35,532

Table 2. Testing dataset information

Test video	Test patch number
IPMN_1	4,977
IPMN_2	6,397
IPMN_3	1,890
IPMN_4	1,890
IPMN_5	5,697
MCN_1	1,359
MCN_2	1,890
MCN_3	10,764
SCN_1	1,890
SCN_2	26,730
SCN_3	1,638
SCN_4	2,304
NET_1	1,773
NET_2	1,890
NET_3	6,147
NET_4	12,528
Pseudocyst_1	5,112
Pseudocyst_2	1,890

On the other hand, 18 test videos are used to evaluate the network performance. We only use the Gaussian filtering as the preprocessing scheme in the test stage. We cut the test image into nine patches with an overlapping of 50%, as the same method used in the training stage. After we cut the test image into patches, the VGG19-trained model predicts each patch and gives the prediction result. We will obtain nine prediction results, each prediction for each patch. We use a voting system among the patches to determine the final prediction result of the corresponding fame. Table 2 shows the number of frames that need to be predicted in the test videos.

3.3   System Overview

The proposed method was divided into the training and test stages in Fig. 3 and Fig. 4, respectively. In the training stage, we first performed data augmentation, namely circular image selection and image rotation and Gaussian filtering for NET lesions type. We attempted patch patch-based extraction method. Finally, we utilized the deep learning algorithm, VGG19, as our classifier of subtypes.

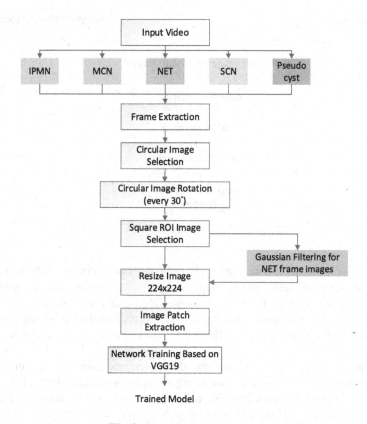

Fig. 3. Training stage overview

In the test stage, we applied the Gaussian filtering preprocessing on the test video frames to enhance image contrast. Before the preprocessing, the filth pattern detection was applied to the test image patches. We discard the image patches that contain filth patterns according to the filth threshold. Then the trained VGG19 algorithm was used to classify the pancreatic cysts subtype patch by patch of the test set videos. The final classification of pancreatic cysts subtype for the whole test video was then determined by the highest percentage calculation from the label voting system.

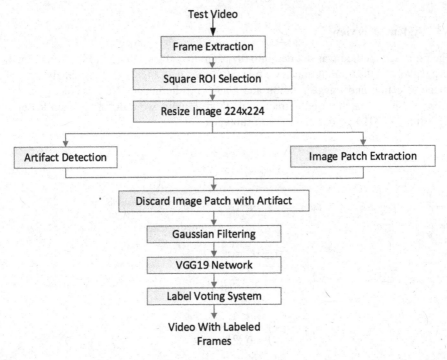

Fig. 4. Test stage overview

In our prior research [16], we employed a manual region of interest (ROI) to segregate the cystic region in various frames, subsequently utilizing this isolated area for prediction. However, this methodology has a drawback because of the potential for numerous and inconsistent results originating from the same frame, attributed to individual variability in selecting the ROI or isolated area. This necessitates a meticulous manual examination of each test video.

In contrast, the novel approach delineated in the current study involves selecting the maximal square of the frame and conducting an analysis of the entirety of the frame. The benefits of this method are twofold: it obviates the necessity for manual selection of the isolated area for prediction, and it ensures that results derived from the same frame are consistently reproducible.

3.4 Gaussian Filtering

Gaussian filtering has been intensively studied in image processing and computer vision [19]. For example, a Gaussian filter can be used to detect the edges and suppress the noise in an image. The variance can be used to smooth out the noise when we use a Gaussian filter. Equation (1) shows the definition of a two-dimensional Gaussian function [19]:

$$G(x, y) = \frac{1}{\sqrt{2\Pi\sigma}} \exp\left(-\left(x^2xy^2\right)/2\sigma^2\right) \tag{1}$$

where σ is the variance of the Gaussian function, x is the distance from the origin of the horizontal axis, and y is the distance from the origin of the vertical axis. We use a 7×7 filter kernel in the training and test stage of this research. Figure 5(a) shows the original image without applying the Gaussian filtering. Figure 5(b) shows the result after applying the Gaussian filtering in Fig. 5(a). Some details and noise in the image have been removed.

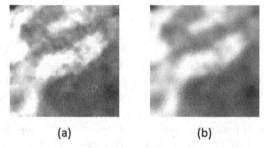

(a)   (b)

Fig. 5. Implementation of Gaussian Filtering: (a) Original image; (b) Filtered result

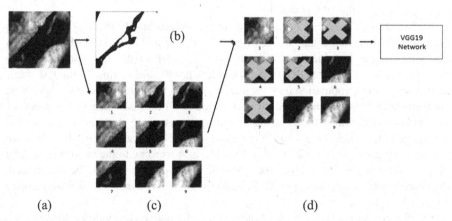

(a)   (c)   (d)

Fig. 6. Filth Pattern Detection: (a) original image; (b) filth pattern label; (c) image patch; (d) image selection

3.5 Filth Pattern

Some test videos contain certain filth pattern on the lens of endoscopy fiber. Filth is an unidentified object that does not belong to the cystic and it stays on the videos for the whole time. After we extract the frames from the test videos. We filter all the images and discard an image that contains the filth pattern. We can obtain nine patches from one original image in this step. Finally, the scheme will automatically search for all the filth pattern pixels in the patches, and only patches without containing the filth pattern, whose pixel number is greater than a threshold value, will be predicted by the VGG19 model. Figure 6(a) to 6(d) show the procedures of how the filth pattern detection works. Figure 6(a) shows the original image. Figure 6(b) shows a corresponding filth pattern label from the original image. Figure 6(c) shows a corresponding nine patches from the original image. Figure 6(d) shows the selected patches containing filth patterns. We observe that the pixel number of patches, which contain filth patterns is 2,026. This becomes our basis for setting the threshold value we use in this filth pattern detection is 2,000.

4   Experimental Results

In our experiments, we use a PC with Windows 10 operation system, CPU AMD Ryzen 7 5800X 8-Core Processor 3.8 GHz, and 128 GB DDR4 memory. We also use Visual Studio 2017 as the software platform with OpenCV library and Python programming language. As we describe in the proposed method, we use the Gaussian filter (only on NET cystic type), image rotation, and image patch schemes to extract the enhanced feature for each type of pancreatic cyst and to increase the training data amount. In the training stage, we use Adam optimizer with 100 epochs, fixed size 224×224 input images. The whole training process costs around 8 h with an average of 288 s/epoch. The deep learning network VGG19 is trained as the classifier to detect the five types of pancreatic cysts in the 18 test videos.

In the test stage, each test video is segmented into separated frames and these frames will be patched into 9 patches images with a fixed size of 112×112, which are then processed using a Gaussian filter. The advantage of using a patch is we do not need to select the region of interest (ROI) for each video. It will save us time in the test stage. Table 3 shows the computation time for predicting each test video in the test stage. Note that the average computation time for each frame in all the test videos is less than 0.1 s. In addition, the filth pattern caused by a dirty lens surface could always appear in each frame of the whole video. To eliminate the wrong classification result from this, we discarded the patches with contain the filth pattern. According to the maximum among the five values at the output layer, the cyst type of the input frame can be determined. The percentages of correctly classified frames as one of five cyst types in this video are compared.

Finally, the classification result of the cyst type for a given test video is the one with the maximum percentage. Table 4 shows the experimental results of the 18 test videos, which include five IPMN, three MCN, four SCN, four NET, and two Pseudocyst types. From all the test videos, the proposed method can classify the cyst type on each frame using a voting system and determine the greatest percentage of correctly classified frames

Table 3. The computation time in test stage

No	Video's cyst ground truth	Detection time (second)	Processing time (sec/frame)
1	IPMN	45 s (553 frames)	0.08
2	IPMN	47 s (933 frame)	0.08
3	IPMN	19 s (210 frames)	0.09
4	IPMN	19 s (210 frames)	0.09
5	IPMN	45 s (631 frames)	0.07
6	MCN	12 s (151 frames)	0.08
7	MCN	19 s (210 frames)	0.09
8	MCN	60 s (1196 frames)	0.08
9	SCN	20 s (285 frames)	0.07
10	SCN	280 s (2970 frames)	0.1
11	SCN	15 s (182 frames)	0.08
12	SCN	21 s (256 frames)	0.08
13	NET	18 s (197 frames)	0.09
14	NET	19 s (210 frames)	0.09
15	NET	55 s (683 frames)	0.08
16	NET	98 s (1392 frames)	0.07
17	Pseudocyst	40 s (568 frames)	0.07
18	Pseudocyst	19 s (210 frames)	0.09

as the predicted type of each video. For example, Fig. 7(a) shows the overall prediction result of Video 13, which consists of 197 frames. In this figure, the numbers 1, 2, 3, 4, and 5 represent the cyst types IPMN, MCN, NET, SCN, and Pseudocyst, respectively. Figure 7(b) shows that the prediction result of Video 13 is NET. The predicted cyst type is shown as the green text is displayed at the top-left corner of the frame. The 193 frames are correctly classified as the NET type and only the other four frames are classified as Pseudocyst. Therefore, Video 13 is classified as NET because in 98% of its frames are classified as NET.

Table 4 also shows that although the 18 videos are classified into correct cyst types, not all the correctly classified percentages are greater than 50%. In some videos, the percentages are as low as 30%–40% only. One of the main reasons why some videos have a low percentage of correctly detected frames is because there are several features in the video which very similar to other cystic types.

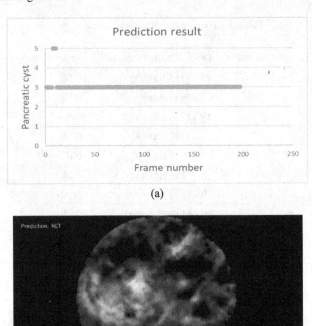

(a)

(b)

Fig. 7. (a) The overall classification result of Video 13; (b) Prediction result of a frame in Video 13.

Table 4. Experimental results of test videos (Gaussian filter = 7x7)

No	Ground truth of cyst	The result of predicted cyst	Correct classification	Prediction percentage from VGG19				
				IPMN	MCN	SCN	NET	Pseudocyst
1	IPMN	IPMN	Yes	51%	16%	31%	1%	1%
2	IPMN	IPMN	Yes	92%	2%	1%	5%	0%
3	IPMN	IPMN	Yes	91%	8%	0%	1%	0%
4	IPMN	IPMN	Yes	52%	31%	12%	5%	5%
5	IPMN	IPMN	Yes	35%	2%	0%	33%	30%
6	MCN	Pseudocyst	No	1%	7%	1%	0%	91%
7	MCN	MCN	Yes	23%	35%	20%	10%	12%
8	MCN	MCN	Yes	18%	70%	1%	6%	5%
9	SCN	NET	No	0%	0%	0%	100%	0%

(*continued*)

Table 4. (*continued*)

No	Ground truth of cyst	The result of predicted cyst	Correct classification	Prediction percentage from VGG19				
				IPMN	MCN	SCN	NET	Pseudocyst
10	SCN	SCN	Yes	3%	1%	59%	37%	0%
11	SCN	SCN	Yes	11%	0%	66%	21%	2%
12	SCN	SCN	Yes	32%	3%	54%	10%	1%
13	NET	NET	Yes	0%	0%	0%	98%	2%
14	NET	NET	Yes	20%	0%	0%	77%	3%
15	NET	NET	Yes	6%	0%	11%	82%	1%
16	NET	NET	Yes	41%	1%	1%	54%	3%
17	Pseudocyst	Pseudocyst	Yes	0%	0%	0%	14%	86%
18	Pseudocyst	IPMN	No	54%	0%	22%	44%	0%

5   Conclusion

We propose a method that utilizes the deep learning neural network VGG19 to classify the pancreatic cystic types with an accuracy of 83% (13 correctly classified videos over 15 test videos). We found that data augmentation and preprocessing on both training and testing images are critical. The selection of kernel in the Gaussian filter on the test videos also becomes a key factor in achieving a highly accurate classification. In our future work, more videos for training and testing are expected to enhance the proposed method. We will also develop an improved method based on the optical flow algorithm.

Acknowledgments. This research is financially supported by the "Intelligent Recognition Industry Service Center" from The Featured Areas Research Center Program within the framework of Higher Education Sprout Project by Ministry of Education (MOE) in Taiwan and Ministry of Science and Technology (MOST), Taiwan, under the contract number MOST 108-2221-E-224-039.

References

1. Sung, H.: Global cancer statistics 2020: GLOBOCAN estimates of incidence and mortality worldwide for 36 cancers in 185 countries. CA Cancer J. Clin. Online Version (2021)
2. Kim, V., Ahuja, N.: Early detection of pancreatic cancer. Chin. J. Cancer Res. **27**, 321–331 (2015)
3. Chiaro, M.D., Segersvard, R., Lohr, M., Verbeke, C.: Early detection and prevention of pancreatic cancer: is it really possible today? World J. Gastroenterol. **20**, 12118–12131 (2014)
4. Pancreatic Cancer: Statistics | Cancer .Net: Trans. Roy. Soc. London **A247**, 529–551 (1955). https://www.cancer.net/cancer-types/pancreaticcancer/statistics
5. Krishna, S.G., et al.: Needle-based confocal laser endomicroscopy for the diagnosis of pancreatic cystic lesions: an international external interobserver and intraobserver study (with videos). Gastrointest. Endosc. **86**, 644–654 (2017)

6. Shah, J., Surve, S., Turkar, V.: Pancreatic tumor detection using image processing. In: Proceedings of 4th International Conference on Advances in Computing, Communication and Control (ICAC3 2015), vol. 49, pp. 11–16 (2015). Procedia Comput. Sci.

7. Dalal, V., Carmichael, J., Dhaliwal, A., Jain, M., Kaur, S., Batra, S.K.: Radiomics in stratification of pancreatic cystic lesions: machine learning in action. Cancer Lett. **469**, 228–237 (2020)

8. Dong, H., Yang, G., Liu, F., Mo, Y., Guo, Y.: Automatic brain tumor detection and segmentation using U-net based fully convolutional networks. In: Proceedings Annual Conference Medical Image Understanding and Analysis, Edinburgh, U.K., pp. 506–517 (2017)

9. Lai, M.: Deep learning for medical image segmentation. https://arxiv.org/abs/1807.04459 (2015)

10. Moeskops, P., et al.: Deep learning for multi-task medical image segmentation in multiple modalities. In: Ourselin, S., Joskowicz, L., Sabuncu, M.R., Unal, G., Wells, W. (eds.) Medical Image Computing and Computer-Assisted Intervention – MICCAI 2016. LNCS, vol. 9901, pp. 478–486. Springer, Cham (2016). https://doi.org/10.1007/978-3-319-46723-8_55

11. Wang, G., et al.: Interactive medical image segmentation using deep learning with image-specific fine-tuning. IEEE Trans. Med. Imag. **37**(7), 1562–1573 (2018)

12. Zhang, Q., Cui, Z., Niu, X., Geng, S., Qiao, Y.: Image segmentation with pyramid dilated convolution based on resnet and U-Net. In: Liu, D., Xie, S., Li, Y., Zhao, D., El-Alfy, E.S. (eds.) Neural Information Processing. ICONIP 2017. LNCS, vol. 10635, pp. 364–372. Springer, Cham (2017). https://doi.org/10.1007/978-3-319-70096-0_38

13. Alom, M.Z., Hasan, M., Yakopcic, C., Taha, M.T., Asari, K.V.: Recurrent residual convolutional neural network based on U-Net (R2UNet) for medical image segmentation. https://arxiv.org/abs/1802.06955 (2018)

14. Oktay, O., et al.: Attention U-Net: learning where to look for the pancreas. https://arxiv.org/abs/1804.03999 (2018)

15. Ahn, E., Kumar, A., Kim, J., Li, C., Feng, D., Fulham, M.: Xray image classification using domain transferred convolutional neural networks and local sparse spatial pyramid. In: Proceedings of 2016 IEEE International Symposium on Biomedical Imaging (ISBI), pp. 855–858. IEEE, Prague, Czech Republic (2016)

16. Lee, T.-C., et al.: Deep-learning-enabled computer-aided diagnosis in the classification of pancreatic cystic lesions on confocal laser endomicroscopy. Diagnostics **13** (2023). https://doi.org/10.3390/diagnostics13071289

17. Simonyan, K., Zisserman, A.: Very deep convolutional networks for large-scale image recognition. http://arxiv.org/abs/1409.1556 (2014)

18. Napoleon, B., et al.: Needle-based confocal laser endomicroscopy of pancreatic cystic lesions: a prospective multicenter validation study in patients with definite diagnosis. Endoscopy **51**, 825–835 (2019)

19. Deng, G., Cahill, L.W.: An adaptive Gaussian filter for noise reduction and edge detection. In: IEEE Conference Record Nuclear Sciences Symposium and Medical Imaging Conference, San Francisco, USA, pp. 1615–1619 (1993)

An Egg Sorting System Combining Egg Recognition Model and Smart Egg Tray

Jung-An Liu[ID], Wei-Ling Lin[✉], Wei-Cheng Hong, Li-Syuan Chen,
and Tung-Shou Chen

National Taichung University of Science and Technology, Taichung, Taiwan
will_ling@nutc.edu.tw

Abstract. Modern agriculture is at the forefront of technological transformation. Smart agricultural technology and mechanical automation are bringing unprecedented opportunities and challenges to the field. This study aims to address the challenges faced by traditional egg production in Taiwan. We have developed an egg sorting system that combines a lightweight robotic arm and a smart egg tray. The system integrates machine vision technology, using the CenterNet technique to rapidly identify the position of eggs and precisely handles them through a lightweight robotic arm. Simultaneously, the smart egg tray, equipped with pressure sensors, monitors the status of the eggs placed on the tray in real-time, ensuring efficient egg positioning. Experimental results show that the system's accuracy rate for egg positioning and egg picking reaches up to 99%. Additionally, the smart egg tray can instantly display the quantity and position of the placed eggs. This system holds the potential to enhance egg production efficiency, reduce costs, and promote the modernization and sustainable development of agriculture.

Keywords: Lightweight Robotic · Machine Vision · CenterNet · Collecting Eggs

1 Introduction

Agriculture has always been a vital industry in human life, providing food and resources while profoundly impacting our living environment. However, modern agriculture is at a pivotal moment of technological transformation. Emerging technologies are presenting unprecedented opportunities and challenges for agriculture. The crux of this transformation lies in the application of new technologies, especially smart agricultural technology and mechanical automation. These technologies are not only changing the way agriculture is conducted but also have profound effects on farmers, production efficiency, the environment, and society at large.

Smart agricultural technology has become one of the primary drivers of modern agriculture. It integrates sensor technology, data analytics, and automation systems to enhance the efficiency and sustainability of agricultural production. Smart agricultural techniques can monitor soil conditions, meteorological data, and crop growth. They can automatically adjust agricultural operations to cater to ever-changing needs. This

C.-Y. Lee et al. (Eds.): TAAI 2023, CCIS 2075, pp. 105–115, 2024.
https://doi.org/10.1007/978-981-97-1714-9_9

not only improves the quality of agricultural products but also contributes to reducing resource wastage, achieving sustainable agricultural production.

Mechanical automation technology has been successfully applied in multiple industries, including manufacturing, logistics, and agriculture. In the agricultural sector, the development of mechanical automation technology allows farmers to manage farm operations more efficiently and increase productivity. This includes using robots and robotic arms to perform various tasks, such as vegetable harvesting robots that can automatically identify and harvest different types of fruits and vegetables [1–3]. Robotic livestock feeders are used for automatic feeding and milking. Drones are employed for monitoring crop growth, irrigation, and fertilization. The advantages of mechanical automation lie in their ability to offer a high degree of precision and efficiency while reducing labor costs and risks.

However, despite significant advancements in modern agricultural technology, many farms in Taiwan still use traditional battery cage methods for egg production. According to the 2022 third-quarter livestock and poultry statistical survey by the Council of Agriculture, Executive Yuan, the total number of laying hens in Taiwan reached 44.92 million. Over 90% of poultry farmers still use this traditional breeding method.

In previous research, mechanical automation technology applied to egg production was relatively limited, mainly focusing on egg collection and classification. In traditional egg production, eggs typically need to be manually collected, classified, and packaged, which requires a significant amount of labor and time. Therefore, this study aims to address the challenges faced by traditional egg production in Taiwan. We have developed an egg sorting system that combines a lightweight robotic arm and a smart egg tray. This system integrates machine vision technology and mechanical automation to enhance the efficiency of egg production, reduce costs, and promote the modernization and sustainable development of agriculture in Taiwan.

2   Research Methods

This paper introduces an egg sorting system based on a lightweight robotic arm and a smart egg tray, aiming to automatically locate and pick up eggs by integrating image recognition technology, the smart egg tray, and the lightweight robotic arm. The system architecture is shown in Fig. 1.

To achieve automatic egg collection and tray sorting, the system structure is primarily divided into four key modules: the system core and egg recognition module, the robotic arm control module, the smart egg tray, and the egg sorting system. Each of these modules plays a distinct role and is responsible for different tasks.

The egg sorting system and egg recognition module are responsible for two tasks: integrating peripheral components and identifying the egg's position, then converting it into corresponding coordinate values. The robotic arm control module primarily receives coordinate values from the egg sorting system and converts them into control parameters for the robotic arm, thereby achieving the goal of positioning and picking up the egg. The smart egg tray incorporates Internet of Things (IoT) devices into commonly used egg trays, allowing it to detect whether eggs are placed on the tray. When eggs are placed on the tray, the smart egg tray can immediately detect this and send this information to the egg sorting system for recording and further processing.

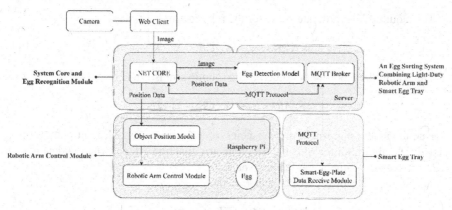

Fig. 1. System architecture diagram.

2.1 Egg Recognition Model

The egg recognition module is tasked with detecting all egg positions within an image and returning these locations as parameters to the egg sorting system. This module employs the CenterNet [4–6] technique, which was chosen for its high accuracy and efficiency when detecting numerous small objects. Unlike traditional object detection methods, CenterNet simplifies the entire process by simultaneously executing keypoint detection and bounding box prediction, reducing operational steps and enhancing efficiency. Moreover, this technology excels in computational efficiency, capable of processing large amounts of image data in a relatively short timeframe, which is crucial for applications requiring real-time data collection and processing. Importantly, the CenterNet technique has broad applications, not only in egg detection but also in target detection for other agricultural and industrial applications, making it an ideal choice to address the challenges of egg recognition.

The recognition process of the model is illustrated in Fig. 2 and can be divided into several primary steps. Initially, it uses the ResNet-50 backbone model to process the input image to extract a feature map with high-level features, such as the edges, textures, and shapes of eggs. These features are vital for subsequent object detection. The core of CenterNet lies in predicting the center points of objects in an image. For each feature point (x, y) in the image, the model predicts whether it contains the center point of an object and generates a center heatmap, marking potential object center positions, indicating potential egg locations. Once the center point positions are predicted, Center-Net further predicts the bounding box corresponding to each center point. This is a key step in achieving object detection by transforming the position of the center point with surrounding pixels to define the size and position of the bounding box.

Firstly, the reference coordinate of the robotic arm is set as:

$$O(Xo, Yo)$$

The detected center point of the egg is denoted as:

$$CE(X\_CE, Y\_CE)$$

The required X-coordinate value for the robotic arm is Eq. (1)

$$X\_ARM = -(X\_CE - X\_O) \tag{1}$$

The required Y-coordinate value for the robotic arm is Eq. (2)

$$Y\_ARM = -(Y\_CE - Y\_O) \tag{2}$$

Due to camera placement discrepancies, a correction error, M, multiplied by it is needed. The algorithm for M is the trigonometric function $Sin(\theta)$, where θ denotes the angle between the camera and the bracket.

The corrected error is calculated as Eq. (3)

$$CM = CE \times M \tag{3}$$

In subsequent steps, the model also predicts the offsets from the center point to the upper-left and lower-right corners of the bounding box. These offsets are used to precisely define the egg's position and bounding box size. These offsets include the horizontal and vertical offsets from the center point to the upper-left corner. Finally, using the position of the center point and offsets, we can compute the actual positions of the bounding boxes of each egg in the image, i.e., the coordinates of the upper-left (dx, dy) and lower-right (dw, dh) corners, achieving accurate egg positioning.

Together, these steps constitute the object detection process, allowing this module to effectively detect and locate egg objects in the image, thereby enhancing the production efficiency and accuracy of the automatic egg sorting system.

2.2 Smart Egg Tray

To ensure whether eggs have been placed in the tray, this study designed a distinctive smart egg tray. By embedding the ESP8266 into commercially available egg trays, the tray can transmit information to the server via a network communication protocol, turning it into an Internet of Things (IoT) device. The architecture is illustrated in Fig. 3.

Initially, the design of this tray emphasizes its physical structure, ensuring it has ample space to accommodate the ESP8266 module, as well as the necessary connections and power facilities, including an appropriate power supply and communication interfaces. In order to detect the status, position, and number of eggs placed on the tray, microswitches are installed inside the tray in this study. When an egg is placed on the tray, the microswitch is triggered. The ESP8266 is responsible for collecting this switch signal and relaying this information back to the egg sorting system. The communication mode between this module and the server uses MQTT as the primary communication protocol, which is also one of the most common protocols in IoT applications. With this design, commercial egg trays can be transformed into smart egg trays that can detect eggs and communicate egg placement information through a network protocol. The information sent by the smart egg tray regarding egg placement is numbered from left to right for each position, with each number corresponding to the position of an egg.

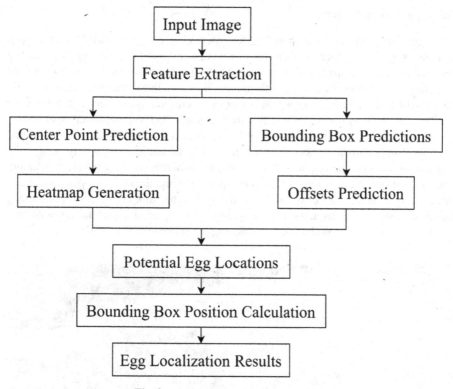

Fig. 2. Model identification flowchart.

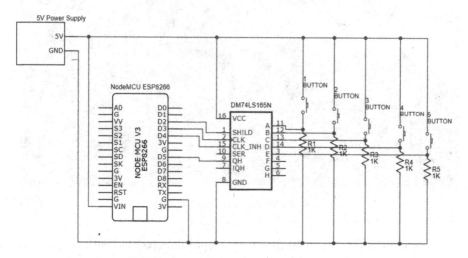

Fig. 3. Circuit diagram of the smart egg tray.

2.3 Egg Sorting System

The egg sorting system is responsible for integrating each peripheral module, such as converting the information from the egg recognition module, receiving egg sorting instructions, and handling user interfaces. The egg recognition module is in charge of detecting the location of each egg in the image. However, these detected positions might have slight deviations from the actual positions. Therefore, this system will convert the positions detected by the egg recognition module into corresponding actual positions for the robotic arm. This ensures that the robotic arm can accurately pick up the eggs while reducing computational stress on the robotic arm. In addition, to accurately achieve the egg sorting function, the system will transmit two sets of robotic arm control information: one for controlling the robotic arm to pick up the egg and the other for placing the egg in the corresponding tray position. Since the system has already received precise egg placement information from the smart tray, eggs will be placed sequentially, prioritizing positions with smaller numbers, thus achieving the purpose of egg sorting (Fig. 4).

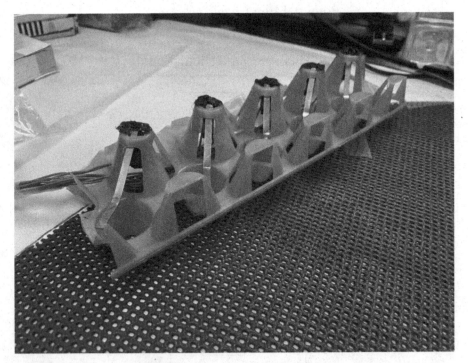

Fig. 4. Schematic of the smart egg tray.

This system provides a user interface for users, presenting egg placement information in an intuitive manner for user reference. The system is hosted on a web server and is a web application system. It adopts a front-end and back-end separation architecture, using Angular as the front-end framework and .NET Core as the backend web framework. The system backend is responsible for receiving real-time tray information and processing and computing this data. It then sends this information to be displayed on the user's page or transmits the data back to the corresponding peripheral devices.

3 Research Results

This study introduces an egg sorting system based on a lightweight robotic arm and a smart egg tray. This system can automatically detect the position of the eggs, and after calculations by the egg sorting system, it sends this information to the robotic arm for the egg-picking function. Additionally, we designed a smart egg tray that sends placement information in real-time to the egg sorting system for recording when eggs are placed on the tray. This data is then displayed on the user interface. We conducted experiments focusing on the robotic arm picking up eggs to calculate its accuracy. The results confirm that our system can accurately pick up eggs and place them in the tray. Furthermore, we will showcase the precise user interface screen and the design of the smart egg tray.

3.1 Experimental Environment

In this research, we established an experimental system to verify the performance of our egg sorting system. We utilized an experimental platform equipped with a lightweight robotic arm with six degrees of freedom, the detailed specifications of which are shown in Table 1. A series of experiments were conducted to evaluate the system's accuracy, efficiency, and stability.

Table 1. ArmPi Hiwonder Raspberry Pi 4B 4GB AI Vision Robotic Arm Specification

Item	Specification
Size	height 291 * width 159 * height 430 mm
Weight	1.2 kg
Material	metal bracket
Power Supply	7.5 V 6A DC adapter
Hardware	Raspberry Pi 4B
Software	PC VNC software
Servo Parameter	single shaft/LX-15D/LX-225 intelligent Bus Servo

The system operates on the Windows 10 operating system and is equipped with a robust hardware setup, providing reliable support for the development and operation of the egg recognition model and the smart egg tray system. The core hardware configuration includes a high-performance Intel Core i7-11800H processor, which has 8 cores and 16 threads, offering outstanding computational capabilities for the system. This is particularly suitable for handling complex computations and large dataset operations. Additionally, to ensure seamless multitasking and efficient operation, the system is equipped with 16 GB of DDR4 memory. This high-frequency memory module contributes to enhancing the system's performance (Fig. 5).

Fig. 5. Physical diagram of the robotic arm.

In terms of data access speed, the system comes with a built-in 512 GB Solid State Drive (SSD), ensuring rapid data access, especially excelling in large model loading and data processing tasks. For graphics processing, the system relies on the NVIDIA GeForce RTX 3050 Ti graphics processor. This high-performance GPU is optimized for graphic computations, computer vision tasks, and deep learning assignments, offering exceptional processing performance.

Regarding software tools, this study employs several highly professional software tools to support the development work. These tools include Visual Studio Code version 1.83, a highly customizable code editor suitable for various programming languages, offering a convenient development environment and a variety of extensions to assist with code editing, debugging, and version control. Moreover, Microsoft Visual Studio 2022 is a comprehensive Integrated Development Environment (IDE) suitable for various application development domains, including desktop, web, and mobile applications, providing a rich set of development tools and powerful integration features. Finally, the Arduino IDE 1.0, designed specifically for the Arduino microcontroller, was used in this study to write, upload, and execute control programs, making it an essential tool for the system.

3.2 Egg-Picking Experiment with Robotic Arm

This experiment tests the egg sorting system by detecting the eggs and converting their positions into coordinates for the robotic arm. After sending the coordinates to the robotic arm, the experiment proceeds to pick up the eggs and calculate the accuracy of the egg-picking process. The schematic diagram of the experimental environment is shown in Fig. 6.

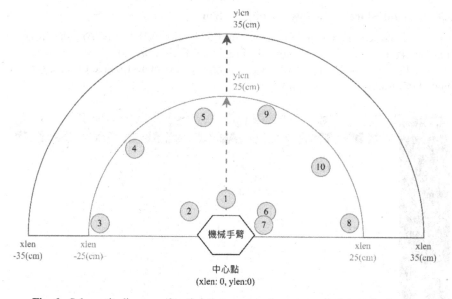

Fig. 6. Schematic diagram of testing the egg grasping accuracy of the robotic arm.

In this experiment, eggs are randomly scattered within the experimental range, and an egg is placed at each position for detection and picking actions. Each position is tested ten times, and the number of successes and failures is recorded to calculate the overall accuracy rate. The results are shown in Table 2.

Table 2. Accuracy test results

Test Coordinate Point		Accuracy	
		Success	Failure
Coordinate 1	(0.86, 14.73)	10	0
Coordinate 2	(−12.57, 10.23)	9	1
Coordinate 3	(−20.14, 8.25)	10	0
Coordinate 4	(−20.86, 12.66)	10	0
Coordinate 5	(−10.71, 22.29)	10	0
Coordinate 6	(12.29, 10.23)	10	0
Coordinate 7	(13.57, 6.54)	10	0
Coordinate 8	(19.43, 8.79)	10	0
Coordinate 9	(12.43, 20.22)	10	0
Coordinate 10	(19.14, 14.64)	10	0
Accuracy		**99%**	

The experimental results indicate that the system has a high egg-picking accuracy of 99%, demonstrating its precision and reliability in picking up eggs and placing them on the smart egg tray.

3.3   User Interface of the Egg Sorting System

The user interface of the egg sorting system was developed using the Angular frontend framework. This interface, as shown in Fig. 7 and Fig. 8, provides real-time feedback on egg placement within the smart egg tray, real-time camera footage of the eggs, and related information.

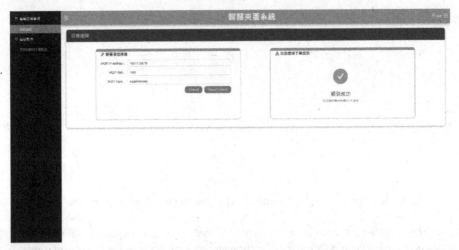

Fig. 7. Connection settings for the MQTT communication protocol of the smart egg tray and the connection status of the Raspberry Pi for the robotic arm.

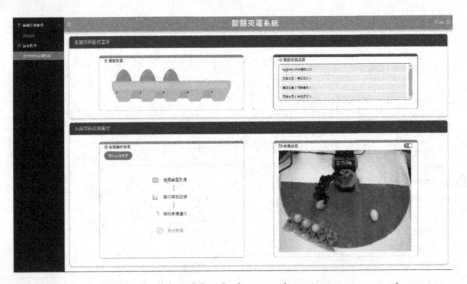

Fig. 8. User interface for the lightweight robotic arm and smart egg tray egg sorting system.

In summary, this system is highly practical and innovative. Not only does it have a complete system architecture, but it can also detect and pick up eggs as intended.

4   Conclusion

The egg sorting system, based on a lightweight robotic arm and smart egg tray, not only offers a clear and distinct user interface but also employs an egg detection model based on CenterNet. Furthermore, it features a unique smart egg tray structure. Based on the results from various tests, this system demonstrates considerable practicality and innovation. We look forward to deploying it in real poultry farms for testing in the future, while also considering integrating it into an autonomous vehicle system for convenient testing and application in real-world scenarios.

References

1. Arad, B., et al.: Development of a sweet. J. Field Rob. **37**(6), 1027–1039 (2020)
2. Li, K., Huo, Y., Liu, Y., Shi, Y., He, Z., Cui, Y.: Design of a lightweight robotic arm for kiwifruit pollination **198**, 0168–1699 (2022)
3. Shi, Y., Jin, S., Zhao, Y., Huo, Y., Liu, L., Cui, Y.: Lightweight force-sensing tomato picking robotic arm with a "global-local" visual servo **204**, 0168–1699 (2023)
4. Duan, K.: CenterNet: keypoint triplets for object detection, 6568–6577 (2019)
5. Zhou, X., Wang, D., Krähenbühl, P.: Objects as points. arXiv preprint arXiv:1904.07850 (2019)
6. Horng, G.-J., Liu, M.-X., Chen, C.-C.: The smart image recognition mechanism for crop harvesting system in intelligent agriculture. IEEE Sens. J. **20**(5), 2766–2781 (2020)

Survival Factors Analysis of Out-of-Hospital Cardiac Arrest Patients via Effective Data Cleaning Techniques and Explainable Machine Learning

Zi-Yi Lu and Hsun-Ping Hsieh$^{(\boxtimes)}$

Department of Electrical Engineering, National Cheng Kung University, Tainan, Taiwan
n26100498@gs.ncku.edu.tw, hphsieh@mail.ncku.edu.tw

Abstract. The purpose of this study is to explore the key survival factors of OHCA (Out-of-Hospital Cardiac Arrest) non-trauma cases through data science methods and machine learning technology. It is expected to provide directions for improvements in first aid procedures and policy advocacy to increase the survival rate of OHCA cases. This study explores the latest data of OHCA cases in Tainan City, Taiwan. To deal with the issue of data mess in the majority category, a suitable data cleaning method is proposed to ensure the rationality of the cleaned data. In addition, due to the insufficient amount of data and extremely imbalanced data, the oversampling technique is used to generate data in the minority category to balance the dataset. Next, a machine learning model is adopted to predict whether OHCA non-trauma patients eventually survive. Finally, SHAP (SHapley Additive exPlanation) is applied to conduct a comprehensive analysis and interpretation of the model training results to gain new insights into the key survival factors.

Keywords: OHCA · Anomaly Detection · Root Cause Analysis · SHAP

1 Introduction

1.1 Background

OHCA (Out-of-Hospital Cardiac Arrest) refers to a situation where the cardiopulmonary function stops before the patient is sent to the emergency room of the hospital. Numerous studies have shown that survival rates drop by about 9% for every minute that passes [1–3]. Therefore, first aid for OHCA patients is a race against time, and it is regarded as the highest priority case in the triage of emergency and severe cases.

CPC (Cerebral Performance Category) refers to the brain function classification of OHCA patients when they are discharged from the hospital. It is divided into five grades: CPC 1 represents good brain function, CPC 2 represents moderate brain function impairment, CPC 3 represents severe brain function impairment, CPC 4 represents coma/persistent vegetative state, and CPC 5 represents brain dead or death. In general medical discussion, CPC 1-2 (CPC 1 to CPC 2) are considered good neurological prognosis and CPC 3-5 (CPC 3 to CPC 5) are poor neurological prognosis [4].

© The Author(s), under exclusive license to Springer Nature Singapore Pte Ltd. 2024
C.-Y. Lee et al. (Eds.): TAAI 2023, CCIS 2075, pp. 116–130, 2024.
https://doi.org/10.1007/978-981-97-1714-9_10

In addition to the professional and complete care given by the medical team after arriving at the hospital, rescue methods before arriving at the hospital are also indispensable. Among them, the response of the first responder and the disposal of EMTs (Emergency Medical Technicians) are the key survival factors of OHCA patients [5].

1.2 Motivation

This study is conducted in collaboration with Tainan City Fire Department, Taiwan. Among the overall OHCA cases in Tainan City, 89% are non-trauma cases and 11% are trauma cases. These patients need to survive for 2 h in the hospital, 24 h in the hospital, and be admitted to the ICU before they have a chance to survive. In the end, only 5% of the patients are CPC 1-2, as shown in Fig. 1.

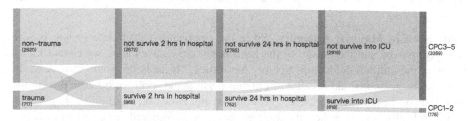

Fig. 1. Overview of OHCA cases in Tainan City

After discussing with Tainan City with the fire department, we learn that for OHCA trauma cases, the actual rescue is mainly about "time to hospital". Because most of the corresponding medical measures are only available at the hospital, it is best for these patients to be got on the ambulance and sent to the hospital as soon as possible. For OHCA non-trauma cases, there are more medical methods that can be performed earlier in the ambulance, and it may also be more related to whether there are witnesses and bystanders performing CPR and other information. In addition, the amount of non-trauma data is larger than that of trauma cases, so this study will only discuss non-trauma cases in OHCA cases. This study will use the perspective of data science and machine learning to find out the key survival factors of OHCA non-trauma cases.

1.3 Related Research

Many of the existing studies have explored the incidence of OHCA cases and found that it is related to geospatial information. For example, OHCA incidents are more likely to occur in communities with a high proportion of the elderly population [6, 7].

In addition, some studies have explored the survival rate of OHCA cases, suggesting that initial heart rhythm, age, early cardiopulmonary resuscitation, EMS (Emergency Medical Services) response time, and location of occurrence are all factors that affect survival rate [5, 8–11].

In these studies of key survival factors analysis, most of the methods used are common statistical analysis methods [5, 8–10], and some are machine learning methods and use the importance of features as the analysis method [11]. Based on the other studies on RCA (Root Cause Analysis), it is known that using machine learning models and adopting SHAP (SHapley Additive exPlanation) to interpret the models globally and locally is a feasible and effective analysis method [12–15].

1.4 Challenge

However, this study faces the following three types of challenges.

Extremely Imbalanced Data. Since the emergency rescue data system in Tainan City has been established in recent years, there is only data from 2020/01/01 to 2022/08/31. There are only 2,820 OHCA non-trauma cases with relatively complete records. Among these cases, the proportion of CPC 1-2 is only 4.5%, with a total of 158 cases. The amount of data in the two categories differs too much, which will lead to poor model training results.

Data Mess in Majority Category. Since the emergency rescue data system is still being improved and the design of the form is not rigorous enough, we cannot know whether the unfilled fields are "No" or "Not Filled". In addition, some OHCA cases may not be given first aid because of obvious death at the scene, or because the family members or the patients themselves give up first aid. However, these types of cases are not specifically labeled in the dataset. Since these types of majority category cases (CPC 3-5) are recorded similarly to the minority category cases (CPC 1-2) with early ROSC (Return of Spontaneous Circulation), this will affect the performance of the model. Therefore, it is necessary to clean up the majority category data.

Difficulty in Evaluating Data Cleaning Methods. While the data needs to be cleaned, there are no answers to assess whether the data cleaning methods are appropriate. This may significantly affect the final analysis results, so methods need to be developed to indirectly validate the rationality of the cleaned data.

1.5 Method

From the related research, it can be known that spatial information may affect the survival rate of OHCA cases, so this study will also consider population data and weather data for model training. In response to the three challenges, the oversampling method is used to generate data of minority category (CPC 1-2). Furthermore, this study proposes a sampler-based algorithm to clean up data. The rationality of the cleaned data is indirectly validated by comparing the analysis results with the exploratory data analysis and related medical research. Next, a machine learning model is adopted to predict whether each OHCA non-trauma case is CPC 1-2. Finally, SHAP is applied to analyze the results of model training to obtain the key survival factors of OHCA non-trauma cases and conduct in-depth discussions on these key survival factors.

1.6 Contribution

To the best of our knowledge, this study has the following contributions.

- The latest data of OHCA cases in Tainan City are explored to gain new insights.
- While most medical research discusses trauma and non-trauma cases together, this study focuses only on non-trauma cases to explore the key survival factors.
- A variety of features are considered. In addition to medical treatment methods, patient information, case time, case location, and other rescue data, external data such as population and weather are also considered.
- A data cleaning method that is suitable for this dataset is proposed and validated.
- A comprehensive analysis and interpretation of the model training results is conducted by SHAP to gain in-depth insights into the impact of key survival factors.
- This study provides the directions for Tainan City Fire Department to improve first aid procedures and policy advocacy, which is expected to increase the survival rate.

2 Preliminary

2.1 Dataset

OHCA Non-trauma Data. The data is provided by Tainan City Fire Department, and the time range is from 2020/01/01 to 2022/08/31, a total of 32 months. There is a total of 4,038 OHCA non-trauma records in the overall data, of which only 2,820 records are relatively complete.

Population Data. Open data from the government are used to calculate the monthly population density and the proportion of the elderly population in the village where each OHCA non-trauma case occurs.

Weather Data. Open data from the government are used to calculate the hourly temperature, humidity, rainfall, visibility, PM2.5, day-to-day temperature difference, and day-to-day AQI when each OHCA non-trauma case occurs.

Finally, the above data are integrated, and specific features are processed through one-hot encoding or data standardization. There are 2,820 records and 158 features in the dataset, of which 158 records are CPC 1-2 and 2,662 records are CPC 3-5.

2.2 Exploratory Data Analysis

The correlation of EMT (Emergency Medical Technician) levels and lay rescuers with CPC values are explored in this section. These two types of features are selected for exploratory data analysis because these are the common factors that affect the survival rate of OHCA cases in much related medical research, and the data records of these two types of features are relatively correct and complete.

Correlation of EMT Levels with CPC Values. EMT is divided into three levels: EMT-1 is a junior ambulanceman, EMT-2 is an intermediate ambulanceman, and EMT-P is a senior ambulanceman. The proportion of EMTs at different levels in Tainan City is 2% for EMT-1, 79% for EMT-2, and 19% for EMT-P. Furthermore, it can be observed that in the presence of EMT-P, the probability of OHCA non-trauma cases ending up as CPC 1-2 is higher (6.3% with EMT-P and 5.1% without EMT-P). This result is consistent with related medical research [5].

Correlation of Lay Rescuers with CPC Values. In the chain of survival, a lay rescuer is considered important. It can be observed that in the case with witnesses or bystanders CPR, the probability of OHCA non-trauma cases ending up as CPC 1-2 is higher (9.6% with witnesses and 2.2% without witnesses; 6.8% with bystanders CPR and 4.2% without bystanders CPR). This result is consistent with related medical research [5].

3 Methodology

3.1 Overall Workflow

The overall workflow of this study is shown in Fig. 2, which consists of three stages. In the first stage, the outlier detection algorithm and the sampler-based algorithm proposed in this study are used to remove anomalies respectively. Based on the output of the first stage, the second stage uses the machine learning model to predict the survival rate of OHCA non-trauma cases. Finally, the third stage evaluates the specific impact of each feature by interpreting the model trained in the second stage, and then analyzes the root cause. The details of each stage will be explained below.

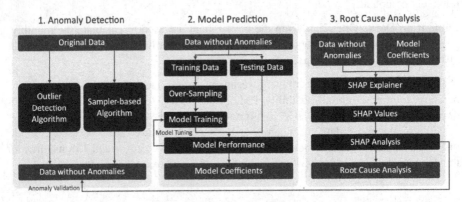

Fig. 2. The overall workflow

3.2 Anomaly Detection

In this stage, the outlier detection algorithm and the sampler-based algorithm which is proposed in this study are used to detect anomalies in majority category (CPC 3-5).

Outlier Detection Algorithm. Five common outlier detection algorithms are used to detect anomalies in majority category, including Isolation Forest [16], Local Outlier Factor [17], Robust Covariance using Elliptic Envelope [18], One-Class SVM [19], and

One-Class SVM with SGD [20]. According to the experimental results, the algorithm and the ratio of anomalies with the best performance are selected.

However, this method only considers the majority category itself and does not interact with the minority category. Therefore, the removed anomalies may not be appropriate enough, which may lead to unreasonable analysis results.

Sampler-Based Algorithm. To deal with the above issue, this study draws inspiration from sampling techniques that are used to solve the problem of data category imbalance, and then designs an anomaly detection method that can consider both majority and minority categories. Due to the data mess issue mentioned in Sect. 1.4, it is reasonable to assume that some majority category data have similar properties to minority category data. Therefore, it is necessary to delete some majority category data that are close to the minority category data.

NearMiss [21], an undersampling technique that selects majority category samples based on their distance from minority category samples, can achieve the goal. NearMiss selects samples by heuristic rules, which can be divided into three versions, namely NearMiss-1, NearMiss-2, and NearMiss-3. According to the goal, adopting NearMiss-1, which selects majority category samples with the smallest average distance to the k nearest minority category samples, is the most appropriate. However, since NearMiss is an undersampling method that deletes the majority category data to the same amount as the minority category data, the amount of cleaned data will be severely insufficient, making it difficult for the model to learn.

Therefore, SMOTE [22], the most mainstream oversampling technique, is adopted to generate more minority category data before NearMiss-1. In this process, the amount of data generated is based on the proportion of anomalies. Assuming that there are 30% anomalies in the majority category data, the minority category data is oversampled to as many as 70% of the majority category data. Next, NearMiss-1 is used to undersample the majority category data. Finally, the undersampled majority category data is concatenated with the unsampled minority category data to obtain data without anomalies.

The complete procedure for the sampler-based algorithm is summarized below.

1. **Input**: The sequence of all OHCA non-trauma data $S_i, \forall i \in \{1, \ldots, I\}$, the ratio of anomalies R_a, and the ratio of neighbors in NearMiss-1 R_b.
2. Separate the sequence S_i, and obtain the sequence of majority category data $S_{i(maj)}, \forall i(maj) \in \{1, \ldots, N\}$ and the sequence of minority category data $S_{i(min)}, \forall i(min) \in \{1, \ldots, I - N\}$.
3. Apply SMOTE algorithm to the sequence S_i with the ratio R_a, and obtain the sequence $S_m, \forall m \in \{1, \ldots, N * (2 - R_a)\}$.
4. Apply NearMiss-1 algorithm to the sequence S_m with the ratio R_b, and obtain the sequence $S_n, \forall n \in \{1, \ldots, N * 2 * (1 - R_a)\}$.
5. To preserve the original minority category data in the sequence S_i, concatenate the majority category data in the sequence S_n and the sequence $S_{i(min)}$. Finally, obtain the sequence $S_r, \forall r \in \{1, \ldots, I - N * R_a\}$.
6. **Return**: $S_r, \forall r \in \{1, \ldots, I - N * R_a\}$.

According to the experimental results, the ratio of anomalies and the ratio of neighbors in NearMiss-1 with the best performance are selected.

3.3 Model Prediction

In this stage, machine learning models are used to predict survival, i.e., CPC1-2 or not.

Feature Selection. Since the goal of this study is to identify key survival factors, no feature deletion or dimensionality reduction will be performed. In other words, the machine learning model will be trained using all 158 features from the data.

Data Sampling. Sampling is a technique commonly used to deal with the problem of data category imbalance. It can be roughly divided into two types: undersampling and oversampling. Among them, the oversampling method usually performs better than the undersampling method and is more suitable when the minority category data is insufficient [23]. Some common oversampling techniques are compared, including Random oversampling, ADASYN [24], and SMOTE [22]. According to the experimental results, the oversampling technique with the best performance is selected.

Model Selection. Several common machine learning models are compared, including Lasso [25], KNN [26], SVM [27], Logistic [28], Decision Tree [29], Random Forest [30], Gradient Boosting Decision Tree (GBDT) [31], LightGBM [32], XGBoost [33], and MLP. During training, the gridsearch method is used to find the best parameters, and k-fold cross-validation is used to evaluate the performance, in which the training data is randomly shuffled and divided into four folds. According to the experimental results, the model with the best performance is selected for subsequent experiments.

Evaluation Criteria. Due to imbalanced data, it is difficult to evaluate the performance by accuracy, so f1-score is used as the comprehensive evaluation criteria in this study.

3.4 Root Cause Analysis

In this stage, SHAP is chosen as the explanation model to make a comprehensive and partial explanation of feature importance [34].

SHAP (SHapley Additive exPlanations) is a novel feature importance calculation method that demonstrates a powerful ability to explain the output of machine learning models in a large number of tasks. In recent years, SHAP has become a popular method for explaining feature contributions in machine learning models.

Compared with feature importance scores, the most used method in the past, SHAP can provide a more comprehensive explanation, such as the impact of each feature on the prediction result as positive or negative. In addition, SHAP can also provide local interpretation of the model on a single prediction result and on a single feature.

4 Experiment

4.1 Experimental Setup

Dataset and Data Splitting. The uncleaned data, the data cleaned by the outlier detection algorithm, and the data cleaned by the sampler-based algorithm are experimented respectively. 80% of the data is for the training set, and 20% is for the test set.

Oversampling Method Selection. The performance of the oversampling method is compared with the prediction results of the XGBoost model. It is found from Table 1 that SMOTE performs best, so SMOTE is used for subsequent experiments.

Table 1. Performance of oversampling methods

	Accuracy	F1-score	Amount of majority category data	Amount of minority category data
no sampling	94.9%	71.3%	2,130	126
Random	93.6%	76.8%	2,130	2,130
ADASYN	95.9%	81.2%	2,130	2,145
SMOTE	**96.6%**	**83.5%**	2,130	2,130

Model Selection. The f1-scores of each classification model in k-fold cross-validation and test set are compared. It is found from Table 2 that the XGBoost model performs best, so the XGBoost model is used for subsequent experiments.

Table 2. Performance of models

	Average f1-score for k-fold cross-validation	F1-score for test set
guess majority category	48.6%	48.5%
Lasso	73.1%	68.3%
KNN	65.0%	64.7%
SVM	72.0%	72.5%
Logistic	74.0%	72.4%
Decision Tree	67.3%	77.0%
Random Forest	74.5%	81.8%
GBDT	78.1%	79.6%
LightGBM	75.1%	78.8%
XGBoost	**78.1%**	**83.5%**
MLP	76.4%	75.2%

4.2 Experimental Result

Figure 3 shows the SHAP summary plots using the uncleaned data, the data cleaned by the outlier detection algorithm, and the data cleaned by the sampler-based algorithm.

Uncleaned Data. The f1-score of the model prediction results is 83.5%.

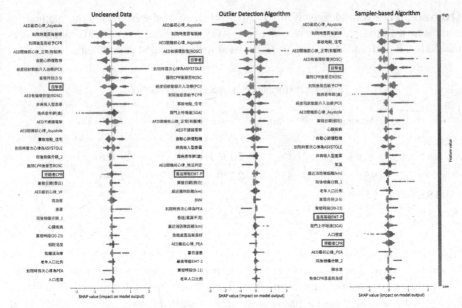

Fig. 3. Summary plots with the top 30 features using the uncleaned data, the data cleaned by the outlier detection algorithm, and the data cleaned by the sampler-based algorithm

Data Cleaned by Outlier Detection Algorithm. Figure 4 shows that the Isolation Forest algorithm performs the most stable and best, and the best performance occurs when 45% of the majority category data are anomalies. Figure 5 shows the process of anomaly detection. It can be observed that the distribution of the majority category data after cleaning is more concentrated. The f1-score of the model prediction results is 92.4%.

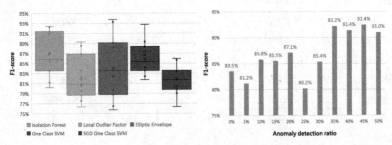

Fig. 4. Performance of five outlier detection algorithms and different ratios of anomalies using the outlier detection algorithm

Data Cleaned by Sampler-based Algorithm. Figure 6 shows that the best performance occurs when 45% of the majority category data are anomalies and when the ratio of neighbors is 14%. Figure 7 shows the process of anomaly detection. It can be observed

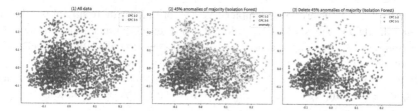

Fig. 5. The process of anomaly detection using the outlier detection algorithm

that the majority category data after cleaning is farther away from the minority category data. The f1-score of the model prediction results is 88.6%.

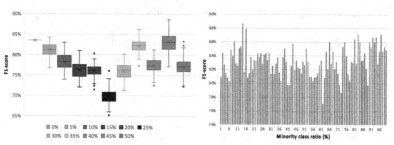

Fig. 6. Performance of different ratios of anomalies using the sampler-based algorithm and different ratios of neighbors in NearMiss-1

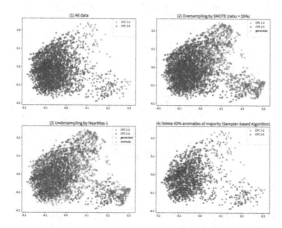

Fig. 7. The process of anomaly detection using the sampler-based algorithm

Compared with the exploratory data analysis in Sect. 2.2, it is found that only the SHAP summary plot of the data cleaned by the sampler-based algorithm is reasonable, since "with witnesses", "with bystanders CPR", and "with EMT-P" are indeed considered key survival factors by the model.

This proves that the proposed sampler-based algorithm is a more suitable method for cleaning the data in this study. In addition, it is also observed that although the model prediction results of the data cleaned by the outlier detection algorithm are better, this does not indicate that the detected anomalies are appropriate.

In the next section, further SHAP analysis will be conducted with the best settings, that is, using the sampler-based algorithm and removing 45% of anomalies.

5   Discussion

5.1   Summary Plot and Waterfall Plot

The summary plot combines feature importance and feature effects. It can be observed in Fig. 3 that, for example, when "the initial heart rhythm by AED is not asystole", "there is a pulse when arriving at the hospital", and "the case location is not a residence", etc., the model will consider that the case has a higher probability of survival.

From the waterfall plot, it can be observed which features affect and how they affect the prediction results of the model for a single case. Figure 8 shows how the model predicts the survival of case 37, which is predicted as CPC 1-2.

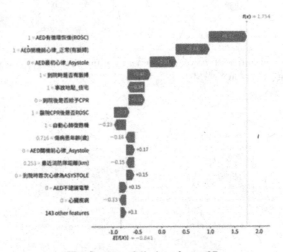

Fig. 8.   Waterfall plot of case 37

5.2   Aggregated Force Plot

From the aggregated force plot shown in Fig. 9, the specific influence of each feature on the model can be observed. The features of the following four examples are the key survival factors considered by the model, and the trend affecting the model is relatively obvious. For example, when "age is less than 68.3 years old", "temperature is less than 28.1°C", "the proportion of the elderly population is from 11.0% to 18.2%", and "the population density is from 3,280 to 11,542 people per square kilometer", it has a positive impact on the survival rate.

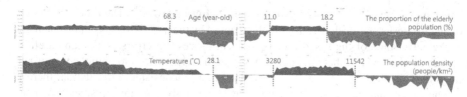

Fig. 9. Aggregated force plot with features of age, temperature, the proportion of the elderly population, and the population density

5.3 Dependence Plot

From the dependence plot shown in Fig. 10, the interaction of two features on the model can be observed. In the dependence plot, the most relevant features for each feature are selected using SHAP calculations.

Take the following four groups of features that have relatively obvious trends affecting the model as examples. First, people with heart disease have a higher survival rate when they are younger than 68.3 years. Second, when the temperature is from 17°C to 29°C, if the heart rhythm is asystole before the AED shuts down, the survival rate is lower, and vice versa. Third, the survival rate of the cases with witnesses is high when the distance to the nearest fire station is less than about 0.9 km. At the distance of approximately 0.9 to 2.3 km, there is no apparent trend in the influence of witnesses. When the distance is greater than about 2.3 km, even if there are witnesses, the survival rate is low. Fourth, the survival rate of the residential cases is higher in places where the proportion of the elderly population is less than about 18.2%.

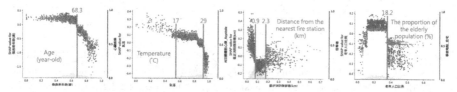

Fig. 10. Dependence plot with features of age, temperature, the distance to the nearest fire station, and the proportion of the elderly population

6 Threat to Validity and Future Work

6.1 Threat to Validity

Insufficient Amount of OHCA Data. Since there are only OHCA case data for the past three years in the emergency rescue data system, about 95% of which are CPC 3-5, it is difficult to conduct a more in-depth and accurate analysis of the key survival factors leading to CPC 1-2. In addition, since there is currently only data from the fire department and a lack of detailed information from the hospital, such as the correct cause of disease diagnosed by the hospital, the quality of medical treatment at the hospital, etc., it is still impossible to explore each case more comprehensively.

The Emergency Rescue Data System is Still Being Improved. The time information of many cases is obviously wrong, which is caused by the lack of fool-proof mechanisms in the early stage of the system, or by manual processing errors. Although carefully compared and revised, there are still many data that are difficult to completely correct. In addition to the issues of lack of information and inconsistent information, there is another issue that the "case type/details" feature is only a rough classification at the moment of phone reporting. It would be more accurate to classify cases based on the symptom categories recorded by EMTs or hospitals. Regarding the above form design issues, if the classification of cases could be automatically corrected according to the records by EMTs or hospitals, and the cases of obvious death at the scene and the cases of abandonment of first aid could be specially labeled, the analysis results would be more accurate and helpful.

7   Future Work

Although there are still limitations at present, some potential directions for future development could be observed from this study. In addition, the Taiwan Emergency Medical Services Information System (TEMSIS) started construction in 2022. As the amount of data gradually increases and becomes more robust, future research could consider more external features (such as transportation, humanities, etc.) and connect hospital systems for further exploration. It is anticipated that these advancements will bring novel discoveries and make significant contributions to the field of emergency medical services.

8   Conclusion

This study explores OHCA non-trauma cases in Tainan City in recent years. In addition to considering diverse features, this study also proposes a data cleaning method suitable for this dataset. Finally, complete analysis and interpretation are performed using the machine learning model and SHAP to gain new insights into key survival factors of OHCA non-trauma cases.

Acknowledgments. This work was partially supported by National Science and Technology Council (NSTC) under Grants 111-2636-E-006 -026 -, 112-2221-E-006 -100 - and 112-2221-E-006 -150 -MY3. The authors are grateful to Tainan City Fire Department for providing the data of OHCA cases.

References

1. Kun-Fu, C.: Pre-hospital ambulance emergency service time and prognosis of out-of-hospital cardiac arrest patients (2021). https://hdl.handle.net/11296/fr3x6w
2. Sladjana, A., Gordana, P., Ana, S.: Emergency response time after out-of-hospital cardiac arrest. Eur. J Int. Med. **22**, 386–393 (2011). https://doi.org/10.1016/J.EJIM.2011.04.003

3. Ko, S.Y., Shin, S.D., Song, K.J., Park, J.H., Lee, S.C.: Effect of awareness time interval for out-of-hospital cardiac arrest on outcomes: a nationwide observational study. Resuscitation **147**, 43–52 (2020). https://doi.org/10.1016/j.resuscitation.2019.12.009
4. Jennett, B., Bond, M.: Assessment of outcome after severe brain damage: a practical scale. The Lancet **305**, 480–484 (1975). https://doi.org/10.1016/S0140-6736(75)92830-5
5. Berg, D.D., Bobrow, B.J., Berg, R.A.: Key components of a community response to out-of-hospital cardiac arrest. Nat. Rev. Cardiol. **16**(7), 407–416 (2019). https://doi.org/10.1038/s41 569-019-0175-4
6. Wong, P.P., Low, C.T., Cai, W., Leung, K.T., Lai, P.-C.: A spatiotemporal data mining study to identify high-risk neighborhoods for out-of-hospital cardiac arrest (OHCA) incidents. Sci. Rep. **12**(1), 1–9 (2022). https://doi.org/10.1038/s41598-022-07442-7
7. Tierney, N.J., et al.: Evaluating health facility access using Bayesian spatial models and location analysis methods. PLoS One. **14**, e0218310 (2019). https://doi.org/10.1371/JOU RNAL.PONE.0218310
8. Sirikul, W., et al.: A retrospective multi-centre cohort study: pre-hospital survival factors of out-of-hospital cardiac arrest (OHCA) patients in Thailand. Resusc Plus. **9**, 100196 (2022). https://doi.org/10.1016/J.RESPLU.2021.100196
9. Lai, C.Y., et al.: Survival factors of hospitalized out-of-hospital cardiac arrest patients in Taiwan: a retrospective study. PLoS One. **13**, e0191954 (2018). https://doi.org/10.1371/JOU RNAL.PONE.0191954
10. Chen, C.C., Chen, C.W., Ho, C.K., Liu, I.C., Lin, B.C., Chan, T.C.: Spatial variation and resuscitation process affecting survival after out-of-hospital cardiac arrests (OHCA). PLoS One. **10**, e0144882 (2015). https://doi.org/10.1371/JOURNAL.PONE.0144882
11. Al-Dury, N., et al.: Identifying the relative importance of predictors of survival in out of hospital cardiac arrest: a machine learning study. Scand. J. Trauma Resusc. Emerg. Med. **28**, 60 (2020). https://doi.org/10.1186/S13049-020-00742-9
12. Cilinio, M., Duarte, D., Vieira, P., Queluz, M.P., Rodrigues, A.: Root cause analysis of low throughput situations using boosting algorithms and the TreeShap analysis. In: IEEE Vehicular Technology Conference. 2022-June (2022). https://doi.org/10.1109/VTC2022-SPRING 54318.2022.9860734
13. Hao, S., Liu, Y., Wang, Y., Wang, Y., Zhe, W.: Three-stage root cause analysis for logistics time efficiency via explainable machine learning. Proc. ACM SIGKDD Int. Conf. Knowl. Disc. Data Mining. **22**, 2987–2996 (2022). https://doi.org/10.1145/3534678.3539024
14. Conradsson, E., Johansson, V.: A model-independent methodology for a root cause analysis system : a study investigating interpretable machine learning methods (2019). https://urn.kb. se/resolve?urn=urn:nbn:se:umu:diva-160372
15. Ritala, M.: Detection and data-driven root cause analysis of paper machine drive anomalies (2019). https://lutpub.lut.fi/handle/10024/160631
16. Liu, F.T., Ting, K.M., Zhou, Z.H.: Isolation forest. In: Proceedings - IEEE International Conference on Data Mining, ICDM, pp. 413–422 (2008). https://doi.org/10.1109/ICDM.200 8.17
17. Breuniq, M.M., Kriegel, H.P., Ng, R.T., Sander, J.: LOF: identifying density-based local outliers. ACM SIGMOD Record. **29**, 93–104 (2000). https://doi.org/10.1145/335191.335388
18. Rousseeuw, P.J.: Least median of squares regression. J. Am. Stat. Assoc. **79**, 871 (1984). https://doi.org/10.2307/2288718
19. Schölkopf, B., Williamson, R., Smola, A., Shawe-Taylor, J., Platt, J.: Support vector method for novelty detection. In: Proceedings of the 12th International Conference on Neural Information Processing Systems, pp. 582–588. MIT Press, Cambridge, MA, USA (1999)
20. Shalev-Shwartz, S., Singer, Y., Srebro, N., Cotter, A.: Pegasos: primal estimated sub-gradient solver for SVM. Math Program. **127**, 3–30 (2011). https://doi.org/10.1007/S10107-010-0420-4/METRICS

21. Mani, I., Zhang, I.: kNN approach to unbalanced data distributions: a case study involving information extraction. In: Proceedings of Workshop on Learning from Imbalanced Datasets, pp. 1–7 (2003)
22. Chawla, N.V., Bowyer, K.W., Hall, L.O., Kegelmeyer, W.P.: SMOTE: synthetic minority over-sampling technique. J. Artif. Int. Res. **16**, 321–357 (2002)
23. Buda, M., Maki, A., Mazurowski, M.A.: A systematic study of the class imbalance problem in convolutional neural networks. Neural Netw. **106**, 249–259 (2018). https://doi.org/10.1016/j.neunet.2018.07.011
24. He, H., Bai, Y., Garcia, E.A., Li, S.: ADASYN: adaptive synthetic sampling approach for imbalanced learning. In: Proceedings of the International Joint Conference on Neural Networks, pp. 1322–1328 (2008). https://doi.org/10.1109/IJCNN.2008.4633969
25. Tibshirani, R.: Regression shrinkage and selection via the Lasso. J. R. Statist. Soc. Ser. B (Methodol.) **58**, 267–288 (1996). https://doi.org/10.1111/J.2517-6161.1996.TB02080.X
26. Taunk, K., De, S., Verma, S., Swetapadma, A.: A brief review of nearest neighbor algorithm for learning and classification. In: 2019 International Conference on Intelligent Computing and Control Systems, ICCS 2019, pp. 1255–1260 (2019). https://doi.org/10.1109/ICCS45 141.2019.9065747
27. Hearst, M.A., Dumais, S.T., Osuna, E., Platt, J., Scholkopf, B.: Support vector machines. IEEE Intell. Syst. App. **13**, 18–28 (1998). https://doi.org/10.1109/5254.708428
28. Dreiseitl, S., Ohno-Machado, L.: Logistic regression and artificial neural network classification models: a methodology review. J. Biomed. Inform. **35**, 352–359 (2002). https://doi.org/10.1016/S1532-0464(03)00034-0
29. Quinlan, J.R.: Induction of decision trees. Mach. Learn. **1**(1), 81–106 (1986). https://doi.org/10.1007/BF00116251
30. Breiman, L.: Random forests. Mach Learn. **45**, 5–32 (2001). https://doi.org/10.1023/A:101 0933404324/METRICS
31. Friedman, J.H.: Greedy function approximation: a gradient boosting machine. Ann. Statist. **29**, 1189–1232 (2001)
32. Ke, G., et al.: LightGBM: a highly efficient gradient boosting decision tree. Adv. Neural Inf. Process. Syst. **30**, 1–9 (2017)
33. Chen, T., Guestrin, C.: XGBoost: a scalable tree boosting system. In: Proceedings of the ACM SIGKDD International Conference on Knowledge Discovery and Data Mining. 13-17-August-2016, pp. 785–794 (2016). https://doi.org/10.1145/2939672.2939785
34. Lundberg, S.M., Allen, P.G., Lee, S.-I.: A unified approach to interpreting model predictions. Adv. Neural Inf. Process. Syst. **30**, 1–10 (2017)

Automatic Identification of Table Contents in Electronic Component Specifications of EDA

Tzung-Pei Hong[1]([✉]), Yi-Zhen Xu[1], Shi-feng Huang[2], Yi-Ting Chen[3], and Ming-Han Lee[4]

[1] Department of Computer Science and Information Engineering,
National University of Kaohsiung, Kaohsiung, Taiwan
tphong@nuk.edu.tw
[2] Graduate Institute of Statistics, National Central University, Taoyuan, Taiwan
huangsf@ncu.edu.tw
[3] Footprintku Inc., Kaohsiung, Taiwan
ytchen@footprintku.com
[4] Department of Applied Mathematics, National University of Kaohsiung, Kaohsiung, Taiwan

Abstract. With the rapid advancement of technology, the electronics industry has flourished in recent decades. Electronic products such as computers, mobile phones, and smart televisions are ubiquitous in our daily lives. In the design, manufacturing, and maintenance processes of electronic products, a large number of electronic components are required. The relevant information of these components is usually recorded in the tables of electronic component specifications. In this paper, we design methods to recognize and extract contents from tables, which typically contain vital information about electronic components, such as their characteristics and packaging methods. Our approach utilizes text processing techniques to structurally process and analyze the extracted table content, enabling us to obtain the specific information we need. We categorize tables in PDFs into different types and explore relevant information from them using the procedure of each type. The experimental results demonstrate that our method can achieve a high accuracy rate of over 90% in recognizing table contents.

Keywords: Electronic Component Datasheets · Image Recognition · Table Recognition · Text Processing

1 Introduction

With the continuous advancement of technology, modern electronic products are evolving rapidly, leading to a greater diversity and complexity in the electronic components they require. Manufacturers of electronic components may produce similar types of components, but due to inconsistencies in standards and formats, the electronic component datasheets written by each manufacturer may vary significantly. Engineers often need to manually search for specific component information from a large number of datasheets, which can be a time-consuming process. In the electronics industry, an increasing number of companies are attempting to introduce the concept of artificial intelligence (AI) to achieve the digitization of electronic data and even to automate the entire design process of electronic components. During this process, it is often necessary to identify and extract specification documents containing information about electronic component specifications. These electronic component specification documents contain rich part information and are typically stored in PDF format. We have observed that engineers typically need to extract information and data about electronic component characteristics from tables of the specification documents. For example, Table 1 shows a table about the electrical characteristics of an electric component.

Table 1. A table in an electronic component specification document.

Electrical Characteristics Over the Operating Range

Parameter	Description	Test Conditions		7C138-25		Unit
				Min	Max	
V_{OH}	Output HIGH voltage	V_{CC} = Min., I_{OH} = –4.0 mA		2.4	–	V
V_{OL}	Output LOW voltage	V_{CC} = Min., I_{OL} = 4.0 mA		–	0.4	V
V_{IH}				2.2	–	V
V_{IL}	Input LOW voltage			–	0.8	V
I_{IX}	Input leakage current	GND $\leq V_I \leq V_{CC}$		–10	+10	µA
I_{OZ}	Output leakage current	Output disabled, GND $\leq V_O \leq V_{CC}$		–10	+10	µA
I_{CC}	Operating current	V_{CC} = Max., I_{OUT} = 0 mA, Outputs disabled	Commercial	–	180	mA
			Industrial	–	190	
I_{SB1}	Standby current (Both ports TTL levels)	CE_L and $CE_R \geq V_{IH}$, $f = f_{MAX}^{[5]}$	Commercial	–	40	mA
			Industrial	–	50	
I_{SB2}	Standby current (One port TTL level)	CE_L and $CE_R \geq V_{IH}$, $f = f_{MAX}^{[5]}$	Commercial	–	110	mA
			Industrial	–	120	
I_{SB3}	Standby current (Both ports CMOS levels)	Both ports CE and $CE_R \geq V_{CC}$ – 0.2 V, $V_{IN} \geq V_{CC}$ – 0.2 V or $V_{IN} \leq 0.2$ V, f = 0[5]	Commercial	–	15	mA
			Industrial	–	30	
I_{SB4}	Standby current (One port CMOS level)	One port CE_L or $CE_R \geq V_{CC}$ – 0.2 V, $V_{IN} \geq V_{CC}$ – 0.2 V or $V_{IN} \leq 0.2$ V, Active Port outputs, $f = f_{MAX}^{[5]}$	Commercial	–	100	mA
			Industrial	–	115	

This kind of information is often displayed in tables of PDF specification documents. Therefore, in this paper, we aim to extract electronic component characteristics within tables in the specification documents. This can significantly reduce the substantial amount of time engineers spend in organizing this information.

As shown in Table 1, a table contains relevant data about electrical components. Besides, there may be subscripts, supersubscripts, and merged cells within a table. That will make the analysis more difficult. We thus categorize tables in PDFs into different types and design individual procedures for these types to explore relevant information from tables.

The rest of this paper is organized as follows. We review related work in Sect. 2, and in Sect. 3, we introduce the proposed framework in detail. Then, we present the experimental results in Sect. 4. Finally, we conclude and suggest future work in Sect. 5.

2 Related Work

In this section, we review some previous works related to this paper. These include the PDF file format and table mining.

2.1 PDF File Format

PDF, which stands for Portable Document Format, was designed and developed by Adobe Company. It has been a mainstream format for storing documents due to its platform-independent nature, making it convenient for both storage and transmission. There are researches focusing on content recognition within PDFs [5], enabling the interpretation of content from the file structure [4].

Besides, machine learning and heuristic methods are also employed to extract content from PDFs [6]. The structure of a PDF file can be divided into four main parts[9]: the header, body, cross-reference table, and trailer. The header primarily declares the version of the PDF specification that the PDF adheres to. The cross-reference table serves as an index table to allow objects to be randomly accessed and referenced. The trailer is used to indicate the location of the cross-reference table and stores security information, such as whether the PDF file is encrypted. The body is the most significant part of the PDF file and is composed of a series of objects. The objects include two kinds: document-outline objects and page-group objects. Document-outline objects are similar to bookmarks in a PDF. It can assist users in organizing the content of a document. Page-group objects contain information about the number of pages in the document and the identification numbers of page objects, which are the most crucial elements in a PDF. Page objects include all the useful information on a page, including fonts, page size, and content (text, images, etc.).

For working with PDF files, many Python libraries are available to support PDF operations, such as PyMuPDF, PDFminer, PDFplumber, and more.

2.2 Table Mining

There are some researches proposed for table mining. Earlier studies typically divided table mining into two stages [11]: (1) table discovery and (2) table-content recognition. In the first stage, researchers identify whether a document contains table objects, followed by the second stage, where the content within the tables is recognized. This may involve detecting merged cells or dividing internal gridlines within tables. Traditionally, these two stages were achieved using separate methods. Recently, there has been a growing trend in research to combine these two stages into a single unified process. For example, Schreiber et al. developed a system that integrated table discovery and structure recognition [3]. Their research employed a fast RCNN for table discovery and adopted deep-learning semantic segmentation for table structure identification. They combined these two stages into a single model [7], making it faster and more versatile.

Prasad et al. proposed an end-to-end table recognition method called CascadeTabNet, based on deep learning [1]. They designed the model to achieve excellent performance with minimal training data. CascadeTabNet, as illustrated in Fig. 1, is composed of two methods, utilizing the Cascade RCNN developed by Cai and Vasconcelos [8] and the modified HRNet by Wang et al. [2]. Both of the methods had demonstrated high accuracy in object detection.

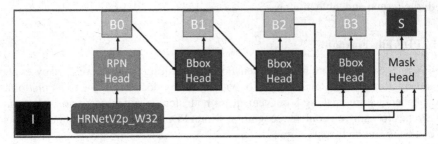

Fig. 1. The CascadeTabNet model architecture

From Fig. 1, it can be observed that CascadeTabNet utilizes HRNetV2p_W32 as its backbone network. It primarily extracts features from the input image. Subsequently, the RPN Head is employed to predict regions within the image that may contain tables. Once candidate regions are identified, the Bbox Heads are responsible for predicting the bounding boxes for each candidate region, including the position and class of the objects contained. In addition to bounding boxes, CascadeTabNet also features a Mask Head, which is used to predict masks for each table in the image. These masks provide precise pixel-level information about the tables, facilitating table discovery.

There are many open-source table-related packages available. These packages help users fast and freely detect tables and analyze their content.

3 Proposed Approach for Extracting Table Contents

Figure 2 depicts the workflow of our approach, which consists of several modules. It uses text processing and image processing techniques, respectively, to extract the content of the tables in electronic-component specification PDFs according to the table gridlines. When a table does not have gridlines, it is not easily recognized as a table by PDF libraries and needs to be processed by image processing techniques. Both the results from text-based and image-based strategies are compared and integrated to produce more accurate results.

3.1 Extracting Text Tables from PDFs

There are various Python libraries designed for recognizing tables in PDFs. In order to rapidly identify tables within electronic component specification sheets, which are usually stored in PDF format, we use PDFplumber because it is not only efficient and convenient for text extraction but also excels in table detection and recognition. When identifying tables, PDFplumber can directly determine the positions of tables and store the content within the tables as lists. Each row of a table is stored as a separate list, and cells within a row are recorded as strings with commas separating them. Figure 3 shows an example of the output from a table by the PDFplumber.

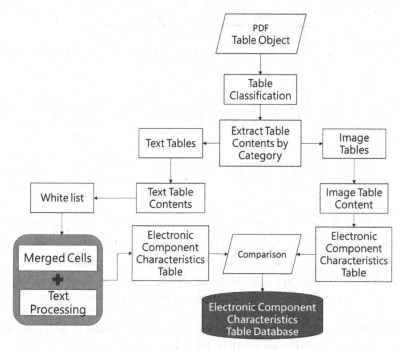

Fig. 2. Flowchart of the proposed approach

['Order code',   'Marking',   'Package',   'Weight',   'Base qty',   'Delivery mode']
['STTH15S12D',   'STTH15S12D',   'TO-220AC',   '1.9 g',   '50',   'Tube']
['STTH15S12W',   'STTH15S12W',   'DO-247',   '4.46 g',   '50',   'Tube']

Fig. 3. Extracted content from a table

Compared to recognizing text by image-based approaches, PDFplumber can identify text very well because it can directly get the text in the table without character recognition. This contributes to its high accuracy in table text recognition. On the contrary, utilizing image recognition for text extraction can sometimes lead to errors, particularly in distinguishing between characters like 'O' and 'o' or 'I' and 'l'. Therefore, PDF-plumber can offer faster extraction of table content with higher accuracy than image recognition methods. Besides, PDFplumber can extract the text positions and cell coordinates within a table, facilitating subsequent processing of superscripts, subscripts, and merged cells in a table. However, Pdfplumber may struggle with complex tables and tables with unclear gridlines. For example, Fig. 4 shows a table without gridlines. For this kind of tables, PDFplumber cannot correctly extract it as a table but as ordinary text. Therefore, the tables that Pdfplumber cannot be correctly recognized are processed with the assistance of optical character recognition (OCR). For the remaining tables, we can use Pdfplumber to extract the textual content from them.

Capacitance (F)	Part number
0.1	KW-5R5C104-R
0.1	KW-5R5C104H-R
0.22	KW-5R5C224-R
0.22	KW-5R5C224H-R
0.33	KW-5R5C334-R
0.33	KW-5R5C334H-R
0.68	KW-5R5C684-R
0.68	KW-5R5C684H-R
1.0	KW-5R5C105-R
1.0	KW-5R5C105H-R

Fig. 4. A table that PDFplumber regards as ordinary text

There are many tables in a PDF document, and not each table is of interest to EDA engineers. Thus, we filter out the desired tables containing electronic component specifications for analysis using a whitelist. Since the electronic component specifications required by engineers fall within a defined range, we have compiled these specifications and put them into a whitelist, as shown in Table 2.

Table 2. A whitelist

Whitelist			
Passive Component	Capacitor	Manufacturer	Package Type
RoHS	Series	Mounting Style	Tolerance
...			

We search for tables containing electronic component specifications based on the words appearing in the whitelist. If a table contains any of the strings in the whitelist, we consider it to have electronic component specifications.

3.2 Text Processing

While PDFplumber is quick and convenient for table text recognition and detection, it may not always present the text in the desired format to engineers. Especially, the processing is complex for subscripts, subscripts, and merged cells. We can thus classify the tables into four types as follows:

(a) Regular tables without subscripts, superscripts, and merged cells. Basically, the PDFplumber can correctly process this kind of table. An example is shown in Table 3.

Table 3. A standard table

Order code	Marking	Package	Weight
STTH15S12D	STTH15S12D	TO-220AC	1.9 g
STTH15S12W	STTH15S12W	DO-247	4.46 g

(b) Tables with merged cells but without subscripts and superscripts. An example is shown in Fig. 5, which shows the text-extraction results for a table with merged cells.

Ref.	Dimensions					
	Millimeters			Inches		
	Min.	Typ.	Max.	Min.	Typ.	Max.
A	4.85		5.15	0.191		0.203
D	2.20		2.60	0.086		0.102

```
['Ref.',   'Dimensions',    None,    None,    None,    None,    None]
[None,     'Millimeters',   None,    None,    'Inches', None,    None]
[None,     'Min.',          'Typ.',  'Max.',  'Min.',   'Typ.', 'Max.']
['A',      '4.85',          '',      '5.15',  '0.191',  '',     '0.203']
['D',      '2.20',          '',      '2.60',  '0.086',  '',     '0.102']
```

Fig. 5. The recognition results of merged cells

In Fig. 5, it can be observed that PDFplumber correctly extracts the content of each cell in the tables except for merged cells. The content of the merged cells is displayed correctly in the first cell and is marked as the "None" value in the other cells. It may lead to confusion for engineers when interpreting the column positions. For example, the "None" cell above the cell of "Typ." in Fig. 5 should be interpreted as Millimeters. For a cell with the "None" value, its neighboring cell without the "None" value can be copied to it according to some judgements.

(c) Tables with subscripts and superscripts, but without merged cells. Normally, PDF-plumber does not handle superscripts and subscripts in text well. For example, Table 4 contains subscripts and the words with subscripts are not marked clearly by PDFplumber.

This is the result of extracting the text with superscripts and subscripts from the PDF using Pdfplumber, as shown in Fig. 6.

Table 4. A table containing subscripted text

Symbol	Value
IF	15A
VRRM	1200V
t_{rr}(typ)	27ns
V_F(typ)	1.9V
V_F(typ)	175 °C

```
['Symbol',      'Dimensions']
['I\nF(AV)',    '15 A']
['V\nRRM',      '1200 V']
['t  (typ)\nrr',  '27 ns']
['V (typ)\nF',   '1.9 V']
['T (max)\nj',   '175 °C']
```

Fig. 6. The Pdfplumber result of extraction

PDFplumber will misinterpret subscript text as text in the next line, displaying '/n,' and the position of the subscript text is shifted to the rear of the string. This deviation from the original text string can be judged by comparing the font sizes and coordinates to distinguish between normal words and their superscript or subscript characters. As a result, we extract the text in each cell, and if there are variations in font size, we identify this as potentially having superscript or subscript content.

(d) Tables with subscripts, superscripts, and merged cells. An example is shown in Table 4. Normally, we can handle this kind of tables by using the two mechanisms for (b) and (c).

3.3 Extracting Tables Using Image Recognition

As mentioned above, for the tables without gridlines, PDFplumber cannot correctly extract it as a table, We thus employ image recognition approaches to find the tables and extract bounded boxes representing a list of words [9]. These words need to be recognized by using optical character recognition (OCR) to extract text content [10]. Besides, even for tables correctly extracted from PDFplumber, we can also use the approach to extract the text content and then compare and correct the content. These two sets of recognition results can thus be cross-referenced and mutually corrected to enhance the accuracy of recognizing the textual content of the tables in electronic component specification documents.

4 Experimental Results

We conducted tests using electronic-component specification documents from a Taiwanese electronic design automation company. There are 51 tables with a total of 1582 cells. We compared the fields among them, aiming for both text and position accuracy in the final results. We conducted dedicated testing on these 1582 cells, utilizing the Python 3.7 environment in conjunction with pdfplumber 0.10.1. Out of the 1582 cells, we first focused on text accuracy without considering positioning or superscripts/subscripts. We found that only 22 cells (1.39%) had inaccuracies in the recognized text. This discrepancy could be attributed to special symbols stored in different encoding formats and a few instances where the text couldn't be recognized by the software. The actual situation is as shown in Fig. 7.

THERMAL RESISTANCE RATINGS					
Parameter		Symbol	Typical	Maximum	Unit
Maximum Junction-to-Ambient (MOSFET)[a]	t ≤ 10 s	R_{thJA}	34	40	°C/W
	Steady State		71	85	
Maximum Junction-to-Foot (Drain)	Steady State	R_{thJF}	18	22	

```
['', '', '', '', '', '']
['Parameter ', 'Parameter ', 'Symbol ', 'Typical', 'Maximum', 'Unit ']
['Maximum Junction-to-Ambient (MOSFET)a^^', 't ≤ 10 s', 'RthJA', '34', '40', '°C/W']
['Maximum Junction-to-Foot (Drain)', 'Steady State', 'RthJF', '18', '22', '°C/W']
['Maximum Junction-to-Ambient (MOSFET)a^^', 'Steady State', 'RthJA', '71', '85', '°C/W']
```

Fig. 7. The text not correctly recognized

In Fig. 7, it can be seen that some columns where text should have been extracted do not have the correct text placement. However, this kind of situation is very rare. Additionally, we utilized a whitelist to filter tables containing electronic-component characteristics. When we considered the correctness of superscripts/subscripts as part of our evaluation criteria, we found 31 cells where superscripts/subscripts were not recognized correctly. This may have been due to the difficulties in determining font sizes and other factors. Furthermore, when we included the accuracy of positioning in our assessment, we found that 68 columns had accurate text but were misplaced within the tables due to some errors, they are placed in the wrong position within the table. Our experimental results, as shown in Fig. 8.

It can be observed from the figure that our method achieves excellent accuracy in recognizing table content. However, challenges persist, particularly in addressing issues related to layout and formatting. Further improving accuracy will be a primary goal in the future.

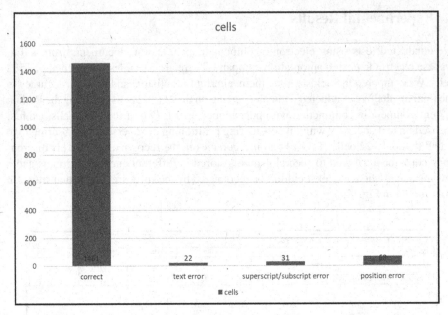

Fig. 8. Experimental results

5   Conclusion and Future Work

This paper primarily discusses utilizing PDF table analysis packages to extract content effectively from electronic component specification documents. We have used the PDF-plumber library to extract tables and their text, and employed text processing techniques to obtain the content in the tables. We have divided the tables extracted from the PDF-plumber into four types and used different processing mechanismd for handling them. We can also employ image recognition approaches to process the tables that cannot be extracted by PDFplumber. These two kinds of processing strategies can cooperate closely to cross-reference and correct the results to enhance the accuracy.

The results obtained from this work have practical applications in the automation of electronic component specification document recognition. By automatically identifying table content within electronic component specification documents, the efficiency of engineers in data retrieval is significantly improved. This expedites the analysis process, aids in engineering workflow, and helps prevent errors that may arise from manual operations. Utilizing such packages not only streamlines the recognition process but also allows for flexible adjustments based on real-world observations.

There is room for further development in the extraction and recognition of table content. For example, once the text is identified, subsequent steps can involve associating it with part numbers and extracting crucial information related to electronic component packaging or other specifications. This further advances the automation of electronic component specification document recognition. We may also attempt to integrate ChatPDF, enabling faster organization of component characteristics, and even entire specification documents, thereby enhancing the automation of electronic component specification document recognition.

Acknowledgments. This research is supported by The National Science and Technology Council, Taiwan, under the grant of NSTC 111-2622-E-390-002 and by Footprintku Inc., Taiwan.

References

1. Gadpal, D.A., Kapadni, K., Visave, M., Sultanpure, K.A.: CascadeTabNet: an approach for end to end table detection and structure recognition from image-based documents. In: IEEE/CVF Conference on Computer Vision and Pattern Recognition Workshops, pp. 2439–2447 (2020)
2. Wang, J., et al.: Deep high-resolution representation learning for visual recognition. IEEE Trans. Pattern Anal. Mach. Intell. **43**(10), 3349–3364 (2020)
3. Schreiber, S., Agne, S., Wolf, I., Dengel, A., Ahmed, S.: DeepDeSRT: deep learning for detection and structure recognition of tables in document images. In: IAPR 14th International Conference on Document Analysis and Recognition, pp. 1162–1167 (2017)
4. Luong, M.T., Nguyen, T.D., Kan, M.Y.: Logical structure recovery in scholarly articles with rich document features. Int. J. Digital Libr. Syst. **1**(4), 1–23 (2010)
5. Kern, R., Jack, K., Hristakeva, M., Granitzer, M.: TeamBeam - meta-data extraction from scientific literature. D-Lib Mag. **18**(7), 1–11 (2012)
6. Klampfl, S., Kern, R.: An unsupervised machine learning approach to body text and table of contents extraction from digital scientific articles. In: Aalberg, T., Papatheodorou, C., Dobreva, M., Tsakonas, G., Farrugia, C.J. (eds.) Research and Advanced Technology for Digital Libraries. LNCS, vol. 8092, pp. 144–155. Springer, Heidelberg (2013). https://doi.org/10.1007/978-3-642-40501-3_15
7. Zhou, X., Koltun, V., Krähenbühl, P.: Probabilistic two-stage detection. arXiv:2103.07461 (2021)
8. Cai, Z., Vasconcelos, N.: Cascade R-CNN: delving into high quality object detection. IEEE Conference on Computer Vision and Pattern Recognition, pp. 6154–6162 (2018)
9. Hanumanthappa, M., Nagalavi, D. T.: Identification and extraction of different objects and its location from a Pdf file using efficient information retrieval tools. In: International Conference on Soft-Computing and Networks Security, pp. 1–6 (2015)
10. Hong, T.P., Chiu, H.W., Huang, S.F., Chen, Y.T.: Deep-learning-based extraction of electronic component parameters from datasheets. In: 2021 IEEE International Conference on Big Data, pp. 5501–5506 (2021)
11. Fang, J., Gao, L., Bai, K., Qiu, R., Tao, X., Tang, Z.: A table detection method for multipage PDF documents via visual seperators and tabular structures. In: International Conference on Document Analysis and Recognition, pp. 779–783 (2011)

Air Pollution Source Tracing Framework: Leveraging Microsensors and Wind Analysis for Pollution Source Identification

Chih-Chieh Hung[1] , Hong-En Hsiao[1], Chuang-Chieh Lin[2] ,
and Hui-Huang Hsu[2(✉)]

[1] National Chung Hsing University, Taichung, Taiwan
{smalloshin,hnhsiao}@nchu.edu.tw
[2] Tamkang University, Taipei, Taiwan
{josephcclin,hsu}@gms.tku.edu.tw

Abstract. In the context of rapid urbanization, air pollution has become a significant concern, particularly in densely developed urban areas. This pollution stems from various sources, including traffic, industry, and external contributors. Its implications go beyond ecological disruption, posing a substantial threat to human health, with prolonged exposure leading to chronic ailments and increased mortality risks. Current air pollution monitoring methods, centered on air quality indices and forecasting, often lack the ability to pinpoint pollution sources. To address this, our study employs Smart City and Rural Air Quality Microsensors deployed across Taiwan. By analyzing pollution movement patterns through continuous time series data and integrating wind data, we utilize backtracking to identify emission sources and create innovative air pollution corridors to assess pollution's extent. This paper introduces the Air Pollution Source Tracing Problem (APSTP), proposing the APSTF (Air Pollution Source Tracing Framework) to address this challenge. The APSTF encompasses three key phases: Identification, Matching and Backtracking, and Pathway Generation. It effectively identifies stations experiencing air pollution, correlates affected areas across different time slots, and predicts pollution impact areas, thereby shedding light on pollution dynamics and aiding in source identification and future pollution prediction. The APSTF stands as a valuable tool for understanding and mitigating air pollution, leveraging data from air quality micro-sensors, meteorological stations, and advanced mathematical algorithms.

Keywords: air pollution · source tracking · hungarian algorithm · trajectory analysis

1 Introduction

With rapid urban development, air pollution has become an increasingly severe issue. Developing urban areas are susceptible not only to intrinsic air pollution factors, such as high traffic zones, densely populated areas, and emissions from industrial zones, but they also experience the impact of external air pollution sources [1]. The impact of air pollution extends beyond ecological disruptions, posing a significant threat to human health. Prolonged inhalation of contaminated air and prolonged exposure to airborne particulate matter in polluted environments intensify the severity of chronic diseases and elevate the risk of mortality.

Currently, common methods for observing air pollution involve monitoring air quality indices and providing forecasts. However, these methods of air pollution observation are unable to detect the sources responsible for the observed air pollution phenomena. Here, leveraging the densely deployed Smart City and Rural Air Quality Microsensors throughout Taiwan, we monitor areas affected by air pollution. By analyzing the movement paths of pollution groups using the continuous time series of air pollution data and considering wind factors, we backtrack to identify the emission sources causing air pollution. Additionally, we formulate innovative air pollution corridors to observe the extent of air pollution impact. Therefore, when air pollution occurs, this method can present the emission sources causing the pollution at that location, the propagation and movement paths during the emission process, and the warning zones that may be affected by pollution in the near future.

This paper develops a methodology to identify pollution sources for air pollution incidents, say Air Pollution Source Tracing Problem, which is defined as follows:

Definition. (Air Pollution Source Tracing Problem): Given a query $Q = (S, T)$ where S represents the monitoring station detecting air pollution in time slot T and the historical readings of air-quality monitoring stations in time slot T, T-1, ..., T-ΔT, derive the potential pollution source G, the set of stations, and the pathway P, the sequence of stations detected air pollution from G.

In this paper, we proposed a framework APSTF (stands for Air Pollution Source Tracing Framework) to solve the air pollution source tracing problem. The process of APSTF involves three phases: Identification Phase, Matching and Backtracking Phase, and Pathway Generation Phase. In the Identification Phase, stations experiencing air pollution within the time slots T, T-1, ..., T-ΔT are identified. The stations with suspended particulate matter concentration above 36 μg per cubic meter are considered stations experiencing air pollution. The entire map is divided into grids, and the mean concentration of particulate matter from all stations in a grid represents the pollution level for that grid. The output of this phase comprises the centroids of groups for each time slot. In the Matching and Backtracking Phase, the centroids from different time slots are matched using the Hungarian algorithm, aiming to trace the trajectory from the query point to the pollution source. This matching is modeled as an assignment problem, efficiently solved using the Hungarian algorithm. Wind factors are integrated into this phase to identify the pollution source from the previous time slot. The Pathway Generation Phase utilizes linear regression on the sequence of correlated affected areas to generate air pollution pathways. The pathway width is determined by the distance between the regression line and the furthest centroids. This pathway represents the area affected by air pollution and aids in predicting potential air pollution occurrences in the future. In summary, the APSTF effectively traces air pollution sources by utilizing the rich data from air quality micro-sensors, meteorological stations, and mathematical algorithms.

It identifies pollution-affected stations, correlates affected areas in different time slots, and generates pathways to predict pollution impact areas. This methodology provides valuable insights into air pollution dynamics, aiding in pollution source identification and future pollution prediction.

The remainder of this paper is structured as follows: Sect. 2 presents a review of relevant literature. Section 3 outlines the backtracking methodology for identifying pollution sources. Section 4 provides details on case studies and compares our proposed approach with other baseline methods. Finally, Sect. 5 presents the conclusions drawn from this paper.

2   Related Works

Selecting specific observation points to observe air pollution phenomena is the most common and straightforward approach. In this approach, an observation point is chosen, and a certain number of air pollution sensors are installed in the surrounding environment. The information on air pollution substance concentrations observed by each sensor is analyzed to determine the areas around the observation point where air pollution is being emitted. Suwimon et. al used a polar coordinate approach to locate air pollution sources [2] by observations in Bangkok, Thailand. Statistical techniques, variable polar coordinates, and conditional probability methods were employed to observe potential air pollution source areas around the environment. In this method, an initial fixed observation point is selected, and the observation point serves as the center of a polar coordinate system. This method segregates the data into different azimuth and distance ranges by computing the conditional bivariate probability function defined as $CBPF_{\Delta\theta,\Delta v} = \frac{m_{\Delta\theta,\Delta v|C\leq x}}{n_{\Delta\theta,\Delta v}}$ where $\Delta\theta$, Δv represent the number of monitoring stations in different blocks and the number of polluted monitoring stations within those blocks and $C \leq x$ indicates that the concentration standard meets a threshold of x or above [3].

Chao Yu et. al identified non-stagnant air pollution phenomena over the middle reaches of the Yangtze River in China [4]. In mainland China, there are numerous industrial areas that can cause widespread air pollution. This not only affects the local areas but can also spread to other regions influenced by monsoons. The article used the observation of the northeast monsoon during winter to examine this phenomenon. It was discovered that air pollution originated in the northeast direction at the observation site. Over time and due to wind propagation, it gradually extended southwestward to the observation point. These research works have addressed wind as the important medium driving the movement of air pollution. Therefore, in our proposed method, wind strength will be a factor in the variations of air pollution phenomena, aiming to analyze whether air pollution is influenced by wind-driven factors. However, there are still limitations in the aforementioned methods. Using wind to deduce the primary air pollution source in a particular direction may be influenced by various other factors, such as rainfall and changes in wind direction. This observation inspires us to develop the method of backtracking air pollution sources through trajectory analysis step by step.

Observing the surrounding air pollution through fixed-point monitoring may not always originate locally but could be transported to the area through environmental factors like wind and convection. If tracking the source of air pollution emissions is necessary, it is essential to simultaneously observe the pathways of air pollution movement. By using a backtracking approach along these pathways, we can more precisely determine from which direction the air pollution is originating. The method proposed by Pouyaei Arman and other scholars for observing air pollution sources and polluted areas utilizes a community multiscale air quality model for research analysis [5]. This method begins by observing the hourly movement pattern of air pollution plumes using meteorological systems. Through this temporal observation, pollution nodes in different locations can be obtained. The Lagrangian interpolation method is then employed to connect the pollution nodes of pollution sources and polluted areas, forming the pathway of air pollution movement. However, the Lagrange interpolation polynomial has a limitation: the x-coordinates must be distinct, or else the subtraction in the denominator during calculations will result in zero, rendering the computation invalid. Moreover, Lagrangian interpolation method can generate smooth curves when connecting a small number of pollution nodes. However, when there are many nodes in between, connecting the pathways can result in a significantly increased computational load and produce pathways with noticeable and unnatural fluctuations in the nodes. This is because the Lagrange formula produces higher powers in the polynomial as more points are introduced.

Zhen Li et. al. Observed in China during the year 2020, amidst the impact of the COVID-19 pandemic, that many people spent extended periods indoors, significantly reducing the impact of air pollution related to transportation. However, industrial areas continued to operate, primarily emitting pollutants from sources such as coal combustion. Consequently, it was inferred that continuously operating industrial areas were the source of air pollution [6]. This method also involves analyzing the movement pathways of air pollution events through air pollution pathway analysis. Grid coordinates are added to the map to observe and statistically analyze the number of times each grid is traversed by a pathway. Formula 3 represents the calculation method for Concentration Weighted Trajectories [7], which is used to calculate each grid. This method allows for the identification of grids traversed by a higher number of pathways. The statistical analysis method can confirm the location of long-term air pollution sources. However, this method requires extended periods of observation and data collection, making it time-consuming. Moreover, relying solely on air pollution and meteorological data for observing long-term pollution sources is less helpful. This is because the detected pollution sources are mostly known industrial areas or traffic hotspots, and it's challenging to detect sudden events like fires and burning incidents.

The literature mentioned above highlights the influence of wind speed on the dispersion and spread of air pollution. He Jianjun et. al. Conducted experimental observations in China, demonstrating that wind speed significantly affects the dispersion and spread of air pollution [8]. The experimental results show a strong negative correlation between air pollution and wind speed. When the wind speed is weak, air pollution tends to accumulate and rise in a specific area, making dispersion difficult. Conversely, with stronger wind speeds, the concentration of air pollution decreases in a particular area, but it spreads to other locations following the wind direction. This illustrates the continuous and mobile characteristics of air pollution dispersion. Therefore, this study incorporates a wind verification mechanism to examine whether the movement of air pollution is influenced by wind speed and the distance of pollution spread. The wind speed limitations are dynamically adjusted based on time intervals to reflect the varying levels of air pollution dispersion associated with wind speed.

3 Methodology

3.1 Overview

Figure 1 illustrates the workflow of APSTF. The input is the query $Q = (S, T)$ where S represents a station experiencing air pollution and T is the time. There are three phases: Identification Phase, Matching and Backtracking Phase, and Pathway Generation Phase. In Identification phase, stations experiencing air pollution in time slot T, T-1, ..., T-ΔT are identified. In Matching and Backtracking Phase, the affected areas, a group of nearby affected stations, at each time slot are derived and Hungarian algorithms are used to correlated the affected areas in different time slots. In Pathway Generation Phase, the potential source of air pollution G and the pathway P can be generated by using regression on the sequence of correlated affected areas in different time slots derived in the phase above.

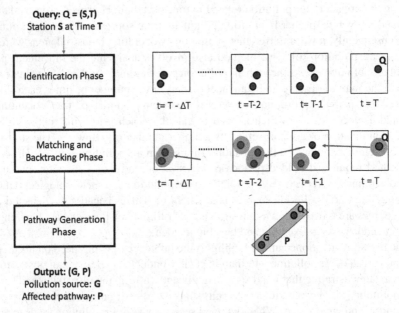

Fig. 1. Workflow of APSTF

3.2 Identification Phase

This phase identifies stations experiencing air pollution in time slot T, T-1, ..., and T-ΔT are identified.

In each time slot, the station experiencing air pollutions are the stations which the suspended particulate of fine matter concentration indicator exceeds 36 μg per cubic meter. In this study, stations include the intelligent air quality micro-sensors provided by the Environmental Protection Administration of the Executive Yuan [9], and automatic meteorological stations by the Central Weather Bureau [10]. A record in both data is generated per 5 min. According to the Environmental Protection Administration's fine particulate matter classification table [11], when the particulate of fine matter concentration indicator exceeds 36 μg per cubic meter, it poses a threat to individuals with heart, respiratory, and cardiovascular diseases. Therefore, all stations with suspended particulate matter concentration values above 36 μg per cubic meter are considered as the stations experiencing air pollution. Stations with suspended particulate matter concentration values below 35 μg per cubic meter at each station are then not considered.

The whole map is divided into grids. If the level of air pollution of a grid is the mean concentration of particulate matter of all stations in this grid. Figure 2 gives an illustrative example by given $\Delta T = 2$. The whole map is divided into 10 x 10 grids. Purple indicates the most severe pollution, followed by red, then yellow, and green represents no serious pollution. The adjacent grids in red and yellow are grouped into groups and the *centroid* of a group is derived to represent this group. Finally, the output of this phase are the centroids of groups in time slot T, T-1, ..., and T-ΔT.

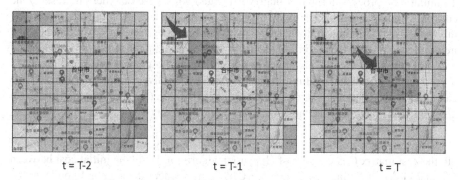

t = T-2   t = T-1   t = T

Fig. 2. The output of Identification Phase in time slot T-2, T-1, and T

3.3 Matching and Backtracking Phase

Given the centroids of each time slots, this phase aims at matching the centroids between centroids at different time slots so that the trajectory tracing from the query point to the pollution source can be found. Figure 3 shows an illustrative example where G_{ti} represents the i-th centroid found in time slot t. The line between the centroid represents two centroids are matched by a specific criterion, which will be described later. Tracing back from Q at t = 5 along the links, we can derive the trajectory is $< G_{0,3}, G_{1,3}, G_{3,2}, G_{4,2}, G_{5,1} >$ where $G_{0,3}$ can be identified as the potential pollution source.

Matching centroids in adjacent time slots can be modeled as the assignment problem: for each centroid G_{ti} in slot t, finding the centroid $G_{(t-1),j}$ that is most possible locations of

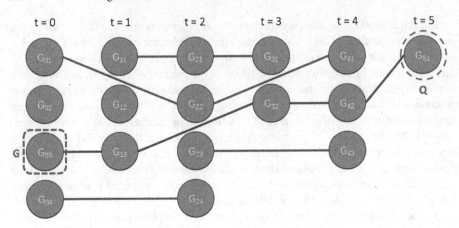

Fig. 3. Source-tracing trajectory from Q to G

$G_{t,i}$ in time slot t-1. That is, $G_{t,i}$ is most likely the same air pollution group moving from $G_{(t-1),j}$. In this case, the *Hungarian algorithm* is a method for solving the assignment problem, which involves assigning m tasks to n people in a way that minimizes the total cost. Suppose there are *m* centroids in time slot *t* and *n* centroids in time slot *t-1*. To initiate the process, an m x n matrix is created where each element represents the cost of assigning a centroid in time t to a centroid in time t-1. By iteratively modifying this matrix and utilizing strategic steps involving line covering, zero assignments, and iterative adjustments, the algorithm identifies the best assignment that minimize the total cost, providing an efficient and effective solution to the assignment problem. Interested readers can find the detail of Hungarian algorithm in [12]. Given the query Q at time T, we can find the *source-tracing trajectory* from G to Q by repletely applying the Hungarian algorithm for matching centroids in adjacent time slots, say T-(i-1) and T-i for i = 0, 1, ..., ΔT.

There are some implementation detail of Hungarian algorithm in this paper. First of all, the cost matrix C is the core of Hungarian algorithm. Here, the initial cost between $G_{t,i}$ and $G_{(t-1),j}$ is defined as $C_{i,j} = dist(G_{t,i}, G_{(t-1),j})$ where distance is Euclidean distance. Secondly, upon completing the pairing using the Hungarian algorithm, in terms of air pollution mobility, the methodology incorporates wind factors by referencing the sectorial wind observation approach proposed by researchers such as Foy [13]. Here, we build a *matching sector* to identify the pollution source from the previous time slot. Historical pollution group centroids are utilized to design the potential locations for a wind sector based on real-time wind direction and speed. A *matching sector* is generated to identify the pollution source from the previous time slot. Using the wind speed S_{t-1} and the wind direction vector $\overrightarrow{v_{t-1}}$ measured by the closest meteorological station to the centroid $G_{t,I} = (x_{t,i}, y_{t,i})$, as indicated in Fig. 4, we construct the matching sector. The sector is centered at $(x_{t,i}, y_{t,i})$ with a radius $r = S_{t-1} \times T_{unit}$ where T_{unit} represents the length of a time slot. The sector's direction is opposite to $-\overrightarrow{v}$, and the opening angle is determined by a user-defined parameter θ. Finally, for each centroid $G_{t,i}$, only the centroids of the previous time slots being inside M can be the candidates of potential locations of $G_{t,i}$ in the previous time slot. Otherwise, the centroids outside M will be omitted in the matching of the Hungarian algorithm.

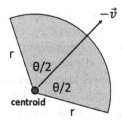

Fig. 4. Matching sector

3.4 Pathway Generation Phase

After completing centroid matching in continuous time, assuming multiple sets of continuous time data have been collected, with each set containing centroids of continuously moving groups that form a moving trajectory. In this phase, all centroids of an event and a simple linear regression method are used to generate air pollution pathways. Formally, let all the centroids in the source-tracing trajectory be: $\{(t_1, x_1, y_1), ..., (t_n, x_n, y_n)\}$ where (x_i, y_i) is the coordinate of the i-th centroid in time slot t_i. In the context of simple linear regression, where we're predicting a target variable y based on a single predictor variable x, the matrix form can be expressed using linear algebra notation. Define the matrices and vectors involved:

$$X = \begin{bmatrix} 1 & t_1 \\ 1 & t_2 \\ ... & ... \\ 1 & t_n \end{bmatrix}, y = \begin{bmatrix} x_1 & y_1 \\ x_2 & y_2 \\ ... & ... \\ x_n & y_n \end{bmatrix}, \beta = \begin{bmatrix} \beta_{1,1} & \beta_{2,1} \\ \beta_{2,1} & \beta_{2,2} \end{bmatrix}$$

The goal of linear regression is to find the coefficient vector β that minimizes the sum of squared differences between the predicted values $X\beta$ and the actual target values y. This can be expressed as the least squares objective function: minimize $||y - X\beta||^2$. The coefficients β can be computed using the normal equation: $\beta = (X^T X)^{-1} X^T y$. Finally, the regression line is $y = X\beta$.

The starting point of the pathway is considered as the source of air pollution G. Then, linear regression is applied to derive the line for all centroids in a moving trajectory and and the width of the pathway is the distance from the regression line to the furthest centroids. The pathway represents the area affected by air pollution and can be used to derive the warning area where potential air pollution may occur in the future.

4 Case Study

This study aims to detect air pollution mobility events and identify pollution sources. Due to the various types of air pollution, including traffic zones, industrial areas, traffic fire incidents, and others, the study observes different types of air pollution events based on whether they exhibit dispersion and are influenced by wind. This section presents case studies of stationary, industrial zone incident and fire incident pollution utilizing the method proposed in this paper.

Case I: Stationary Pollution. Figure 5 illustrates a stationary air pollution event that occurred in Xinzhuang District, New Taipei City. The entire event lasted for 23 min, during which a total of 4 centroids were connected. At that time, the wind was weak to calm, resulting in all centroids overlapping at the red coordinates on the map, and the average reliable matching score was also considerably high. Figure 5 presents the temporal changes in air pollution impact for this event. Three figures in the bottom of Fig. 5 corresponds to the beginning from the end of this event. It is evident that both the air pollution boundary framework and the centroids remained at the same location throughout the event.

Date: 2021/07/07
Direction: 168°
Speed: 0.7 m/s

Fig. 5. Stationary pollution (Case I)

Case II: Industrial Zone Incident. Figure 6 depicts an air pollution event that occurred in Yong'an District, Kaohsiung City. The surrounding environment belongs to the industrial zone category, characterized by noticeable exhaust pollution from factories and other sources. The entire event lasted for 44 min, during which a total of 5 centroids were connected. The wind was in a gentle breeze state at that time. Figure 6 shows the temporal changes in air pollution impact for this event. Figure 6 also shows the evolution of this pollution in the bottom three figures. It is observed that the regional extent of air pollution and the centroids moved in the southeast direction following the wind.

Case III: Fire Incident. Figure 7 illustrates an air pollution event in an industrial zone. The event occurred in a factory in Xiaogang District, Kaohsiung City. According to a news report by Liberty Times on July 23, 2021 [14], there was an explosion incident in the factory at noon on that day. The impact of the explosion was carried by the wind towards multiple administrative districts in the northeast. The event lasted for 57 min, during which a total of 4 centroids were connected. The wind was in a gentle breeze state at that time. Figure 29 shows the temporal changes in air pollution impact for this event. The bottom three figures in Fig. 7 corresponds to the beginning of the event to the end of the event. It is observed that the regional extent of air pollution and the centroids moved in the southeast direction following the wind. The reason for the significant distance

Date: 2021/07/23
Direction: 301°
Speed: 4.1 m/s

Fig. 6. Industrial Zone Incident (Case II)

between centroids is the fewer air quality micro-sensors installed in the intermediate region. Despite this uneven spatial distribution, this method can still identify potential air pollution sources at a greater distance.

Date: 2021/07/07
Direction: 234°
Speed: 4.0 m/s

Fig. 7. Fire Incident (Case III)

To evaluate the effectiveness of our research methodology, the Air Pollution Mobility Corridor, in comparison to two alternative approaches proposed by Pouyaei Arman employing Lagrange interpolation to link air pollution centroids [5] and by Zhen Li using event statistical analysis [6], we present a comparative analysis of their outcomes. In the shared legend, the red coordinates depict air pollution sources, the black coordinates indicate air pollution detection points, and the black and blue lines represent the paths of air pollution movement. In the Air Pollution Mobility Corridor approach, the red box illustrates the generated air pollution corridor through linear regression, while the orange box represents the warning zone. In the Lagrange interpolation method, the black path illustrates the connected movement path using Lagrange interpolation. In the event statistical analysis method, multiple events occurring at the same location require observation and statistical analysis to confirm the air pollution event.

Upon comparing these methods, it becomes apparent that our research methodology offers a comprehensive and effective solution, encompassing air pollution sources, impacted areas, and warning zones. The first column in Fig. 8 portrays stationary pollution, where the pollution remains localized and does not spread. In this scenario, all three methods yield similar results, and the corridor and impact areas are not distinctly discernible using our approach. The second column in Fig. 8 showcases pollution in an industrial zone. The output path from the Lagrange interpolation method displays more significant fluctuations due to the relatively dispersed distribution of centroids. Lastly, the third column illustrates a fire incident case. The statistical analysis method tends to generate fewer paths for abnormal events, potentially overlooking sporadic paths in such cases.

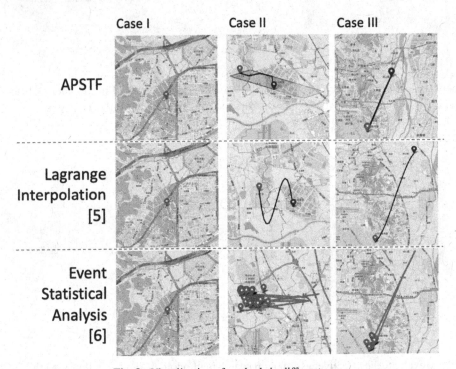

Fig. 8. Visualization of methods in different cases

5 Conclusion

In conclusion, this study underscores the escalating issue of air pollution amidst rapid urban development, emphasizing its profound implications for both the environment and human health. As urban areas expand and face increasing pollution challenges, encompassing intrinsic factors like traffic congestion and industrial emissions, they are further impacted by external sources of pollution. The consequences extend beyond environmental disruptions, posing a substantial threat to public health by exacerbating chronic illnesses and raising mortality risks.

The prevailing monitoring methods primarily center around air quality indices and forecasting, albeit falling short in identifying pollution sources. Addressing this gap, the study leverages the extensive deployment of Smart City and Rural Air Quality Microsensors, employing a methodical approach to trace and pinpoint pollution sources. By analyzing pollution movement paths through continuous time series data and integrating wind factors, the study successfully identifies emission sources contributing to air pollution. The proposed Air Pollution Source Tracing Framework (APSTF) unfolds as a comprehensive solution, effectively tracing air pollution sources and predicting its future impact areas. Through innovative approaches and leveraging cutting-edge technology, APSTF brings forth a sophisticated methodology to comprehend the dynamics of air pollution. By correlating affected areas across various time slots, this framework aids in pollution source identification and provides invaluable insights for future pollution prediction and mitigation. In essence, the study sheds light on the pressing need for proactive measures to tackle air pollution, advocating for further research and technological advancements to achieve cleaner and healthier urban environments. The APSTF exemplifies a promising step towards addressing the complex challenge of air pollution and offers a paradigm for future studies in environmental science and public health.

References

1. Seddon, J., Contreras, S., Elliott, B.: Under-recognized. Impacts of Air Pollution (2019)
2. Kanchanasuta, S., Sooktawee, S., Patpai, A., Vatanasomboon, P.: Temporal variations and potential source areas of fine particulate matter in Bangkok. Air Soil Water Res. **13**, 1178622120978203 (2020)
3. Uria-Tellaetxe, I., Carslaw, D.C.: Conditional bivariate probability function for source identification. Environ. Model. Softw. **59**, 1–9 (2014)
4. Chao, Y., et al.: Heavy air pollution with a unique "non-stagnant" atmospheric boundary layer in the Yangtze River middle basin aggravated by regional transport of $PM_{2.5}$ over China. Atmos. Chem. Phys. **20**(12), 7217–7230 (2020). https://doi.org/10.5194/acp-20-7217-2020
5. Pouyaei, A., Choi, Y., Jung, J., Sadeghi, B., Song, C.H.: Concentration trajectory route of air pollution with an integrated Lagrangian model (C-TRAIL Model v1.0) derived from the community multiscale air quality model (CMAQ Model v5.2). Geosci. Model Dev. **13**(8), 3489–3505 (2020). https://doi.org/10.5194/gmd-13-3489-2020
6. Li, Z., et al.: Non-stop industries were the main source of air pollution during the 2020 coronavirus lockdown in the North China Plain. Environ. Chem. Lett. **20**(1), 59–69 (2022)
7. Hsu, Y.K., Holsen, T.M., Hopke, P.K.: Comparison of hybrid receptor models to locate PCB sources in Chicago. Atmos. Environ. **37**(4), 545–562 (2003)
8. He, J., et al.: Air pollution characteristics and their relation to meteorological conditions during 2014–2015 in major Chinese cities. Environ. Pollut. **223**, 484–496 (2017)
9. Civil IoT Taiwan Data Service Platform, Air EPA Dataset. https://ci.taiwan.gov.tw/dsp/dataset_air_epa_micro.aspx
10. Civil IoT Taiwan Data Service Platform, CWB Dataset. https://ci.taiwan.gov.tw/dsp/dataset_cwb_auto.aspx
11. Civil IoT Taiwan Data Service Platform, Air Quality Indicator Dataset. https://airtw.epa.gov.tw/cht/Information/Standard/AirQualityIndicator.aspx
12. Kuhn, H.W.: The Hungarian method for the assignment problem. Naval Res. Logist. Q. **2**(1–2), 83–97 (1955)

13. Foy, B., Heo, J., Kang, J.Y., Kim, H., Schauer, J.J.: Source attribution of air pollution using a generalized additive model and particle trajectory clusters. Sci. Total Environ. **780**, 146458 (2021)

14. Chen, W.: Factory Explosion and Fire in Xiaogang, Kaohsiung Causes Air Pollution Affecting Seven Districts Including Fengshan. Liberty Times. https://news.ltn.com.tw/news/life/breakingnews/3595036. 7 July 2021

Prediction of Execution Probabilities and Attack Probabilities of Werewolf Game Using Machine Learning of Game Logs

Ryo Saito[1], Keita Ushida[1(✉)], and Tatsuya Arakawa[2]

[1] Kogakuin University, 1-24-2 Nishi-Shinjuku, Shinjuku-ku, Tokyo, Japan
ushida@cc.kogakuin.ac.jp
[2] National Institute of Technology, Gunma College, 580 Toriba-Machi, Maebashi, Gunma, Japan

Abstract. The topic of this paper is an analysis of Werewolf game. In this game, the players are divided into the villagers' side and the werewolves' side. The players erasure the opposite side's players through discussion and inference. In this paper, execution probabilities and attack probabilities are predicted using machine learning. Five-player games are adopted as the fundamental setting. Game logs were collected from an online chat-style Werewolf game server and analyzed as training data using logistic regression. The authors then analyzed the test data (game logs) with the calculated partial regression coefficients. For both execution and attack probabilities, predictions were appropriate when the self-proclaimed seer appeared. Since the appearance of the seer(s) is an objective piece of information about the situation, it is properly reflected in the prediction. In these predictions, the probabilities indicate which players are certainly executed/attacked otherwise which players are certain to survive. When no seers appeared, because there was little objective information, the execution/attack probabilities of each player changed little. In these situations, since the players can't decide who to execute/attack, the predictions are not irrational. In short, when the seer(s) (who provide objective information to the field) appear, the predictions tend to be appropriate. In addition, the predictions in this paper are stable with not much (50–80) training data, which is one of the characteristics of this method.

Keywords: Werewolf game · logistic regression · execution probabilities · attack probabilities

1 Introduction

Werewolf game is one of the popular party games. The players are divided into the villagers' side and the werewolves' side, and the players erasure the opposite side's players through discussion and inference. The werewolves hide their identities and attack the villagers' side players. The villagers execute the werewolves lurking in the village with their votes.

. Werewolf game is not only a party game but is now also studied as an incomplete information game. Program agents that play Werewolf game (Werewolf AIs) are developed and there are competitions for Werewolf AIs. Among the various research topics of this game, the authors are interested in studies on the analysis of the game itself.

In this paper, the authors attempt to predict execution probabilities and attack probabilities using machine learning.

2　Related Works

In this section, works on the analysis of Werewolf game are introduced. They are related to the topic of this paper.

There are studies on probabilities concerning Werewolf game. The win ratio of Mafia game, the origin of Werewolf game, was analyzed under a simplified condition (the executed player is chosen randomly) [1–3]. As for Werewolf game, the win ratio was calculated provided that the werewolves did not attack each other [4]. A mathematical model of the games which introduced execution probabilities and attack probabilities was constructed [5].

The conversation of Werewolf game is also analyzed. The relation between the tendency of conversation and victory or defeat was examined using the game logs of online Werewolf game [6]. There is an attempt to analyze the structure of the discussion in the game [7]. What is the best utterance for each player is analyzed using game theory focused on five-player games [8].

Statistics are also a research topic of Werewolf game. The regulation in which the win ratio was even was analyzed from the statistics of the games [9]. The prediction of the trustworthy players was attempted [10].

While the approach of most of the above works is mathematical, the one of this paper is machine learning (logistic regression). Though the idea of execution/attack probabilities in this paper is derived from [5], the approach in this paper is analysis using machine learning, not mathematical modeling.

3　Analysis of the Logs of the Werewolf Game

3.1　Collecting Logs and Configuring Features

The authors collected the game logs of Werewolf game played in online chat style on *Ruru-saba (server)*. Following the previous works on Werewolf game analysis, as a simple and basic regulation, five-player games (three villagers, one seer, and one werewolf) were focused on. Logs of the games in which the player acted violations were excluded.

In this paper, the following three probabilities were analyzed:

- The execution probability of the first day
- The attack probability of the first day
- The execution probability of the second day

Features were prepared for the conversations and the situations of the games. They were calculated for each game. The authors added the features to the logs manually. Tables 1, 2 and 3 show the features used in this paper, which were selected based on the previous works [6, 11, 12] and which were able to be extracted from a sufficient number of games.

Table 1. Features and regression coefficients for calculating the execution probability of the first day.

Feature	Value	Coefficient
Whether only s/he is the player that claims to be the seer	0 or 1	−2.247
Whether s/he and the other player claim to be the seers	0 or 1	0.816
The number of players who are identified as humans by the seers	0 or over	−21.283
The number of players who are identified as werewolves by the seers	0 or over	2.871
The amount of idle talk	1–5	−0.090
The amount of conversation on divination	1–5	0.107

Table 2. Features and regression coefficients for calculating the attack probability of the first day

Feature	Value	Coefficient
Whether only s/he is the player that claims to be the seer	0 or 1	48.836
Whether any players claim to be the seers	0 or 1	−19.765
The number of players who are identified as humans by the seers	0 or over	0.806
The amount of idle talk	0 or over	0.120
The amount of conversation on suspicion	1–5	−0.133
The amount of conversation on the revelation of the role	1–5	−0.635

Table 3. Features and regression coefficients for calculating execution probability of the second day

Feature	Value	Coefficient
Whether s/he and the other player claims to be the seers	0 or 1	53.901
The number of players who are identified as humans by the seers	0 or 1	−23.619
The amount of idle talk	1–5	2.508
The amount of conversation on divination	1–5	−0.800

3.2 Analysis with Logistic Regression

A subset of the game logs with the features were analyzed using logistic regression as the training data. The authors calculated the partial regression coefficients by increasing the number of game logs. The authors confirmed that the coefficients were calculated stably with 50 or more game logs. In other words, 50 or more logs are enough to predict the probabilities stably. Considering this trial and the amount of game logs collected, the authors set the number of training data:

- 80 for the execution probability of the first day
- 50 for the attack probability of the first day
- 50 for the execution probability of the second day.

Tables 1, 2 and 3 show the calculated partial regression coefficients. As the value increases, the feature has a more positive effect on increasing the execution/attack probability, and vice versa. When the value is near zero, the feature has little effect on the probability.

4 Analysis of the Game Logs (Test Data)

4.1 The Execution Probability of the First Day

From Table 1, the game situation mainly affects the execution probability of the first day. The following are the predictions by test data in different situations.

- When no self-proclaimed seers appeared
- When one self-proclaimed seer appeared and identified a player as a human
- When one self-proclaimed seer appeared and identified a player as the werewolf
- When two self-proclaimed seers appeared

In this paper, the appearance of the seer(s) is considered as one of the main factors impacting the game situation because the seer is the player with an important role. The seer can identify whether the selected player is a werewolf or not. The seer's divination brings logical cues to the players. Since the seer is an important player, the werewolves may claim to be the seers to confuse the game.

When No Self-proclaimed Seers Appeared. Table 4 shows the predicted execution probabilities using a game log in which no self-proclaimed seers appeared. The table also shows each player's vote.

Table 4. Execution probabilities and votes (first day, no seers)

Player	#1 villager	#2 villager	#3 seer	#4 werewolf	#5 villager
Exec. Prob.	0.228	0.216	0.228	0.201	0.226
1st vote	2	1	4	1	2
2nd vote	2	4	2	2	2

In this situation, the players need to infer who the werewolf is from the conversation because there are no logical clues. The calculated probabilities are almost the same for all players. According to the log, the players also said that they could not guess who the werewolf was. As well as the players, the predictor in this paper requires events as logical cues to calculate the probabilities. In the actual game, the players seemed to vote with intuition. The votes were split, and then player #2 was executed after the second vote.

When One Self-proclaimed Seer Appeared and Identified a Player as a Human. Table 5 shows the execution probabilities and the votes when one self-proclaimed seer appeared and identified a player as a human.

Table 5. Execution probabilities and votes (first day, one seer, identified as a human)

Player	#1 villager	#2 villager	#3 seer	#4 werewolf	#5 villager
Exec. Prob.	0.187	0.000	0.039	0.187	0.276
Vote	5	1	4	1	1

In this game, player #3 claimed to be the seer and told that player #2 was a human. According to Table 5, the execution probabilities of the self-proclaimed seer (player #3) and the identified human (player #2) decreased. There were no votes for them in the game. By comparing the game and the prediction, it can be said that who would survive was appropriately predicted.

However, there were few clues about the other players (player #1, #4, and #5), and in the game, the players said they had no idea who the werewolf was. The execution probabilities of them changed little, which is similar to the situation described above (no seer appeared). The players seemed to vote with intuition.

When One Self-proclaimed Seer Appeared and Identified a Player as the Werewolf. Table 6 shows the execution probabilities and the votes when one self-proclaimed seer appeared and identified a player as the werewolf.

Table 6. Execution probability and votes (first day, one seer, identified as the werewolf)

Player	#1 werewolf	#2 seer	#3 villager	#4 villager	#5 villager
Exec. Prob.	0.834	0.036	0.216	0.222	0.216
Vote	2	1	1	1	1

In the game, player #2 claimed to be the seer and told that player #1 was the werewolf. The execution probability of player #1 increased, while that of player #2 decreased. In the game, player #1 was executed. By comparing the game and the prediction, it can be said that the prediction of who would be executed was appropriate.

When Two Self-proclaimed Seers Appeared. Table 7 shows the execution probabilities and the votes when two self-proclaimed seers appeared. In this game, player #4 and player #5 claimed to be the seers and told that player #1 and player #2 were humans.

Table 7. Execution probabilities and votes (first day, two seers)

Player	#1 villager	#2 villager	#3 villager	#4 werewolf	#5 seer
Exec. Prob.	0.000	0.000	0.201	0.466	0.323
Vote	4	4	4	5	4

In such a situation, it is logical that one of the self-proclaimed seers is the werewolf (there is no benefit for the villagers to lie and claim to be the seer). The increase in the execution probabilities of both seers reflects the logic. In this game, player #4, one of the self-proclaimed seers, was executed. In this situation, since the villagers win by executing player #4 (werewolf) on the second day, it is also logically valid to execute player #5. Thus, the prediction that player #4 or #5 would be executed is appropriate.

4.2 The Attack Probability of the First Day

Table 2 shows that the attack probabilities of the first day are also strongly influenced by the game situation. Similar to Sect. 4.1, the following are the predictions by test data in different cases.

- When no self-proclaimed seers appeared
- When one self-proclaimed seer appeared
- When two self-proclaimed seers appeared

When No Self-proclaimed Seers Appeared. Table 8 shows the attack probabilities and the attacked player when no self-proclaimed seers appeared. Player #2 (villager) was executed as the conclusion of the inference from the players' conversation.

Table 8. Attack probabilities and the attacked player (first day, no seers)

Player	#1 villager	#2 villager	#3 seer	#4 werewolf	#5 villager
Attack Prob	0.351	executed	0.162	N/A	0.244
Attacked			3		

There was no objective information about the seer. The werewolf has an advantage if s/he can attack the seer. However, it is not a disadvantage even if s/he attacks a villager. As the consideration indicates, the difference between the attack probabilities in Table 8 is modest. In the game, the werewolf successfully attacked the seer. As for this attack, it is not sure that the werewolf is convinced that player #3 is the seer. Features that are not picked up in this paper may be clues to predict. This issue is to be considered as one of future works.

When One Self-proclaimed Seer Appeared. Table 9 shows the attack probabilities and the attacked player when one self-proclaimed seer appeared. Player #5 claimed to be the seer and told that player #2 was a human. Player #4 was then executed.

Table 9. Attack probabilities and the attacked player (first day, one seer)

Player	#1 werewolf	#2 villager	#3 villager	#4 villager	#5 seer
Attack Prob	N/A	0.000	0.000	executed	1.000
Attacked			5		

In this situation, the werewolf must attack the seer because s/he will inevitably reveal who the werewolf is if the seer survives on the second day. The prediction is appropriate as it reflects logic. In the game, the seer was attacked after all.

When Two Self-proclaimed Seers Appeared. Table 10 shows the attack probabilities and the attacked player when two self-proclaimed seers appeared. Player #2 and player #5 claimed to be the seers and told that player #1 and player #4 were humans. Player #2 (seer) was then executed. Since the werewolf (player #5, the other self-proclaimed seer) survived, the game continued.

Table 10. Attack probabilities and the attacked player (first day, two seers)

Player	#1 villager	#2 seer	#3 villager	#4 villager	#5 werewolf
Attack Prob	0.357	executed	0.379	0.254	N/A
Attacked			4		

In this situation, the werewolf will lose because the continuing game means that the players executed the genuine seer and that the surviving seer is the werewolf. The werewolf can do nothing but randomly attack a villager. The slight difference in the predicted probabilities reflects this circumstance.

4.3 The Execution Probability of the Second Day

The execution probabilities of the second day are calculated based on the coefficients shown in Table 3. In this paper, to simplify the analysis, the log of the second day is analyzed independently from the log of the first day in the same game. Similar to Sects. 4.1 and 4.2, the following are the predictions by test data in different situations.

- When no self-proclaimed seers appeared
- When one self-proclaimed seer appeared
- When two self-proclaimed seers appeared

When No Self-proclaimed Seers Appeared. Table 11 shows the execution probabilities and the votes when no self-proclaimed seers appeared. On the first day, player #2 was executed, then player #4 was attacked. By the second day, no self-proclaimed seers appeared.

Table 11. Execution probabilities and votes (second day, no seers)

Player	#1 villager	#2 seer	#3 werewolf	#4 villager	#5 villager
Exec. Prob.	0.450	executed	0.228	attacked	0.226
Vote	3	N/A	5	N/A	3

In this situation, there are still no objective clues about the werewolf. According to the game log, the players said there was no information about the werewolf. As for the prediction, because of few logical clues as described above, the probability of player #1 was slightly higher than the others. After all, the werewolf (#3) was successfully executed. However, from the game log, the villagers did not seem convinced that player #3 was the werewolf. They seem to have voted with intuition.

When One Self-proclaimed Seer Appeared. Table 12 shows the execution probabilities and the votes when one self-proclaimed seer appeared. On the first day, player #2 claimed to be the seer and told that player #1 was a human. After that, player #4 was executed, then player #2 was attacked. On the second day, another self-proclaimed seer did not appear.

Table 12. Execution probabilities and votes (second day, one seer)

Player	#1 villager	#2 seer	#3 villager	#4 villager	#5 werewolf
Exec. Prob.	0.000	attacked	0.586	executed	0.454
Vote	5	N/A	5	N/A	3

In this situation, there was no objective information as to which of player #3 and player #5 was the werewolf. Since player #1 was identified as a human, player #3 voted for player #5, and player #5 voted for player #3, inevitably (even if player #5, the werewolf, voted for player #1, player #1 would not be executed because player #1 could not get two votes). Thus, player #1's vote was the deciding factor between victory and defeat. However, the players said they had no idea which player (player #3 or #5) was the werewolf. In the end, the werewolf (player #5) was successfully executed.

As for the prediction, the execution probability of player #1 was zero. Considering the circumstances and the prediction, it is appropriately predicted that player #1 will survive.

When Two Self-proclaimed Seers Appeared. Table 13 shows the execution probabilities and the votes when two self-proclaimed seers appeared. On the first day, player #2 and player #5 claimed to be the seers and told that player #1 and player #4 were humans. After that, player #2 was executed, then player #4 was attacked.

Table 13. Execution probabilities and votes (second day, two seers)

Player	#1 villager	#2 seer	#3 villager	#4 villager	#5 werewolf
Exec. Prob.	0.000	Executed	0.321	attacked	1.000
Vote	5	N/A	5	N/A	3

In this situation, the werewolf, the other self-proclaimed seer, is necessarily executed. The reason for this has been described in Sects. 4.1 and 4.2. As for the prediction, the execution probability of player #5 (werewolf) was the highest.

5   Discussion

Comparing the predictions to the actual game log in the previous section indicates the predictions are appropriate in most cases when the seers appear. In these situations, who will be executed or attacked or who will survive is predicted appropriately. The player whose execution/attack probability increases will be executed/attacked, and the player whose execution/attack probability decreases will survive. Especially when the players' behavior is logically decided, the calculated probabilities reflect the situations (e.g., when two self-proclaimed seers appeared), although the predictor was built by machine learning. These predictions are made using machine learning, not with manual model building. Furthermore, the training data for prediction were less than 100 for each probability. Little time and labor will be needed to construct predictors for other regulations and settings of Werewolf game.

When objective clues such that the seers appear are few, the probabilities' change is slight. In the game, one of the players with almost equal probabilities will be executed or attacked.

These predictions can be used to analyze the situation of games. Adding this prediction function to Werewolf AIs will be effective for their development. Besides, by displaying the analyzed situation to the audience, watching Werewolf games will be supported and enjoyable.

Some issues are to be considered to improve the prediction. In the current implementation, to simplify the problem, the analysis of the second day is independent of that of the first day. Taking the first day into account will improve the prediction of the second day. Taking the evaluation of situations from each player's point of view into account will also be effective. At present, the viewpoint of the features is objective. Analyzing what a player thinks about other players will be useful to improve the prediction.

6 Conclusion and Future Works

In this paper, execution probabilities and attack probabilities of Werewolf game were calculated using machine learning (logistic regression). The probabilities have been calculated appropriately, and who will be executed/attacked or who will survive is almost certainly predicted when the seers appear.

Improving the prediction is one of the significant future works. The issues described in Sect. 5 and further investigation of the features should be considered. As described in Sect. 4.3, analyzing the logs through the game (not by a day) will increase information for prediction. Analyzing games with more players (players of other roles such as doctor join) is also one of the next steps. Supporting game-watching with situation analysis with probability prediction is an interesting work. Furthermore, cooperation with Werewolf AIs is also expected.

References

1. Braverman, M., Etesami, O., Mossel, E.: Mafia: a theoretical study of players and coalitions in a partial information environment. Ann. Appl. Probab. **18**(3), 825–846 (2008)
2. Yao, E.: A theoretical study of Mafia games. arXiv:0804.0071 (2008)
3. Migdal, P.: A mathematical model of the Mafia game. arXiv:1009.1031 (2013)
4. Nishino, J.: A natural winning percentage of the werewolf game. IPSJ Technical Report, vol. 2015-GI-33, no. 18 (2015). (in Japanese)
5. Miyata, H., Arakawa, T.: Mathematical models of Werewolf with execution probabilities and attack probabilities. In: Game Programming Workshop, vol. 2019, pp. 161–164 (2019). (in Japanese)
6. Inaba, M., Ohata, N., Takahashi, K., Toriumi, F.: You will be executed if you keep chatting —development of tag sets for utterances in the werewolf game and analysis of action and winning or losing using the tags. J. IPSJ **57**(11), 2392–2402 (2016). (in Japanese)
7. Inaba, M., Osawa, H., Katagami, D., Shinoda, K., Toriumi, F.: Analysis of werewolf game based on discussion structure. In: Game Programming Workshop, vol. 2014, pp. 61–66 (2014). (inJapanese)
8. Shimizu, D., Hasebe, K.: Game theoretic analysis of best utterance in Werewolf game. In: The 37th JSSST Annual Conference, 55-L (2020). (in Japanese)
9. Inaba, M., Toriumi, F., Takahashi, K.: The statistical analysis of Werewolf game data. In: Game Programming Workshop, vol. 2012, pp. 144–147 (2012). (in Japanese)
10. Sonoda, A., Toriumi, F.: Analysis of trust in "are you a werewolf?" In: The 31st Annual Conference of JSAI, 2H1-1in1 (2017). (in Japanese)
11. Konno, N., Otsuki, T.: Improvement of team estimation in AIWolf player using machine learning. In: Entertainment Computing Symposium, vol. 2017, pp. 64–69 (2017). (in Japanese)
12. Kimura, Y., Ito, T.: Improvement of role estimation using machine learning in Werewolf AI. In: The 32nd Annual Conference of JSAI, 1H1-OS-13a-03 (2018). (in Japanese)

Using Strongly Solved Mini2048 to Analyze Players with N-tuple Networks

Shunsuke Terauchi, Takaharu Kubota, and Kiminori Matsuzaki[✉] [iD]

School of Informatics, Kochi University of Technology, Kami, Japan
{250348z,240312k}@ugs.kochi-tech.ac.jp,
matsuzaki.kiminori@kochi-tech.ac.jp

Abstract. *2048* is a stochastic single-player game and there have been many studies of computer players for 2048. The authors believe that 2048 and its players can be useful for analyzing, comparing, and characterizing AI techniques. Yamashita et al. (2022) showed that a smaller variant of 2048, called Mini2048, can be strongly solved, and used the game to analyze some properties of AlphaZero-based players. In this study, we continue the work to deepen the analysis of the properties of the game itself and of the players. We first reproduce the retrograde analysis and then use the results to investigate the properties of the game, including the usefulness of the tile downgrading technique. We also develop four N-tuple networks following some of the state-of-the-art training methods and try to analyze the properties of N-tuple networks. We find several similarities and dissimilarities among the N-tuple networks. This is an important first step towards deep analysis of various AI techniques applied to 2048.

Keywords: Game 2048 · Strongly Solving · N-tuple Networks

1 Introduction

2048 [2] is a stochastic single-player game categorized in slide-and-merge games. 2048 is considered *easy to play but difficult to master*, and has attracted so many people to play. There have been many studies of computer players that have achieved quite high scores [1, 3–5, 7, 8, 11, 17]. Many of them were developed based on N-tuple networks trained with TD learning [11] and Expectimax search [17], and also several techniques have also been innovated to improve the performance. The state-of-the-art player [3] achieves an average score of 625,377. In recent years, several computer players based on neural networks and deep learning have also been developed [1, 5, 8, 14]. Against this background, the authors believe that game 2048 and its player can be useful for analyzing, comparing and characterizing deep learning technologies.

Strongly solving (a.k.a. prefect analysis) of a game is to compute the values of all the states when the players make the best moves. Several relatively simple two-player games, such as Dobutsu shogi (a Japanese chess played on 3×4 board) [13], Chinese checkers [10], and Quixo [12], have recently been strongly solved. For 2048, strongly solving is to compute the expected values for all the states, but it is very hard due to the

C.-Y. Lee et al. (Eds.): TAAI 2023, CCIS 2075, pp. 165–178, 2024.
https://doi.org/10.1007/978-981-97-1714-9_14

excessive state space size. Yamashita et al. [16] strongly solved the game 2048 played on a 3 × 3 board, called *Mini2048*. They also studied some properties of the game and its variants, as well as the computer players developed using an AlphaZero-style training method.

In this study, we continue the work of Yamashita et al. We first reproduce the value DB obtained by the strongly solving of Mini2048 and a perfect player (a greedy player using the value DB) to study other properties of the game. We then develop multiple computer players based on N-tuple networks and TD learning with extensions, to investigate the properties of the players with respect to the perfect player. The main contributions of the paper are summarized below.

- Sect. 3: We have independently reimplemented a program of retrograde analysis to create value DB, and a perfect player that greedily selects a move with the value DB. We also implement retrograde analysis under the setting that we try to maximize the sum of the tile values (we call the half of the sum *progress* in the paper).
- Sect. 4: We investigate properties of Mini2048 by using the value DB and the perfect player. The investigation includes the performance of the greedy player using value DB with noise, the correctness of the tile downgrading technique.
- Sect. 5: We develop several N-tuple players of Mini2048. Several improvements proposed in existing works are applied such as multi-staging [17], TC learning [4], and optimistic initialization [3]. We expect the developed players to be nice counterparts to those for the standard 2048.
- Sect. 6: The play logs of these N-tuple players were analyzed in two main ways. We found several similarities and dissimilarities among the networks. More detailed experiments and analysis would be needed to explain these results.

2   Mini2048: 2048 on 3 × 3 Board

In this study, we use *Mini2048* as the target game. Mini2048 is a smaller variant of game 2048 that is played on a 3 × 3 board. The rules are the same as those of 2048 except for the board size.

2.1   Rules

In an initial state, two tiles each having a value of either 2 (with a probability of 0.9) or 4 (with a probability of 0.1) are randomly placed. At each turn, the player selects a direction (either up, right, down, or left), and all the tiles will slide in the selected direction. When two tiles of the same number collide, they merge into one with the sum value, and the score increases by the sum. Merging is done from the far side and newly created tiles do not merge again at the turn: sliding to the right from _2_, 222, and 422 results in ___2, _24, and _44, respectively. The player cannot select a direction in which no tiles slide nor merge. After each move, a new tile will randomly appear in an empty cell with a value of either 2 (with a probability of 0.9) or 4 (with a probability of 0.1). If there is no legal direction to select, the game ends. The goal is to get as high a score as possible before the game ends.

2.2 Notions

Since a move in Mini2048 consists of two steps, we introduce the two notions of *state* and *afterstate*, defined as follows [11]. We also introduce the notion of *progress* to compensate for the difference in values of new tiles. Figure 1 illustrates these concepts.

- **state**: A *state* is a board (and score) at which the player selects a move.
- **afterstate**: An *afterstate* is a board (and score) obtained after the slide-and-merge step.
- **progress**: *Progress* is defined as the sum of tile values divided by two. Note that this value remains constant during the slide-and-merge step but increases by one or two respectively when a 2- or 4-tile is randomly added in the new-tile step. Therefore, the progress monotonically increases by one or two for each turn.

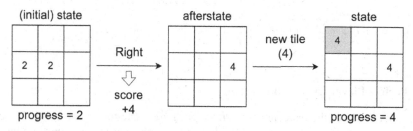

Fig. 1. Introduction of notions of state, afterstate, and progress.

3 Strongly Solving Mini2048

3.1 Depth-First Retrograde Analysis

Yamashita et al. [16] showed that Mini2048 can be strongly solved. Their implementation was based on a two-phase retrograde analysis algorithm. In the first phase, all reachable afterstates are enumerated from the initial states using breadth-first search. After initializing the values of all the terminal states with 0, the second phase iteratively assigns expected values to afterstates when the values of all the next afterstates have been computed.

In this study, we have implemented a depth-first retrograde analysis program that simultaneously lists up the reachable afterstates and computes their values; Algorithm 1 shows the pseudocode of the depth-first retrograde analysis algorithm for Mini2048. To reduce the computation cost, *afterstate.id* is assumed to have a unique value modulo the rotation and/or reflection symmetry of boards. Also, *valueDB* stores the expected values from the states to end games.

After running the program, we obtain 41,325,017 unique states and 31,431,374 unique afterstates[1]. The expected score of the initial states is 5468.49 on average.

---

[1] Yamashita et al. [16] reported that they obtained 48,713,519 states/afterstates in total and 31,431,370 afterstates. For some reasons we had four more afterstates than Yamashita et al.'s.

Algorithm 1 Depth-first retrograde analysis of Mini2048

```
 1:  def RECS(state) :
 2:      maxv ← −∞;
 3:      for each d in state.legalmove :
 4:          r, afterstate ← PLAY(state, d)
 5:          maxv ← MAX(r + RECA(afterstate), maxv)
 6:      return maxv
 7:
 8:  def RECA(afterstate) :
 9:      if valueDB[afterstate.id] is None :
10:          val ← 0
11:          for each i in afterstate.emptycells :
12:              for each j in {2, 4} :
13:                  state ← ⟨add a j-tile at position i of afterstate⟩
14:                  .if ISENDSTATE(state) : continue
15:                  val ← val + RECS(state) * ⟨probability of a j-tile⟩
16:          valueDB[afterstate.id] ← val;
17:      return valueDB[afterstate.id]
```

3.2 Perfect Player Using Value DB

The *valueDB* stores the expected score from each afterstate to the end game. We can develop a perfect player by using the *valueDB*: we greedily select a move that maximizes the sum of the expected score and the reward given by the move.

We can study some properties of Mini2048 from the play logs of the perfect player. In this study, we played 10,000 games with the perfect player and statistically processed them after grouping them by the progress. Figure 2 shows the score of the games and the alive ratio with respect to the progress. Table 1 shows the progress, score, and alive ratio when the perfect player successfully reached 256-, 512-, and/or 1024-tiles. Even for the perfect player, the game is hard after reaching a 512-tile and before reaching a

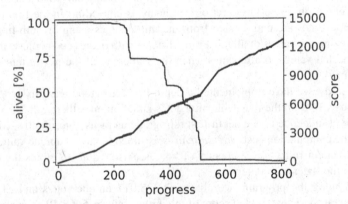

Fig. 2. Average score (blue, right axis) and alive ratio (red, left axis) with respect to progress. (Color figure online)

1024-tile: we can see several very hard timings in Fig. 2 where the line of the alive ratio drops quickly.

Table 1. Progress, score, and alive ratio of perfect player.

Condition	Progress	Score	Alive
256-tile	136	1750	99.53%
512-tile	263	4000	73.84%
512-tile & 256-tile	391	5750	54.40%
512-tile & 256-tile & 128-tile	456	6500	40.49%
1024-tile	511	9000	1.07%

3.3 Strongly Solving in Terms of Progress

We modified Algorithm 1 to compute the values based on the progress. The results of the retrograde analysis were almost the same (in terms of the best move for each state): (1) only 2.03% of the states have different best move between two retrograde analyses; (2) the perfect player using the values achieved an average score of 5459.03 (-9.46).

From these results, we conclude that we can use either the score or the progress in the training and playing. Using the progress (or the number of actions) as a reward would have advantages for stabilizing the training since it increases almost linearly.

4   Analysis of Mini2048 Using Perfect Analysis

4.1   Average Score of Players with Noise

In general, an evaluation function of states/afterstates cannot be fully accurate. Therefore, we first examined the changes in scores by simulating inaccurate evaluation functions by adding noise to the value DB. Here, we pick up the noise from a normal distribution with mean zero and variance σ^2 where the standard deviation σ was varied from 0 up to 500. Figure 3 plots the average scores (out of 10,000 games) of the players that greedily select the moves.

As can be seen in the figure, the average score decreases monotonically as the noise size σ increases. For instance, the average scores of 5000, 4000, 3000, and 2000 are obtained when we have the noise σ being $\sigma \approx 25$, 75, 145, and 270.

4.2   States Reachable by Perfect Player

Exploration and exploitation are the key to the success of tree search and reinforcement learning methods. Consider the case where we always select the optimal moves (a random tile is still placed randomly), resulting in the number of reached afterstates being smaller

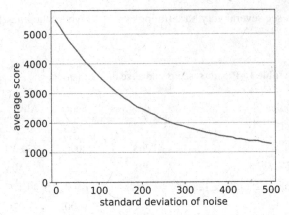

Fig. 3. Average score of players with noise.

than that in the original retrograde analysis. We enumerated all the reachable states with a perfect player using a program similar to Algorithm 1, and found 9,415,456 afterstates. This number is 29.96% of the total number of states/afterstates.

This number suggests that even if we only select the best moves we have enough variation of states/afterstates for reinforcement learning (this was claimed in [8]). The number also suggests that there is some room for improvement in terms of exploration, since the optimal initialization technique was successful [3].

4.3 Tile Downgrading

One of the difficulties in performing reinforcement learning for 2048 is that the game becomes more difficult in later turns, resulting in fewer opportunities to sample the training data from later turns. Weight promotion [4] and tile downgrading [3] have been proposed to address this issue. Both project a state/afterstate containing tiles with large values onto a state consisting of tiles with smaller values.

In this study, we tested the following two methods (Fig. 4).

- **Full Downgrading** [4]: Halve all the tile values except 2s. The tiles with value 2 are removed. Note that this downgrading method can map an afterstate to a non-afterstate as shown in the example in Fig. 4.
- **Partial Downgrading** [3]: Starting from the largest value v of the tiles, the tiles with values v, v/2, v/4, ... are halved. If there is no tile with value $v/2^k$, the processing stops. In the example, the tile values 1024, 512, 256, and 128 are halved, and the processing stops since there is no 64-tile.

To empirically analyze the effects of tile downgrading, we randomly selected 3000 afterstates from the perfect player's game records containing either one 512 or one 1024, and then plotted the original values and the values of the downgraded board. Figures 5(a) and 5(c) includes the cases marked with orange dots when the downgraded state becomes a non-afterstate. We found that 37% of the states are not afterstates for both cases with a 512- or 1024-tile. Note that there are a few ($\leq 1\%$) outliers in the experiment results that fall outside the plot range.

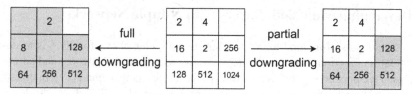

Fig. 4. Two tile downgrading methods. The shaded cells show the changes.

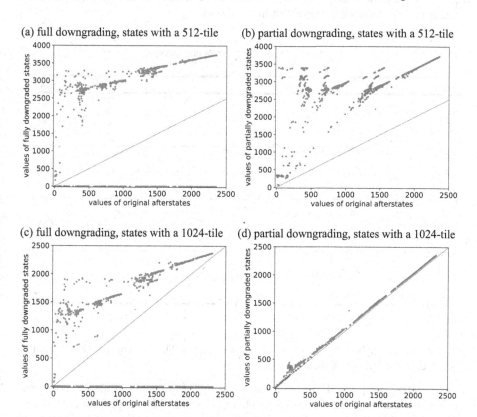

Fig. 5. Relationship of values before and after tile downgrading. The orange dots show the cases when the results of downgrading are not afterstates.

When downgrading a state with one 512-tile, both methods resulted in points far from the $y = x$ line. Full downgrading seems to yield a better result as seen in the results with a (roughly) single line, while there exists the problem of non-afterstates. In the resulting plot of the partial downgrading, we can see three lines in the graph, which performs worse when we compare the values of states.

When downgrading a state with one 1024-tile, the partial downgrading performs quite well and the dots are plotted near $y = x$. This partial downgrading was used by Guei et al. [3] to compute the evaluation values for the states with 32768 or 65536 tiles. The success is supported by the experiment results in Fig. 5(d).

5 Developing Mini2048 Players with N-tuple Networks

The most successful method to create a strong computer player for 2048 is to design an evaluation function (functional approximator) with N-tuple networks and adjust the weights in the networks using an extension of the TD learning method [11]. In this study, we designed four N-tuple networks covering the 3×3 board. Table 2 shows the design of the N-tuple networks used in this paper. Note that we sample eight symmetric positions for each tuple to reduce the number of tuples needed.

Table 2. Design of N-tuple networks.

Name	Tuples	Number of weights
NT6		7,086,244
NT4a		175,692
NT4b		87,846
NT3		13,310

The weights of N-tuple networks are adjusted by a TD learning method, which is enhanced by the following techniques.

- **Symmetric sampling**: For each tuple, we sample from eight symmetric positions. This allows us to extract features from the entire board with a small number of tuples.
- **Multi-staging**: We switch the look-up table of weights as the game progresses. In this study, we set the number of stages to be two as in Guei et al. [3]: the first stage is for the states without a tile of 512 or larger; the second stage is for the state with such a tile.
- **Temporal coherent learning** (TC learning): TC learning is a TD learning equipped with automatic learning-rate adjustment, which was first used for 2048 in the development of the previous state-of-the-art [4].
- **Optimistic initialization**: To ensure the exploration in the training phase, we initialize the weights with large values (instead of zeros). In this study, based on the expected values of the states computed from strongly solving, we decided to initialize the weights so that the initial values of all the afterstates are 1200.

We carried out the training with the methods described above until training with 5×10^8 actions. We believe that our training was sufficient: in a previous work [4] networks with 1.3×10^9 weights were trained to 4×10^{10} actions while our largest NT6 network has only 7.1×10^6 weights.

Figure 6 shows the progress of the training, where we plot the results of the training episodes with a moving average with a window size of 10,000. We can see that the training of networks NT4a, NT4b, and NT3 almost converged in the early stages of training. The network NT6 seems to improve a little, we consider that the training is almost converged. As expected, the performance of the players depends strongly on the number of weights in the N-tuple networks. Note that the NT6 player is close to the perfect player: the average score of NT6 was 4905.27 and the theoretical best average score is 5468.49.

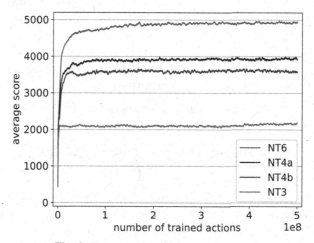

Fig. 6. Progress of training: average scores.

6   Analysis of N-tuple Networks

We developed a greedy player for each N-tuple network trained with 5×10^8 actions. We then investigated the properties of those networks from the play logs of 10,000 games.

For each state in the play logs, we computed the evaluation values of all the moves using the N-tuple networks and the value DB from the retrograde analysis. The following three values are calculated after grouping the states by their progress.

- **Accuracy**: The ratio when the N-tuple player selects the (true) best move.
- **Absolute error**: The averaged difference between the N-tuple player's move and the (true) best move measured in terms of true values.
- **Relative error**: The averaged ratio between the absolute error and the difference between the best and worst move measured in terms of true values.

Figures 7, 8, and 9 show the accuracy, absolute errors, and relative errors. Note that we applied smoothing with the moving average (window size 20).

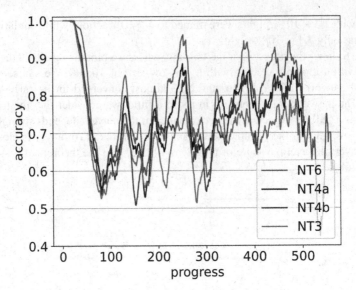

Fig. 7. Accuracy of players' selection.

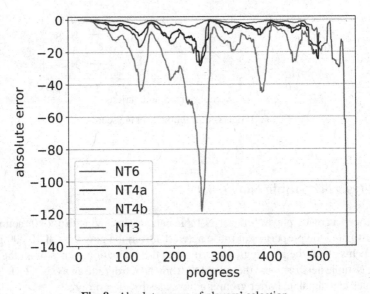

Fig. 8. Absolute errors of players' selection.

For NT6, although the accuracy drops similarly to the other networks, the absolute errors are very small for states with progress ≤450. After that it has large absolute errors, probably due to less training on later turns.

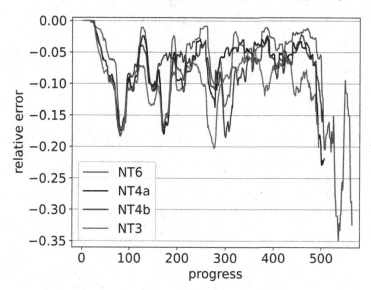

Fig. 9. Relative errors of players' selection.

Roughly speaking, the lines have similar shapes for all the plots. This suggests that there are easy or difficult states for which N-tuple networks accurately evaluate the values. Comparing with the graph of perfect players in Fig. 2, we can see that the peaks appear at different positions between Fig. 2 and Figs. 7, 8, and 9. So far, we do not have an exact reason for this fact, and we leave it as an important open question.

When we look closely, we can see some differences between these plots. The absolute errors have very similar shape to each other. However, the other two plots have some shifts between the lines. It would be interesting if we could analyze the states with progress 250–300 (around the time when the first 512-tile appears).

We also investigate the correctness of the evaluation values themselves. We randomly extracted 3000 afterstates from each play log and plotted their evaluation values using N-tuple networks against the true values. Figure 10 shows the results, one for each N-tuple network.

NT6 achieved an average score of 4905.27 (Fig. 6) and we expect the error to be as small as $\sigma = 30$ (Fig. 3). The evaluation values are, however, much higher than the true values for states with true values ≥ 2500 (a right half). We expect this to be a (bad) effect of optimistic initialization. It is interesting that we have similar plots for Figs. 5(b) and 5(c) even though the number of 4-tuples is different.

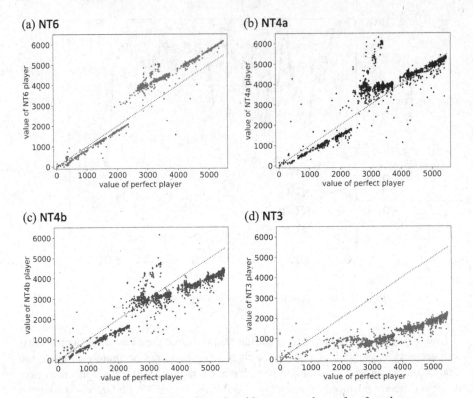

Fig. 10. Values of N-tuple networks with respect to those of perfect player.

7 Related Work

There have been a few studies on the use of strongly solved games as the testbed for reinforcement learning algorithms. Dobutsu Shogi, a small Japanese chess played on 3×4 board with three types of pieces, is one of the strongly solved games [13]. Nakayashiki and Kaneko [9] analyzed the performance of AlphaZero players with respect to their hyperparameters using Dobutsu Shogi as the target game. A previous work by Yamashita et al. [16] analyzed neural-network-based players trained with Proximal Policy Optimization (PPO) and an AlphaZero-like method. In this study we used (almost) the same value DB as Yamashita et al. did. The main difference is in the computer players studied. We investigated the performance and properties of computer players based on N-tuple networks which yield the state-of-the-art players for the original 2048.

The state-of-the-art player of 2048 [3] was developed with eight 6-tuples, two stages, temporal coherent (TC) learning, optimistic initialization, and tile downgrading, and expectimax search techniques. There are some other techniques to improve the performance of N-tuple-network players, such as redundant encoding, carousel shaping [4], restart and jump start [6]. The best computer player based on neural networks and deep learning techniques was by the AlphaZero approach [1]. The second-best neural network player was based on convolutional neural networks trained with TD learning [14]. Our important future work includes a study of the effects of these techniques using Mini2048 as a target game.

8 Conclusion

In this study, we have continued the work of Yamashita et al. on the strongly solving of Mini2048 (2048 on a 3×3 board) and its use to analyze the game. We have investigated the properties of the game based on the true values of all the states to reason the feasibility of existing techniques for developing computer players. In addition, we have conducted a comparative study of the properties of N-tuple networks.

As a result, we obtained several interesting results. In terms of the properties of the game, we confirmed (1) the relationship between the average scores and the quality of evaluation functions and (2) the usefulness of tile downgrading. Regarding the properties of the N-tuple networks, we found (3) some similarities and dissimilarities among neural networks. We need more detailed experiments and analysis to explain the differences between the N-tuple networks.

Our future work includes an extension to cover a variety of techniques for developing 2048 players. For example, we have excluded redundant encoding, carousel shaping [4], restart, and jump start [6] during the training. Another direction of research is to compare two sets of major techniques: N-tuple networks and neural networks, and Expectimax [17] search and Monte-Carlo tree search [15].

Acknowledgments. Part of this work was supported by JSPS KAKENHI Grant Numbers JP20K12124 and JP23K11383.

References

1. Antonoglou, I., Schrittwieser, J., Ozair, S., Hubert, T.K., Silver, D.: Planning in stochastic environments with a learned model. In: International Conference on Learning Representations (2022)
2. Cirulli, G.: 2048 (2014). http://gabrielecirulli.github.io/2048/
3. Guei, H., Chen, L.P., Wu, I.C.: Optimistic temporal difference learning for 2048. IEEE Trans. Games **14**(3), 478–487 (2022)
4. Jaśkowski, W.: Mastering 2048 with delayed temporal coherence learning, multistage weight promotion, redundant encoding and carousel shaping. IEEE Trans. Comput. Intell. AI Games **10**(1), 3–14 (2018)
5. Kao, C.Y., Guei, H., Wu, T.R., Wu, I.C.: Gumbel MuZero for the game of 2048. In: International Conference on Technologies and Applications of Artificial Intelligence (TAAI 2022), pp. 42–47 (2022)
6. Matsuzaki, K.: Developing 2048 player with backward temporal coherence learning and restart. In: Proceedings of Fifteenth International Conference on Advances in Computer Games (ACG 2017), pp. 176–187 (2017)
7. Matsuzaki, K.: A further investigation of neural network players for game 2048. In: Proceedings of Sixteenth International Conference on Advances in Computer Games (ACG 2019), pp. 53–65 (2020)

8. Matsuzaki, K.: Developing value networks for game 2048 with reinforcement learning. J. Inf. Process. **29**, 333–346 (2021)
9. Nakayashiki, T., Kaneko, T.: A survey on AlphaZero algorithm through dobutsu shogi. In: 24th Game Programming Workshop (GPW 2019), pp. 86–93 (2019). (in Japanese)
10. Sturtevant, N.R.: On strongly solving Chinese checkers. In: Cazenave, T., van den Herik, J., Saffidine, A., Wu, I.C. (eds.) Advances in Computer Games (ACG 2019). LNCS, vol. 12516, pp. 155–166. Springer, Cham (2020). https://doi.org/10.1007/978-3-030-65883-0_13
11. Szubert, M., Jaśkowski, W.: Temporal difference learning of N-tuple networks for the game 2048. In: 2014 IEEE Conference on Computational Intelligence and Games, pp. 1–8 (2014)
12. Tanaka, S., Bonnet, F., Tixeuil, S., Tamura, Y.: Quixo is solved. In: Browne, C., Kishimoto, A., Schaeffer, J. (eds.) Advances in Computer Games (ACG 2021). LNCS, vol. 13262, pp. 85–95. Springer, Cham (2022). https://doi.org/10.1007/978-3-031-11488-5_8
13. Tanaka, T.: An analysis of a board game "doubutsu shogi". IPSJ SIG Technical Reports 2009-GI-22(3) (2009). (in Japanese)
14. Wang, W., Matsuzaki, K.: Improving DNN-based 2048 players with global embedding. In: 2022 IEEE Conference on Games (CoG 2022), pp. 628–631 (2022)
15. Watanabe, S., Matsuzaki, K.: Enhancement of CNN-based 2048 player with Monte-Carlo tree search. In: 2022 International Conference on Technologies and Applications of Artificial Intelligence (TAAI 2022), pp. 48–53 (2022)
16. Yamashita, S., Kaneko, T., Nakayashiki, T.: Strongly solving 2048 on 3×3 board and performance evaluation of reinforcement learning agents. In: 27th Game Programming Workshop (GPW 2022), pp. 1–8 (2022). (in Japanese)
17. Yeh, K.H., Wu, I.C., Hsueh, C.H., Chang, C.C., Liang, C.C., Chiang, H.: Multistage temporal difference learning for 2048-like games. IEEE Trans. Comput. Intell. AI GamesGames **9**(4), 369–380 (2016)

Optimizing 3D Object Detection with Data Importance-Based Loss Reweighting

Chun Chieh Chang[1], Ta Chun Tai[1], Van Tin Luu[1], Hong Han Shuai[1],
Wen Huang Cheng[2], Yung Hui Li[3], and Ching Chun Huang[1]([✉])

[1] Department of Computer Science, National Yang Ming Chiao Tung University, Daxue Road,
Hsinchu 300093, Taiwan (R.O.C.)
{chingchun,maxtai.10,hhshuai,chingchun}@nycu.edu.tw
[2] Department of Computer Science and Information Engineering, National Taiwan University,
Taipei 106319, Taiwan
wenhuang@csie.ntu.edu.tw
[3] Hon Hai Research Institute, Taipei, Taiwan
yunghui.li@foxconn.com

Abstract. With the advancement of AI technology, deep learning-based intelligent driving assistance systems have seen substantial growth. However, 3D object detection remains a significant challenge due to LiDAR's characteristics, such as sparse point clouds, varying point cloud density, and object occlusion, resulting in incomplete data. To enhance accuracy, models must be more robust. Past approaches emphasized model design, feature extraction, and obtaining finer features. In contrast, our approach introduces a novel perspective, addressing 3D object detection by focusing on sample processing without altering the model architecture. We found that point cloud variations can be substantial even within the same category. Adding such incomplete/corrupted samples to training does not improve performance; it can lead to model confusion and reduced generalization. This study proposed inferring the importance of samples based on the sample dispersed ratio and model reflection, encompassing classification and regression loss caused by sample variations. We utilize our Important Sample Selection (ISS) module to predict the sample's importance for training and adjust the loss function to prioritize informative samples. We train and evaluate our detectors using the KITTI dataset. The experimental results show that our selection approach enhances overall detection performance without increasing parameter count.

Keywords: 3D object detection · loss reweighting · training sample selection · learn from noisy data

1 Introduction

3D object detection is of growing importance in computer vision because autonomous driving gains more and more attention. Finding out the object and getting its precise 3D location are the primary tasks in 3D object detection. However, the 3D outdoor scenes captured by LiDAR are represented as point clouds and possess several characteristics that render the task challenging. The challenges can be summarized as follows.

© The Author(s), under exclusive license to Springer Nature Singapore Pte Ltd. 2024
C.-Y. Lee et al. (Eds.): TAAI 2023, CCIS 2075, pp. 179–194, 2024.
https://doi.org/10.1007/978-981-97-1714-9_15

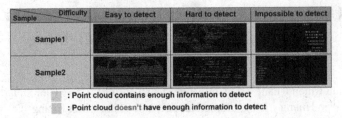

Sample \ Difficulty	Easy to detect	Hard to detect	Impossible to detect
Sample1			
Sample2			

: Point cloud contains enough information to detect
: Point cloud doesn't have enough information to detect

Fig. 1. Samples of point clouds representing cars at different levels are shown in the figure. In this visualization, the 3D points of the cars are projected onto a 2D front view. It is evident that the pattern of point clouds varies significantly even within the same category. Some samples are informative for the model to detect, while others lack the necessary cues for effective detection. We perform an analysis of these varying sample qualities and design a loss function that adjusts the importance of each sample while training the model.

Sparsity of Point Clouds. Despite containing depth information, point clouds generated by LiDAR sensors lack the regular information found in images, such as RGB data. Point clouds exhibit irregular patterns, posing challenges when computing similarity and accurately locating objects.

High Variability Within the Same Category. The density of point clouds varies dramatically with distance, leading to substantial fluctuations even within the same object category. This variability can present challenges for accurate object recognition by the model.

Incomplete Point Clouds due to Occlusion. Objects may become occluded, resulting in incomplete point clouds. LiDAR sensors measure distance by emitting a laser pulse towards the target, causing objects behind obstructions to be obstructed by those in front. This incompleteness increases the variability in point clouds for the same object and impacts the model's performance.

Although many challenges mentioned earlier make achieving perfect 3D object detection difficult, many researchers have been actively exploring various approaches to overcome these obstacles and take them up a notch. Previous solutions have primarily emphasized the design of the model architecture, including the development of more powerful feature extractors, the acquisition of finer features, and the incorporation of additional information, such as images, to enhance object detection performance. For example, BtcDet [1] pre-processes the ground truth to ensure that all samples represent complete object shapes. Subsequently, a shape model is utilized to predict the appearance of objects. Through model learning, additional information about potential object configurations is acquired. These additional insights enable the model to predict object positions more accurately. In approaches like PVRCNN [2] and Voxel-RCNN [3], they first perform an initial detection step to identify regions of interest (RoI). Then, within these bounding boxes, a second refinement step is employed to extract finer and more comprehensive features. Other method like [4–11] merge RGB information with point clouds. VFF [12] maps image information onto 3D space, and by computing the inner product with voxel features, it determines which voxel locations correspond to the image features. Ultimately, it results in a feature space containing both image and point cloud information. This integrated feature space is used by the detection model to obtain precise object positions.

Different from previous methods, in this paper, we first identify that selecting important samples for training is also significant and introduce this issue into 3D object detection. The input samples provided to the model for training are crucial to achieve stronger and more robust features. To address the new issue, we investigate the factors that determine the importance of samples. We incorporate additional information into our Important Sample Selection (ISS) module to assess the significance of each sample. The loss function is then dynamically adjusted based on this importance during training iterations, resulting in training the detection model with more appropriate samples. To be more specific, we first identify the key influential factor called Disperse Ratio by analyzing the ground truth data. By visualizing the point cloud of each car sample, we can readily identify that some samples lack a significant number of points, making it challenging to recognize them as cars. When we divide the 2D projected object box into left and right halves, the disparity in the number of points between the two halves becomes a crucial factor for assessing the sample's quality. We place the larger number in the denominator to form the Disperse Ratio. When the Disperse Ratio is larger, it indicates that the points are evenly distributed between both halves. This ratio can assist the model for sample selection. Furthermore, classification loss and regression loss can

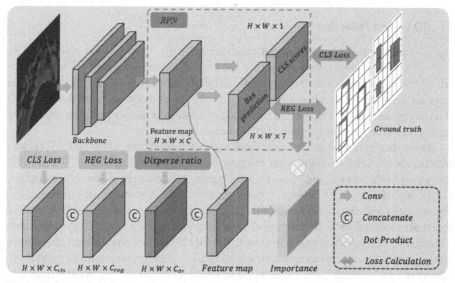

Fig. 2. Pipeline of the training process. The upper part shows the 3D detection model, including the backbone, Region Proposal Network (RPN) block, and detection head. (i.e., Here, we use a 2D map to show the pillar-based 3D detection in the Bird's Eye View (BEV). However, our method can be used in other point-based or voxel-based 3D detection methods. The model's output consists of classification scores (H × W × 1) and box predictions (H × W × 7). The lower parts show the weighting process for each object instance. Each positive sample will be assigned an importance weight by considering its classification loss, regression loss, and Disperse Ratio. This weighting mechanism allows the model to focus on more crucial samples for training.

serve as two additional factors that indicate the importance of a sample because they directly show the model's performance. These three factors are input into our ISS module to reshape the loss, ensuring that the model pays more attention to these crucial samples. Finally, we validate our model's performance on the KITTI dataset [13, 14]. The results demonstrate a performance improvement by integrating our ISS module. In general, our main contributions are as follows.

- We explore a new weighting method by employing an Important Sample Selection (ISS) module to predict the importance of each sample, resulting in a more effective object detector.
- We analyze the sample and then acquire the Disperse Ratio, which is a vital piece of information serving as an indicator of sample importance.
- The ISS module is only involved during the training phase and can be effortlessly plugged into most object detectors. This integration results in performance improvements without affecting inference time.
- We target a new issue in 3D object detection, which concerns the impact of training samples on performance. Our paper might represent an early effort to address this particular challenge.

2   Related Works

2.1   3D Object Detection

The common practice for 3D object detection typically involves first using a backbone network containing several layers of 3D convolutional neural networks (CNNs) to extract features from point clouds, voxels, or pillars and then using an optional region proposal network and detection heads to estimate the object's class and location. 3D object detection can be categorized into three possible approaches based on processing units: Point-based, Voxel-based, and Pillar-based.

Due to the unordered and irregular format of point cloud data, Lidar-based 3D object detection is challenging. Significant progress was initiated by Qi, Charles R et al. [15, 16], who introduced point cloud methods for feature extraction. Point-based approaches, though providing detailed information, are the most time-consuming and computationally intensive. For instance, PointRCNN [17] uses a two-stage process, first identifying potential object regions with foreground points and then refining object proposals, which is computationally demanding. In contrast, 3D-SSD [18] offers an efficient compromise between accuracy and efficiency with improved point sampling and candidate generation, achieving a better prediction. Voxel-based techniques [19, 20] divide the 3D space into regular grid cells (voxels) for point cloud quantization, allowing feature extraction via 3D convolutions. Models like SECOND [19], PartA2 [21], PV-RCNN [2], and Voxel-RCNN [3] fall into this category, offering a balance between detail and computational efficiency. Pillar-based methods use a similar approach but employ pillars or columns instead of voxels, as the height dimension is less critical for 3D detection. Points within pillars are aggregated, and then 2D convolutional operations are used to extract the pillar features over the BEV plan. PointPillars [22] is an example of this direction, aiming to reduce data dimension and enhance detector efficiency. Among the three methods, pillar-based approaches provide the fastest computational speed, albeit with slightly lower performance. In summary, the choice of approach in 3D object detection from LiDAR point clouds depends on the trade-off between detail and computational efficiency. Point-based methods provide detailed information but are computationally expensive, voxel-based methods strike a balance, and pillar-based methods provide an alternative grid structure while maintaining computational efficiency. The approach choice should consider the application's specific requirements and available computational resources. As 3D object detection advances, researchers seek to enhance performance by incorporating texture features from images, providing additional information for 3D models. The fusion approaches can be categorized into three approaches: early fusion, middle fusion, and late fusion. Early fusion, as demonstrated by Vora et al. [4], projects point clouds into images, overlays segmentation scores on points, and feeds them into a feature extractor. In middle fusion methods, such as those by Mahmoud et al. [5], Huang et al. [6], Wang et al. [8], Zhu et al. [9], Li et al. [12], Chen et al. [10], and Wu et al. [11], researchers aim to fuse information during feature extraction, dealing with the challenge of integrating two distinct types of data, i.e., images and point clouds. Late fusion methods, exemplified by CLOCs [7], merge results from separate detection branches. 3D bounding boxes from a 3D detector are projected into 2D space and connected with 2D bounding boxes from a 2D detector. A module considers various results, including 2D classification scores, 3D classification scores, and Intersection over Union (IoU) between projected 3D and 2D bounding boxes, and selects the best results for the final prediction.

2.2 Training Positive Instance/Sample Selection

In this paper, we introduce a sample selection issue that has not been addressed in any 3D detection papers. We preliminarily attempt to treat each sample uniquely. Later, inspired by learning from noisy data for 2D object detection, we delve into the effect of sample quality for training and address this new challenge in 3D object detection. Object detection performance is sensitive to not only the definition of positive and negative samples but also the different sampling strategies. Therefore, many researchers are committed to tackling this challenge. Different anchor assignment approaches try to define the positive and negative samples by considering IoU, classification loss, and box regression loss. Then, these sampling methods assign different weights to positive and negative samples for training.

Anchor Assignment. Anchor assignment methods in 3D object detection can be broadly categorized into two main groups: hard assignment methods and soft assignment methods. In hard assignment methods, the prevalent technique involves using Intersection over Union (IoU) to determine whether an anchor should be considered a positive or negative sample. For instance, RetinaNet [23] defines positive samples when IoU exceeds 0.5 and negative samples when IoU falls below 0.4. FCOS [24] follows a similar approach but includes additional constraints for positive sample assignment. ATSS [25] introduces an adaptive selection method, which identifies candidate positive samples for each ground truth box, calculates their IoU with the ground truth boxes, and dynamically sets the IoU threshold based on the mean and standard deviation of these IoU values. However, this approach may introduce noise when bounding boxes intersect with the target.

In contrast, soft anchor assignment methods consider a broader range of information, including classification cost and model feedback, to optimize anchor assignment. PAA [26] calculates anchor scores to guide model training based on model feedback, fits a probability distribution (typically a Gaussian Mixture Model), and categorizes anchors as positive or negative based on their probabilities. IQDet [27] introduces a Quality Distribution Encoder (QDE) that extracts region features for each ground-truth instance, estimates the quality distribution using a GMM, and assigns positive samples based on this distribution, giving preference to higher-quality anchors. These soft assignment methods offer a more comprehensive and adaptive approach to anchor assignment and inspired us to adopt them in 3D object detection.

Sampling Assignment. Sample assignment in 3D object detection can be challenging due to the unequal contribution of samples. This issue results in imbalanced sample distribution when categorizing them as positive or negative. To address this challenge, two main categories of sampling methods are utilized: hard sampling and soft sampling.

Hard Sampling Methods. In hard sampling, a subset of positive and negative samples is selected during training, often applied in the second stage of two-stage detection models. Various strategies are used for sample selection. For instance, OHEM [28] arranges ROIs in descending order based on their loss, selecting a predefined number of ROIs with the highest loss as hard examples for training.

Soft Sampling Methods. Soft sampling methods focus on adjusting the contribution of each sample without selecting a subset. They aim to address imbalanced samples by altering their importance during training. One well-known approach is the Focal Loss [23], which introduces a weighting factor for each sample, emphasizing hard examples

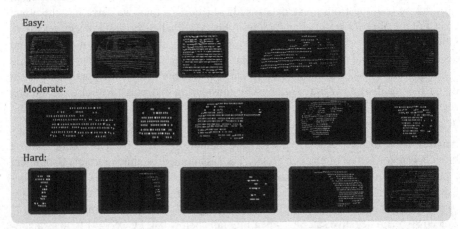

Fig. 3. Projected the point clouds of instance samples on 2D views. We have projected the ground truth points of cars into 2D space across different difficulty levels: easy, moderate, and hard. In the easy level, points are distributed quite evenly. In the moderate level, some samples are slightly occluded (middle left), while others are partially occluded (middle right). In the hard level, most of the samples are significantly occluded (lower left), although some still maintain relatively complete shapes (lower right).

while down-weighting easier ones. GFL [29] extends this concept by considering both classification scores and localization. Other methods like SAPD [30] use the distance between ground truth centers and anchor points to treat samples differently. SWN [31] employs a model to predict weights based on various factors, including IoU scores, classification loss, regression loss, and probability. DW [32] identifies key influential factors for positive and negative weights, dynamically reshaping the loss function.

These sampling methods are crucial for addressing the imbalanced sample issue. We leverage these ideas may improve the training process in 3D object detection models.

3 Proposed Method

3.1 Preliminaries

First, let's start with a brief introduction to 3D object detection, the mechanism of anchor assignment and sampling. Then, we will leverage the insights obtained from the training data to aid the model's learning process.

3D object detection takes point clouds as input, which consists of a collection of (x, y, z) coordinates. Due to the irregular properties of point clouds, it is a common practice to quantize them by dividing the space into voxels or pillars. This allows us to employ 3D convolutional neural networks (CNNs) for feature extraction. In 3D object detection, multiple CNN layers are typically used to extract spatial features, and these features are then fed into a detection head for both class classification score and regression of predicted bounding boxes offsets, which contain $(x_c, y_c, z_c, l, w, h, \theta)$. Here, (x_c, y_c, z_c) represents the center of the bounding box; (l, w, h) indicates the size of the bounding box; θ means the angle between the y-axis of the LiDAR and the bounding box. Anchor assignment is commonly used in dense prediction on feature maps. It involves slicing a dense grid on the feature map extracted through CNNs. Each grid cell on the mesh grid is used for one or multiple object predictions. Anchors are pre-defined sizes that are compared to ground truth to determine which of them should be considered positive samples and which should be considered negative samples. The differences between the predicted bounding boxes and the ground truth are used as the answers (ground truth) of the model's predictions when predicting a grid cell as an object. With these processes, we can train the 3D model with these labels to guide the prediction of the class and location of objects. Because there is a considerable imbalance between the number of foreground and background objects, the sampling method is applied to address this issue. Focal loss [23] is the well-known method used in object detection and is also used in 3D object detection. Each foreground and background are attached by a weight inversely proportional to the number of foreground and background.

On the other hand, AdaFace [33] found that using all training samples under different obscured and degraded levels for face recognition tasks would cause a performance drop. Thus, they proposed a strategy to emphasize that the importance of samples should be adjusted according to their image quality. Inspired by this, we wonder and ask the question if there's the same issue in 3D object detection.

As shown in Fig. 1, we project the point cloud of the car instance into a 2D front view. The distribution of the points varies dramatically. Then, we conduct a simple experiment to see the effect of removing hard samples. In the KITTI dataset [13, 14], according to size, occlusion, and truncation, there are three difficulty levels, i.e., easy, moderate, and hard. We filter out object samples with hard difficulty and train with the remaining data. The results in Table 1 show that the performance surprisingly improved when we trained the model without hard samples. The incomplete shape and detail-lacking samples would harm the generalizability of the model.

Table 1. The mAP of the car in KITTI validation data with different setting. The first column shows the performance of the model trained with whole data. The second column shows that there's a slight improvement in performance when we filter the hard samples.

Voxel-RCNN	Easy	Mod.	Hard
Baseline	92.56	84.83	82.50
Filter Hard	92.57	85.14	82.26

Table 2. The number of samples at various distances and across different difficulty levels.

Distance(m)	Easy	Mod.	Hard
0–10	806	515	300
10–20	2638	1839	1665
20–30	2398	1942	2100
30–40	286	3275	1347
40-inf	4	2237	398

3.2 Factors of Sample Importance

The weight of a sample should reflect its importance. Hence, we try to determine the factors affecting the sample's importance/quality. When it comes to the characteristics of LiDAR, the object distance is a potential factor because the object's density varies with distance. The farther the distance, the lower the point cloud density. Therefore, distance may be one of the criteria for sample importance. Hence, we begin by analyzing the relationship between the number of ground truth points and the level of difficulty with respect to distance. However, in Table 2, we find the distance distributions of moderate and hard samples are similar. It implies distance may not be a primary factor in distinguishing sample quality.

To determine the more predominant influencing factors, we do a statistical analysis of training samples. As shown in Fig. 3, in the case of samples of the easy level, we observe that the point cloud is relatively complete, uniform, and less occluded. For the moderate level, although there is more occlusion and fewer points, it is still possible to identify the sample as a target (i.e., vehicle). On the contrary, in the case of a hard level, most object samples are obscured and have fewer points, making it more challenging to learn discriminative features. Even so, still, a small subset of hard samples contains informative data. Based on these observations, we deduce that one of the influencing factors is the Disperse Ratio, which is defined as follows. First, we project the point cloud of the bounded point cloud of a 3D object box into the 2D frontal view and then split the projected box into left and right parts. Later, we count the points within these two halves. The formula of the Disperse Ratio is then calculated by

$$\text{Disperse Ratio} = \frac{\min(N_l, N_r)}{\max(N_l, N_r) + \lambda} \tag{1}$$

where N_l represents the number of points in the left part, N_r represents the number of points in the right part, and λ is a small number to avoid a zero denominator. As shown in Fig. 3, the samples with a higher Disperse Ratio have more evenly distributed points, and hard examples usually have lower ratios. Thus, the Disperse Ratio may serve as an indicator of sample quality. Here, we also conduct a quick experiment using the Disperse Ratio as the indicator to weigh samples and modify the loss dynamically. The Table 3 shows the results.

Table 3. Reweight the loss function with the disperse ratio directly. The higher performance could tell that the disperse ratio can be an indicator of the sample quality more precisely.

Voxel-RCNN	Easy	Mod.	Hard
Baseline	92.56	84.83	82.50
Filter Hard	92.57	85.14	82.26
Hard Sampling	92.79	85.27	82.52

Apart from the Disperse Ratio being one of the factors influencing importance, the loss values during training iteration are another contributing factor. While the Disperse Ratio can reflect the quality of sample distribution, it may not reveal the model's reflection. During the training phase, classification loss and box regression loss are calculated. These two losses can directly show which samples the current model needs to focus more on to improve learning. In other words, we hope that importance considers the Disperse Ratio and model reflection. With these features, our module automatically predicts each sample's weight automatically and reshapes the total loss accordingly.

3.3 Importance Prediction

In the previous section, we analyzed which information can be used to predict sample importance. This section will discuss utilizing the aforementioned factors (i.e., Disperse Ratios, classification loss, and box regression loss) to predict the sample importance and train 3D detectors with more re-weighted samples. Firstly, we transform these factors through CNNs to get the high-dimensional features and concatenate them with the content features extracted by the detection backbone, as shown in Fig. 2. Subsequently, we pass this combined information through a CNN-based auxiliary network to predict the importance map. By referring to the GT locations of instances, we can find the importance of each sample. Importance map $\mathcal{W} \in R^{H \times W \times N_{anchors}}$ is generally calculated by the following formula.

$$\mathcal{W} = \sigma\left(f^{1 \times 1}[\mathcal{F}_{cls}; \mathcal{F}_{reg}; \mathcal{F}_{dr}; \mathcal{F}_s]\right), \tag{2}$$

where $\mathcal{F}_{\lceil \nabla} \in R^{H \times N \times C_{dr}}$ extracted from the Dispersion Ratio calculated per positive sample. $\mathcal{F}_{\rfloor \uparrow f} \in R^{H \times N \times C_{cls}}$ and $\mathcal{F}_{\nabla \rceil\}} \in R^{H \times N \times C_{reg}}$ are extracted from the classification loss and the regression loss respectively.

As shown in Fig. 2, these predicted importance scores will be used to adjust the regression loss dynamically. If the importance is high, the weight is close to 1, indicating that the model will focus more on these samples. Conversely, the weight would approach 0 if the importance is low, indicating that the model will not learn from these lower-quality samples. Eventually, we select essential samples the model needs; meanwhile, the model helps to filter out samples that harm model generalization, making the feature extractor more robust and improving overall performance.

3.4 Loss Function

The proposed importance prediction module is adaptable and can be seamlessly integrated into most 3D detectors. It harmonizes with our lightweight module, resulting in a refined loss formulation for 3D detection. To elucidate further, as [12], we may divide the total loss $\mathcal{L}_{\sqcup \mathcal{R} \sqcup \dashv \updownarrow}$ for training a 3D detector as classification loss $\mathcal{L}_{\rfloor \uparrow f}$, box regression loss $\mathcal{L}_{\nabla \rceil\}}$, and direction loss L_{dir}. That is

$$\mathcal{L}_{total} = \alpha \mathcal{L}_{cls} + \beta \mathcal{L}_{reg} + \gamma \mathcal{L}_{dir}, \tag{3}$$

where α, β, γ are hyper-parameters to balance these losses, $\mathcal{L}_{\rfloor \uparrow f}$ is the Focal loss [23] for classification and $\mathcal{L}_{\nabla \rceil\}}$ is the Smooth-L_1 loss for the offset regression, $\mathcal{L}_{\lceil \rangle \nabla}$ is a binary entropy loss for the orientation prediction. Next, we detail and rewrite the $\mathcal{L}_{\sqcup \mathcal{R} \sqcup \dashv \updownarrow}$ as

$$\mathcal{L}_{total} = \alpha \sum_{i=1}^{m} \mathcal{L}_{cls}^{i} + \beta \sum_{j=1}^{n} \mathcal{L}_{reg}^{j} + \gamma \sum_{j=1}^{n} \mathcal{L}_{dir}^{j}, \tag{4}$$

where i indicates the i-th anchor, m indicates the number of total anchors, and n indicates the number of positive samples. Finally, considering the importance reweighting, the final loss we used for training is

$$\mathcal{L}_{total} = \alpha \sum_{i=1}^{m} \mathcal{L}_{cls}^{i} + \sum_{j=1}^{n} \left(\beta \omega^{j} \mathcal{L}_{reg}^{j} + \gamma \mathcal{L}_{dir}^{j} - \delta\left(\omega^{j} - 0.5\right)^{2}\right), \tag{5}$$

where ω^{j} is the importance of each anchor, $(\omega^{j} - 0.5)^{2})$ is a regularization term that we want the importance to vary from zero to one, and δ is a hyper-parameter to adjust the regularization term.

4 Experiments

4.1 Dataset and Evaluation Metric

To evaluate the performance of our method, we added our module on the state-of-the-art (SoTA) 3D detection model on the KITTI dataset [14]. The KITTI dataset comprises a training set with a total of 7481 examples. Following the commonly applied setting, this dataset contains 3712 examples for training and 3769 examples for validation. Additionally, the dataset includes a test set with 7518 examples. The benchmark has three difficulty levels: easy, moderate, and hard, based on the 2D bounding box size, occlusion, and truncation levels. Moreover, the average precision (AP) at a moderate level is the official ranking metric for 3D detection. The average precision (AP) metric is the common evaluation method to assess 3D object detection. The equation of AP is as follows.

$$AP = \frac{1}{|R|} \sum_{r \in R} \max_{r' \geq r} p\left(r'\right) \tag{6}$$

Here, $|R| = 40$, r $= \{\frac{1}{40}, \frac{2}{40}, \ldots, 1\}$, and p(r) indicates the precision at recall r. Our detection results include three categories (i.e., Car, Pedestrian, and Cyclist) and are evaluated by AP with standard IoU thresholds 0.7, 0.5, and 0.5.

4.2 Results and Comparisons

In order to demonstrate the effectiveness of our method, we train 3D object detectors with our ISS module. We experiment on three detectors, Voxel R-CNN [3], SECOND [20], and Focals Conv [10]. Table 4 reports the 3D detection results, and Table 5 reports the detection results for the BEV case. For the 3D detection benchmark, Voxel R-CNN + ISS module achieves 93.00%, 85.29%, 82.78% AP3D separately in the easy, mod., hard levels on the KITTI val set. When comparing our results with the original performance, which achieved an AP3D of 92.56%, 84.83%, and 82.50%, we observe a significant improvement of 0.44%, 0.43%, 0.28% without making any alterations to the detection architecture.

In addition to the car category, we conducted comprehensive testing on the model across the pedestrian and cyclist categories, and the results demonstrated remarkable and substantial improvements in performance. We also incorporated our module into Focals Conv [10], a fusion-based method, and the results also indicate that our approach leads to performance improvements.

Besides testing on 3D detection, we also conducted experiments on Bird's Eye View detection. All the BEV detection results demonstrated a performance improvement.

4.3 Ablation Study

In the subsequent experiments, we present the outcomes of alternative configurations to the Important Sample Selection setting. It's worth noting that for these experiments, we employ Voxel-RCNN as the foundational 3D detector, serving as our baseline model for

Table 4. 3D Object Detection Performance. Each model's performance is compared with and without our important sample selection modules. Results show with Easy, Moderate (Mod.) and Hard levels on the three classes. ISS module improves most aspects of the performance.

Method	Car			Pedestrian			Cyclist		
	Easy	Mod.	Hard	Easy	Mod.	Hard	Easy	Mod.	Hard
Voxel R-CNN [3]	92.56	84.83	82.50	66.21	59.61	54.24	90.76	72.30	67.65
Voxel R-CNN [3] + **Ours**	**93.00**	**85.29**	**82.78**	**68.86**	**61.92**	**56.42**	90.61	**72.42**	**68.04**
SECOND [20]	90.83	81.28	77.90	55.62	50.53	45.77	82.02	67.30	63.73
SECOND [20] + **Ours**	**91.10**	**82.00**	**78.69**	**56.18**	**51.26**	**46.20**	**84.76**	**67.44**	63.20
Focals Conv [10]	92.91	85.74	85.22	71.87	64.96	60.58	90.21	72.51	68.62
Focals Conv [10] + **Ours**	**93.03**	**85.98**	**85.51**	**72.78**	**65.85**	**61.22**	**91.92**	72.26	68.32

Table 5. Bird-Eye-View (BEV) object detection Performance. ISS improves the overall performance of all the detectors.

Method	Car			
	Easy	Mod.	Hard	Avg.
Voxel R-CNN [3]	95.81	91.14	88.82	91.92
Voxel R-CNN [3] + **Ours**	**96.27**	**91.34**	**90.55**	**92.72**
SECOND [20]	94.26	89.80	87.23	90.43
SECOND [20] + **Ours**	**94.55**	**90.23**	**87.76**	**90.85**
Focals Conv [10]	95.56	91.45	91.11	92.71
Focals Conv [10] + **Ours**	**95.96**	**91.73**	**91.48**	**93.06**

comparison. In our framework, three factors contribute to the determination of importance. We experiment with various combinations of these factors and present the corresponding results in Table 6. We observe only a slight improvement for the moderate case if we only input the Disperse Ratio into the ISS module. As shown in Fig. 3, the samples in the easy level exhibit a more complete shape and higher Disperse Ratios compared to those in the moderate and hard levels. This may force the network bias to the easy cases. Also, without considering the model losses for dynamic learning, the network loses the chance to improve the model generalizability in a curriculum learning manner (i.e., learning from easy to hard). After integrating with the loss factors, the performance improves in all three cases. Note that only using the loss factors for sample reweighting gives worse results, indicating the importance of Disperse Ratios (Table 7).

Table 6. Ablations on input selection in AP3D (R40) on KITTI val.

Method	Importance Factor	Car		
		Easy	Mod.	Hard
Voxel R-CNN	X	92.56	84.83	82.50
+ ISS	Loss	92.38	84.74	82.44
	Disperse Ratio	92.48	84.99	82.41
	Disperse Ratio + Loss	93.00	**85.29**	82.78

Table 7. Ablations on different regularization terms in AP3D (R40) on KITTI val.

Method	Regularization Term	Car		
		Easy	Mod.	Hard
+ ISS	1.5	91.93	82.98	82.05
	1.0	**93.00**	**85.29**	**82.78**
	0.8	92.50	84.65	82.20
	0.5	92.12	84.48	82.38

Additionally, we introduce an extra term into the loss function, referred to as the regularization term, which effectively drives the predicted scores not toward zero. In this context, we conduct an ablation study, systematically varying the value of this regularization term to assess its impact.

5 Conclusion

In this paper, we launch a new research issue for 3D object detection and claim that not all training samples are equally important. Notably, the point clouds of objects within the same class exhibit substantial variations. When we employ the entire dataset for model training, samples that lack sufficient informative cues can adversely impact the model's generalization. Consequently, the process of selecting data for training becomes vital. To address this challenge, we present a novel ISS method to predict the importance of each sample. We begin by conducting an in-depth analysis of ground truth, leading us to discover a previously overlooked factor, the Disperse Ratio. This ratio plays a pivotal role in indicating the quality of individual samples. With the implementation of our ISS module, each sample is assigned a weight that reflects its significance to the model. Subsequently, the model undergoes training using the data selected by the ISS module. One noteworthy advantage of our framework is that it is integrated into the training phase, ensuring that inference time remains unaffected. Moreover, we demonstrate that training SoTA 3D detectors using our method substantially boosts performance.

Acknowledgments. This work was financially supported in part (project number: 112UA10019) by the Co-creation Platform of the Industry Academia Innovation School, NYCU, under the framework of the National Key Fields Industry-University Cooperation and Skilled Personnel Training Act, from the Ministry of Education (MOE) and industry partners in Taiwan. It also supported in part by the National Science and Technology Council, Taiwan, under Grant NSTC-112-2221-E-A49-089-MY3, Grant NSTC-110-2221-E-A49-066-MY3, Grant NSTC-111- 2634-F-A49-010, Grant NSTC-112-2425-H-A49-001-, and in part by the Higher Education Sprout Project of the National Yang Ming Chiao Tung University and the Ministry of Education (MOE), Taiwan.

References

1. Xu, Q., Zhong, Y., Neumann, U.: Behind the curtain: learning occluded shapes for 3D object detection. In: Proceedings of the AAAI Conference on Artificial Intelligence, vol. 36, pp. 2893–2901 (2022)
2. Shi, S., et al.: PV-Rcnn: point-voxelfeature set abstraction for 3D object detection. In: Proceedings of the IEEE/CVF Conference on Computer Vision and Pattern Recognition (CVPR) (2020)
3. Deng, J., Shi, S., Li, P., Zhou, W., Zhang, Y., Li, H.: Voxel R-CNN: towards highperformance voxel-based 3D object detection. arXiv:2012.15712 (2020)
4. Vora, S., Lang, A.H., Helou, B., Beijbom, O.: Pointpainting: sequential fusion for 3Dobject detection. In: Proceedings of the IEEE/CVF Conference on Computer Vision and Pattern Recognition (CVPR) (2020)
5. Mahmoud, A., Hu, J.S., Waslander, S.L.: Dense voxel fusion for 3D object detection. In:Proceedings of the IEEE/CVF Winter Conference on Applications of Computer Vision, pp. 663–672 (2023)
6. Huang, T., Liu, Z., Chen, X., Bai, X.: Epnet: enhancing point features with image semantics for 3D object detection. In: Vedaldi, A., Bischof, H., Brox, T., Frahm, J.M. (eds.) Computer Vision–ECCV 2020, pp. 35–52. Springer, Cham (2020). https://doi.org/10.1007/978-3-030-58555-6_3
7. Pang, S., Morris, D., Radha, H.: CLOCs: camera-LiDAR object candidates fusion for 3Dobject detection. In: 2020 IEEE/RSJ International Conference on Intelligent Robots and Systems (IROS), pp. 10386–10393 (2020). IEEE
8. Wang, C.-H., Chen, H.-W., Fu, L.-C.: Vpfnet: voxel-pixel fusion network for multi-class3D object detection. arXiv preprint arXiv:2111.00966 (2021)
9. Zhu, H., et al.: VPFNet: improving 3Dobject detection with virtual point based LiDAR and stereo data fusion. IEEE Trans. Multimedia (2022)
10. Chen, Y., Li, Y., Zhang, X., Sun, J., Jia, J.: Focal sparse convolutional networks for3D object detection. In: Proceedings of the IEEE/CVF Conference on Computer Vision and Pattern Recognition, pp. 5428–5437 (2022)
11. Wu, X., et al.: Sparse fusedense: towards high quality 3D detection with depth completion. In: Proceedings of the IEEE/CVF Conference on Computer Vision and Pattern Recognition, pp. 5418–5427 (2022)
12. Li, Y., et al.: Voxel field fusion for 3Dobject detection. In: Proceedings of the IEEE/CVF Conference on Computer Vision and Pattern Recognition, pp. 1120–1129 (2022)
13. Geiger, A., Lenz, P., Stiller, C., Urtasun, R.: Vision meets robotics: the kitti dataset. Int. J. Robot. Res. **32**(11), 1231–1237 (2013)

14. Geiger, A., Lenz, P., Urtasun, R.: Are we ready for autonomous driving? The kittivision benchmark suite. In: 2012 IEEE Conference on Computer Vision and Pattern Recognition, pp. 3354–3361 (2012). IEEE
15. Qi, C.R., Su, H., Mo, K., Guibas, L.J.: Pointnet: deep learning on point sets for 3Dclassification and segmentation. In: Proceedings of the IEEE Conference on Computer Vision and Pattern Recognition (CVPR) (2017)
16. Qi, C.R., Yi, L., Su, H., Guibas, L.J.: Pointnet++: deep hierarchical feature learningon point sets in a metric space. In: Guyon, I., Luxburg, U.V., Bengio, S., Wallach, H., Fergus, R., Vishwanathan, S., Garnett, R. (eds.) Advances in Neural Information Processing Systems, vol. 30. Curran Associates, Inc. (2017)
17. Shi, S., Wang, X., Li, H.: Pointrcnn: 3D object proposal generation and detection from-point cloud. In: Proceedings of the IEEE/CVF Conference on Computer Vision and Pattern Recognition (CVPR) (2019)
18. Yang, Z., Sun, Y., Liu, S., Jia, J.: 3DSSD: point-based 3D single stage object detector. In:Proceedings of the IEEE/CVF Conference on Computer Vision and Pattern Recognition (CVPR) (2020)
19. Zhou, Y., Tuzel, O.: Voxelnet: end-to-end learning for point cloud based 3D objectdetection. In: Proceedings of the IEEE Conference on Computer Vision and Pattern Recognition (CVPR) (2018)
20. Yan, Y., Mao, Y., Li, B.: Second: sparsely embedded convolutional detection. Sensors18(10) (2018) https://doi.org/10.3390/s18103337
21. Shi, S., Wang, Z., Shi, J., Wang, X., Li, H.: From points to parts: 3D object detection from point cloud with part-aware and part-aggregation network. arXiv preprintarXiv:1907.03670 (2019)
22. Lang, A.H., Vora, S., Caesar, H., Zhou, L., Yang, J., Beijbom, O.: Pointpillars: fastencoders for object detection from point clouds. In: Proceedings of the IEEE/CVF Conference on Computer Vision and Pattern Recognition (CVPR) (2019)
23. Lin, T.-Y., Goyal, P., Girshick, R., He, K., Dollár, P.: Focal loss for dense objectdetection. In: 2017 IEEE International Conference on Computer Vision (ICCV), pp. 2999–3007 (2017). https://doi.org/10.1109/ICCV.2017.324
24. Tian, Z., Shen, C., Chen, H., He, T.: FCOS: fully convolutional one-stage objectdetection. In: Proceedings of International Conference on Computer Vision (ICCV) (2019)
25. Zhang, S., Chi, C., Yao, Y., Lei, Z., Li, S.Z.: Bridging the gap between anchor-basedand anchor-free detection via adaptive training sample selection. In: Proceedings of the IEEE/CVF Conference on Computer Vision and Pattern Recognition (CVPR) (2020)
26. Kim, K., Lee, H.S.: Probabilistic anchor assignment with IOU prediction for objectdetection. In: ECCV (2020)
27. Ma, Y., Liu, S., Li, Z., Sun, J.: IQDet: instance-wise quality distribution sampling forobject detection. In: Proceedings of the IEEE/CVF Conference on Computer Vision and Pattern Recognition (CVPR), pp. 1717–1725 (2021)
28. Shrivastava, A., Gupta, A., Girshick, R.: Training region-based object detectors withonline hard example mining. In: Proceedings of the IEEE Conference on Computer Vision and Pattern Recognition (CVPR) (2016)
29. Li, X., et al.: Generalized focal loss: Learning qualified and distributed bounding boxes for dense object detection. Adv. Neural. Inf. Process. Syst. 33, 21002–21012 (2020)
30. Zhu, C., Chen, F., Shen, Z., Savvides, M.: Soft anchor-point object detection. In: Vedaldi, A., Bischof, H., Brox, T., Frahm, J.M. (eds.) Computer Vision–ECCV 2020, pp. 91–107. Springer, Cham (2020). https://doi.org/10.1007/978-3-030-58545-7_6
31. Cai, Q., Pan, Y., Wang, Y., Liu, J., Yao, T., Mei, T.: Learning a unified sample weightingnetwork for object detection. In: Proceedings of the IEEE/CVF Conference on Computer Vision and Pattern Recognition (CVPR) (2020)

32. Li, S., He, C., Li, R., Zhang, L.: A dual weighting label assignment scheme for objectdetection. In: Proceedings of the IEEE Conference on Computer Vision and Pattern Recognition (2022)
33. Kim, M., Jain, A.K., Liu, X.: Adaface: quality adaptive margin for face recognition. In:Proceedings of the IEEE/CVF Conference on Computer Vision and Pattern Recognition (CVPR), pp. 18750–18759 (2022)

Structural Topology Optimization Using Genetic Algorithm and Fractals

Chih-Yi Hsu[1], Yi-Ruei Chen[2], and Chuan-Kang Ting[2(✉)]

[1] Department of Power Mechanical Engineering, National Tsing Hua University,
Hsinchu, Taiwan
[2] Department of Computer Science, National Tsing Hua University, Hsinchu, Taiwan
`ckting@cs.nthu.edu.tw`

Abstract. Structural topology optimization is a recognized technique for designing structures. Genetic algorithm (GA) provides a reliable approach to finding the optimal structure; however, it has been criticized for its high computational cost. Although many studies aim to design the representation to reduce the number of variables and thereby increase search efficiency, the actual computational time in the structure's evaluation by the finite element method (FEM) remains high. This study proposes two methods, i.e., GA with fractal iteration in the loop (GAFI-ITL) and GA with fractal iteration out of the loop (GAFI-OOTL). These two methods combine GA and fractals to address high computational cost. GAFI-ITL leverages the fractals to increase the structural complexity without requiring additional parameters. GAFI-OOTL utilizes the self-similarity information between fractals and enables non-iterative state structures during the GA process, thus saving the time for running the FEM. Once the best non-iterative structure is determined, GAFI-OOTL builds the internal structure with fractal rules. This study uses two test problems to validate the effects of fractal iteration on the structures obtained and the efficiency of algorithms. The results indicate that fractals can reduce the compliance of the original structure while imposing limitations on the distribution of materials during optimization.

Keywords: Structural Topology Optimization · Fractals · Genetic Algorithm · Evolutionary Computation

1 Introduction

Structural topology optimization is a recognized technique for designing structures, which changes geometry's size and shape while serving to be useful for applications. This technique is often implemented to solve the real-life applications such as [2,20]. In the past three decades, researchers have developed algorithms for topology optimization. The widely used algorithms include the solid isotropic material with penalization (SIMP) [3], evolutionary structural optimization (ESO) [17], and level-set methods [14]. In addition, GA [7], a population-based algorithm, also provides an alternative for solving topology optimization problems. However, the high computational cost has been a serious

C.-Y. Lee et al. (Eds.): TAAI 2023, CCIS 2075, pp. 195–208, 2024.
https://doi.org/10.1007/978-981-97-1714-9_16

drawback since a large number of structures need to be generated and analyzed, further intensifying the deficiencies of evolutionary algorithms in computational time [6,12].

'To address this problem, various studies have attempted to reduce the computational time of topology optimization. For instance, [8,15,18,19] present the unit volume with geometric shapes to reduce the number of variables, allowing algorithms to find the optimal solution more quickly. Other methods [4,9,13] use a structural construction rule or formula as a translator to reduce the number of parameters. Utilizing parallel computing to enhance computational capabilities is also commonly applied in large-scale simulations such as crash-worthiness design [1,16].

In this study, we introduce fractals into the GA-based topology optimization process to deal with the issue of computational cost. More specifically, two new topology optimization methods that combine GA and fractals, i.e., GA with fractal iteration in the loop (GAFI-ITL) and GA with fractal iteration out of the loop (GAFI-OOTL), are proposed to optimize structures more efficiently. Fractal structures have the property of infinite iteration and self-similarity, which can increase the complexity of structures without raising the number of parameters and allow the iteration of multiple patterns to be similar with the original geometry. This study attempts to reduce the high computational cost by utilizing these two characteristics of fractals when using GA for structural topology optimization. The experimental results show that the GAFI-OOTL method proposed in this study can perform structural optimization with less computational time.

The main contributions of this study are summarized as follows:

1. Two algorithms that combine GA and fractal structures are developed to save actual computation time for topology optimization.
2. The new representation method, coupled with the Sierpinski triangles, is designed for simplifying iteration through the fractal structure.
3. Discussing whether the fractals can decrease the structural compliance without additional parameter settings through experiments, and whether such a decrease in structural compliance follows a regular pattern.

The remainder of this study is organized as follows. Section 2 reviews the related work about structural topology optimization algorithms. Section 3 describes our proposed methods in detail. Section 4 presents and discusses the experimental results of the proposed methods. Finally, conclusions are drawn in Sect. 5.

2   Related Work

Topology optimization is a hybrid field of mechanical structure and computer science. Successfully completing this work requires background knowledge from both these areas. Up to this point, research has been developed from various perspectives. The method used to address this problem will be introduced in this section.

2.1   Structural Topology Optimization

Compared to size and shape optimization, topology optimization has the ability to adjust both the shape and size during the procedure. Specifically, the topology optimization problem is to find the best the material distribution which can optimize the objective under certain constraints. A standard problem formulation of continuum topology optimization is:

$$\underset{x}{\text{argmin}}\ F(x) \tag{1}$$
$$\text{s.t.}\ G(x) \leq 0$$
$$H(x) = 0$$

where x is the parameters set in the problem, objective function $F(x)$ is to be minimized, functions $G(x)$ and $H(x)$ are inequality and equality constraints about the physical properties, respectively.

In topology optimization, the structural compliance is typically used as the objective function, which is defined by

$$C = U^T KU, \tag{2}$$

where U is the displacement vector corresponding to each element's deflection in every degree of freedom. K is the global stiffness matrix of the structure. The compliance value is the reciprocal of stiffness, which normally acts as the fitness measure in a topology optimization problem.

To measure the compliance of structures, the finite element method (FEM) is adopted to obtain the structure's features in a certain boundary condition. This method uses discretization to deal with this problem. It cuts the domain (geometry) into several sub-domains (elements) and assembles each element's stiffness matrix into the global matrix.

2.2   Fractals

The concept of fractals was proposed by Benoit Mandelbrot in [10]. Fractals are the irregular, infinite, non-Euclidean, and self-similar patterns observed in nature. In other words, a small part of the structure mirrors the whole structure. There are several functions to generate fractal geometry, such as the L-system [5], and iterated function systems (IFS) [11]. Classical fractal models include Koch, Minkowski, and Sierpinski models. The following introduces the Sierpinski models in detail.

The Sierpinski model is a well-known fractal. The traditional Sierpinski model is triangle-based, and its creation involves a series of steps: initially, the triangle is segmented into four equal parts, resulting in three corner triangles. Each of these triangles has half the edge length of the original triangle and yet maintains an identical shape. This procedure is then repeated for these three triangles, with the process continuing until a termination point is reached. Figure 1 displays the first four iterations of the Sierpinski fractal.

Fig. 1. Sierpinski fractal model

2.3   Genetic Algorithm

GA is a popular algorithm that imitates Darwin's evolutionary theory [7]. The main idea of the evolutionary theory is "survival of the fittest." A higher fitness values leads to a higher chance for an individual to survive. GA contains the following operators: initialization, crossover, mutation, and survival selection. Offspring are generated by recombination and mutation. High-quality parents likely make good offspring. These two mechanisms search the landscape through exploration and exploitation and give the chance to find a better solution. As a versatile optimization algorithm, GA is often used in the field of structural optimization.

3   Methodology

In this study, we propose two methods i.e., GAFI-ITL and GAFI-OOTL, which introduce the concept of fractals to reduce the computational cost. The following describes the methods in detail.

3.1   Problem Formulation

The problem formulation in this study is presented as follows:

$$\underset{x}{\text{argmin}}\ C(\boldsymbol{x})$$
$$\text{s.t.}\quad V(\boldsymbol{x}) \leq kV_{\max} \tag{3}$$

where $\boldsymbol{x} \in \mathbb{R}$ is the design variable, $C(\boldsymbol{x})$ is the compliance value, $V(\boldsymbol{x})$ is the volume, $V_{\max}$ is the volume constraints, and k is the ratio of volume constraint. The objective is to minimize the structure's compliance under certain volume constraint. The purpose of volume constraint is to prevent the algorithm from excessively filling the design area with materials for smaller compliance values.

3.2   Representation

This study employs the skeleton shape elements as the structural representation, where lines are used to depict the geometry in the design domain. The triangular structures, referring to as unit-triangles, are fundamental units in the structural representation and serve as the building blocks of the entire structure.

An individual is represented as a one-dimensional real-valued array, each of which represents the coordinate in design space. A single vertex in the design space is formed by a pair of genes representing the x and y coordinates of the point. A unit-triangle is formed by grouping three vertices together, which is constituted by the linkage of three discrete points into a triangular formation. Figure 2 illustrates the genotype and phenotype representations.

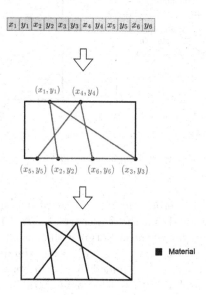

Fig. 2. Example representation of individuals in GA

3.3   Fractal Iteration

Fractal is a geometric form that exhibits self-similarity, which can generate infinite structures using a single rule. In this study, the Sierpinski triangle is used to enhance the resolution of structure without imposing additional parameter settings. The Sierpinski fractal generates structures composed of similar triangles through iteration. This allows the non-fractal triangle shape to be closely related to the structure's performance after iteration. Figure 3 shows an example of the fractal iteration in this work.

3.4   Proposed Methods

This study presents two GA with fractal iteration methods: GAFI-ITL and GAFI-OOTL. Both of them integrate GA with the same fractal iteration process. Their only difference lies in the timing of applying the fractal iteration, thereby enhancing algorithm efficiency in different ways. The details of each method and the design idea are discussed below.

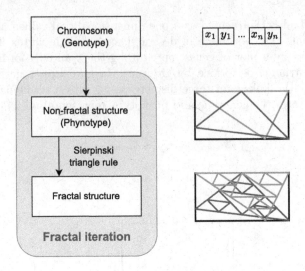

Fig. 3. Example of fractal iteration

GAFI-ITL. GAFI-ITL method integrates fractal iteration into the representation process. Figure 4a shows the flowchart of GAFI-ITL. Fractal iteration occurs during the generation of the structure's phenotype for each individual, so it is within the optimization loop of the GA. After the initialization stage, the phenotype of an individual is determined by its chromosomes, which gives the formation of a non-fractal structure. This non-fractal structure consists of the boundaries of the design area and the unit-triangles. In the GAFI-ITL method, structures undergo fractal iteration using the Sierpinski triangle fractal rules to increase their complexity before entering the evaluation step.

This method enables the generation of structures with higher resolution using shorter chromosomes, compared to GA. With fewer variables, the algorithm's search space is reduced, lowering the level of difficulty for the problem, and thus enhancing the efficiency of the algorithm.

GAFI-OOTL. GAFI-OOTL is a method that performs the fractal iteration step after GA optimization. Figure 4b shows the flowchart of GAFI-OOTL method, where GA optimizes the structure that remains in a non-fractal iteration state, known as a non-fractal structure. The best non-fractal structure obtained by GA will then undergo a fractal iteration to reduce its structural compliance, which is known as a fractal structure. The self-similar characteristics of fractals result in fractal structures composed of multiple similar geometries. Basically, a good geometric shape will also be a good fractal after fractal iteration.

Since only the fitness of non-fractal structures needs to be evaluated instead of directly comparing the quality of fractal structures, this method can avoid directly evaluating the complex structure by FEM and further reduces the computational cost in the structure's evaluation.

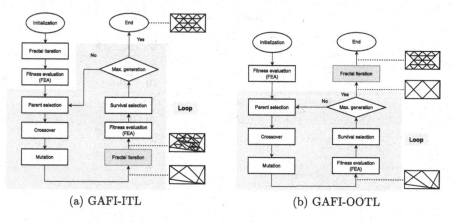

(a) GAFI-ITL (b) GAFI-OOTL

Fig. 4. Flowchart of the proposed methods

4 Experimental Results

In this section, we conducted experiments to examine the proposed methods. Two test problems are used to evaluate their performance: the cantilever beam problem and the bicycle rack structure design problem. The performance of optimized structures, calculation time, and efficiency of the GAFI-ITL and GAFI-OOTL algorithms are compared in the experiments.

4.1 Test Problems

The cantilever beam problem is a simple test problem for topology optimization (see Fig. 5). It is a rectangular area 100 mm long and 50 mm wide. The left side is fixed, and a 1000 Newtons force is applied at the bottom right corner. Table 1 lists the material properties and element settings used in the structure. In addition, the mesh size is uniformly set to 2 mm to ensure fairness in both calculation time and accuracy for each structural analysis. The geometry of the element is shown in Fig. 5b. In this test problem, GAFI-ITL with the first iteration fractal structure (1st iteration) and the second iteration fractal structure (2nd iteration) are compared to the original GA.

The bicycle rack problem is a real-world design problem often used in the field of structural optimization, which has a larger design region and more complex structures than cantilever beam problem. This study simulates the problem of the bicycle frame into a 2D problem, which is shown in Fig. 6. The cyan part is the bicycle rack, which is the region for structural topology optimization. The boundary conditions of this problem are indicated in Fig. 6a, and the geometry of the element is shown in Fig. 6b. Table 1 lists the material properties and element settings used in the structure.

Table 1. Parameter settings of FEM

	Cantilever beam	Bicycle rack
Meshes size	2 (mm)	8 (mm)
Element cross-section	2×1 (mm^2)	10×10 (mm^2)
Material	Steel	Aluminum
Young's modules	210 GPa	69 GPa
Poisson's ratio	0.3	0.33

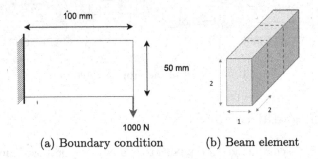

(a) Boundary condition   (b) Beam element

Fig. 5. Illustrations of the cantilever beam problem

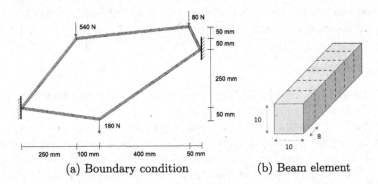

(a) Boundary condition   (b) Beam element

Fig. 6. Illustrations of the bicycle rack problem

4.2   Experimental Setting

Both GAFI-ITL and GAFI-OOTL employ GA and fractals for optimization. Due to the stochastic nature of GA, each experiment includes 30 independent trials. The parameters utilized are listed in Table 2. In this study, we utilized ANSYS as the tool for the FEM calculations. After conducting FEM in ANSYS, the strain energy of each element is summed up to obtain compliance, which is used as the structural fitness value in this study.

Table 2. Parameter settings of GA and fractal

Parameter	Value
Representation	Real value
Population size	20
Selection	3-tournament selection
Crossover	Uniform crossover ($p_c = 0.5$)
Mutation	Uniform mutation ($p_m = 1/\ell$)
Survival selection	$\mu + \lambda$
Termination	60 generations
Fractal type	Sierpinski triangle
Fractal iteration	$1^{st}, 2^{nd}$ (cantilever beam problem) 1st (bicycle rack problem)

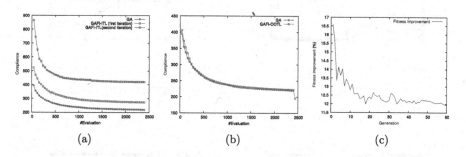

(a)   (b)   (c)

Fig. 7. Performance comparison on the cantilever beam problem: progress of compliance against the number of evaluations for (a) GA and GAFI-ITL, (b) GA and GAFI-OOTL, and (c) fitness improvement if applying fractal iteration on the best individual at each generation of GAFI-OOTL

4.3 Numerical Results

Cantilever Beam Problem. Figure 7 plots the experimental results of the proposed methods on the cantilever beam problem, while Table 3 presents the detailed results. First, we compare the performance of GAFI-ITL and GA to examine the benefit of additional fractals iteration in the GA loop. Table 3 shows that GAFI-ITL uses fewer variables in optimization but performs worse than GA does in terms of the convergence speed and the fitness value (Fig. 7a). Additionally, the fitness value of GAFI-ITL (2nd iteration) is worse than that of GAFI-ITL (1st iteration), indicating that the ability of GAFT-ITL to find good structures decreases as the number of fractal structures increases. Figure 8 plots the stress distribution of optimal structures obtained from GA, GAFI-ITL (1st iteration), and GAFI-ITL (2nd iteration).

Next, we compare the performance of GAFI-OOTL and GA. As Fig. 7b shows, GA and GAFI-OOTL perform very similarly, except the drastic improvement by the fractal iterations executed in the end of the optimization process.

Table 3. Mean best fitness (MBF), number of variables (#Vars), and CPU time (Time) for GA, GAFI-ITL, and GAFI-OOTL on the cantilever beam problem

	MBF	#Vars	Time
GA	219.64	24	1283.58
GAFI-ITL (1st iter)	272.78	18	1315.19
GAFI-ITL (2nd iter)	420.87	12	1575.34
GAFI-OOTL	195.18	24	1262.91

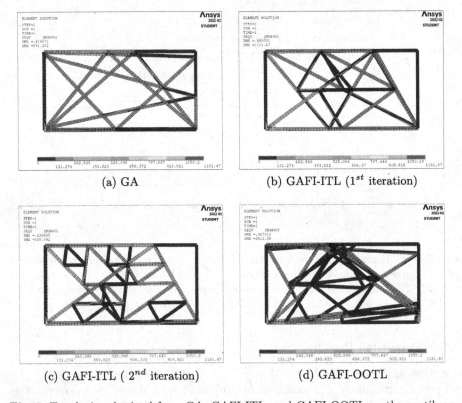

(a) GA

(b) GAFI-ITL (1st iteration)

(c) GAFI-ITL (2nd iteration)

(d) GAFI-OOTL

Fig. 8. Topologies obtained from GA, GAFI-ITL, and GAFI-OOTL on the cantilever beam problem

To investigate the effectiveness of fractal iteration as a post processing, we further examine the fitness improvement if the best individual at each generation is applied with the fractal iteration process. The result in Fig. 7c reveals that the fitness improvement caused by fractal iteration keeps 11.9–16.6% although decreasing with generation. This outcome validates the advantage of fractal iteration as a post process in improving structures.

Figure 8 compares the distributions of stress in the structure obtained from the test algorithms. The figure shows that the stress is distributed around every

Table 4. Mean best fitness (MBF), number of variables (#Vars), and CPU time (Time) for GA, GAFI-ITL, and GAFI-OOTL on the bicycle rack problem

	MBF	#Vars	Time
GA	6.86	36	1435.34
GAFI-ITL	8.79	24	1517.84
GAFI-OOTL	6.48	36	1528.36

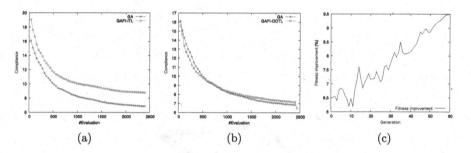

(a)   (b)   (c)

Fig. 9. Performance comparison on the bicycle rack problem: progress of compliance against the number of evaluations for (a) GA and GAFI-ITL, (b) GA and GAFI-OOTL, and (c) fitness improvement if applying fractal iteration on the best individual at each generation of GAFI-OOTL

beam in the structure obtained from GA. By contrast, in the structure obtained from GAFI-ITL, certain internal structures generated by fractal iteration fail to distribute stress uniformly. Although fractal iteration can lower the number of variables in GAFI-ITL, it does not improve the stiffness. The original GA method without incorporating fractal iteration, on the other hand, discovers a more effective material distribution and structural compliance. As for the structure obtained from GAFI-OOTL, it is similar to the result of GA and can disperse the stress. The substructures generated by fractal iteration help to further distribute the stress (Table 4).

Bicycle Rack Problem. This study also investigates the performance of GA, GAFI-ITL, and GAFI-OOTL on a bicycle rack problem, which has a larger design region and more complex structures than the cantilever beam problem. For a fair comparison, GA and GAFI-ITL are set to have the same volume constraints. Note that fractal structures can lead to fewer variables needed and thus a smaller search space under the volume constraints. According to Fig. 9a, GAFI-ITL has slower convergence and worse solution quality than GA. On the other hand, Fig. 9b demonstrates that GAFI-OOTL can achieve bicycle racks with better compliance. Comparing the fitness improvement made by fractal iteration, the improvement is smaller (6.1–9.5%) but increasing on the bicycle rack problem.

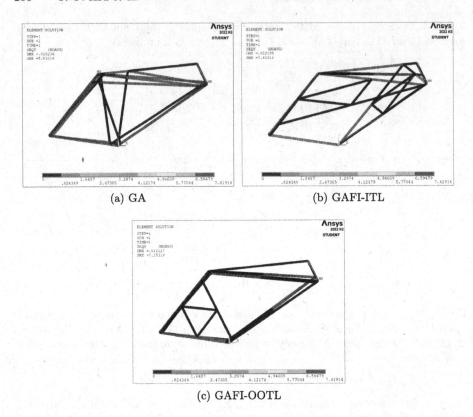

(a) GA

(b) GAFI-ITL

(c) GAFI-OOTL

Fig. 10. Topologies obtained from GA, GAFI-ITL, and GAFI-OOTL on the bicycle rack problem

Observing the structures obtained and their stress distribution (Fig. 10), GA and GAFI-ITL differ much in the distribution of beams used; in particular, the internal triangles iterated by fractals do not disperse stress well in racks generated by GAFI-ITL. It reveals the stress distribution in the structures obtained from GA is directional, whereas that obtained from GAFI-ITL fail to effectively disperse stress, and the directions of substructures are not aligned with the primary stress direction. Figure 10c show that the resultant rack from GAFI-OOTL is similar to that of GA. The main substructures disperse most of the stress; moreover, the substructures generated by fractal iteration disperse less stress.

In this section, we test the performance of GA, GAFI-ITL and GAFI-OOTL on two test problems, i.e., the cantilever beam problem and the bicycle rack problem. The results show that GAFI-ITL performs worse than GA on both test problems in that the materials are wasted on generating the fractal structures that cannot disperse stress well. On the other hand, GAFI-OOTL leads to better performance than GA on both test problems, showing the advantages of using fractal iteration as a post process to improve the design of structures.

5   Conclusions

Structural topology optimization aims to optimally distribute materials within a specific area. GA is often used as a solver for structural topology optimization due to its high ability to find the optimal solutions. However, since GA is a population-based method, it needs to generate a large number of individuals for optimization, and each individual requires fitness evaluation using the FEM, which is very time-consuming. In the past, many studies have tried to reduce the number of variables to decrease the search space in order to improve the search efficiency, but the problem of high calculation time for structure verification has not been improved.

To address this problem, this study proposes a new representation and two methods that combine GA and fractal structures. The new representation method constructs skeletal structures stacked with triangles within the design area, and applies the Sierpinski triangle rule to the structures. The first method GAFI-ITL carries out the fractal iteration before evaluation to increase structural complexity without additional parameters. The second method GAFI-OOTL performs the fractal iteration after the GA optimization process. During the evolutionary process, structures with non-fractal states compete with each other. After identifying the best individual in the population, its internal structure is grown by fractal rules. This method allows the structure to be in a state with less complex structure during the fitness evaluation by FEM, therefore reducing the actual computational time.

This research uses two test problems, i.e., the cantilever beam problem and the bicycle rack problem, to verify the performance of the two methods. The results on the two test problems are consistent. Although the GAFI-ITL method uses fewer variables for optimization, its convergence speed is slower than the original GA. On the other hand, the GAFI-OOTL method adds an additional step of iteration compared to the original GA method. This may lead to an increase in calculation time, but the fractal iteration significantly enhances the quality of the structure.

Future study includes some directions. First, other shapes of fractals can be considered. Second, the representation of individuals that defines a fixed structure at the boundary can be improved. Transforming the boundary structure into a softer material minimizes its impact on structural optimization, which can further enhance the performance of optimization algorithm.

Acknowledgment. This work was supported by the Science Park Emerging Technology Application Program 112AO21B, National Science and Technology Council of Taiwan.

References

1. Aulig, N., Olhofer, M.: State-based representation for structural topology optimization and application to crashworthiness. In: Proceedings of the 2016 IEEE Congress on Evolutionary Computation, pp. 1642–1649. IEEE (2016)

2. Beghini, L.L., Beghini, A., Katz, N., Baker, W.F., Paulino, G.H.: Connecting architecture and engineering through structural topology optimization. Eng. Struct. **59**, 716–726 (2014)
3. Bendsøe, M.P.: Optimal shape design as a material distribution problem. Struct. Optim. **1**(4), 193–202 (1989)
4. Bielefeldt, B.R., Akleman, E., Reich, G.W., Beran, P.S., Hartl, D.J.: L-system-generated mechanism topology optimization using graph-based interpretation. J. Mech. Robot. **11**(2), 020905 (2019)
5. Bielefeldt, B.R., Reich, G.W., Beran, P.S., Hartl, D.J.: Development and validation of a genetic l-system programming framework for topology optimization of multifunctional structures. Comput. Struct. **218**, 152–169 (2019)
6. Guirguis, D., et al.: Evolutionary black-box topology optimization: challenges and promises. IEEE Trans. Evol. Comput. **24**(4), 613–633 (2019)
7. Holland, J.H.: Adaptation in natural and artificial systems (1975)
8. Liu, J., Ma, Y.: A survey of manufacturing oriented topology optimization methods. Adv. Eng. Softw. **100**, 161–175 (2016)
9. Lohan, D.J., Dede, E.M., Allison, J.T.: Topology optimization for heat conduction using generative design algorithms. Struct. Multidiscip. Optim. **55**(3), 1063–1077 (2017)
10. Mandelbrot, B.B., Mandelbrot, B.B.: The Fractal Geometry of Nature, vol. 1. WH Freeman, New York (1982)
11. Salcedo-Sanz, S., Aybar-Ruíz, A., Camacho-Gómez, C., Pereira, E.: Efficient fractal-based mutation in evolutionary algorithms from iterated function systems. Commun. Nonlinear Sci. Numer. Simul. **56**, 434–446 (2018)
12. Sigmund, O.: On the usefulness of non-gradient approaches in topology optimization. Struct. Multidiscip. Optim. **43**(5), 589–596 (2011)
13. Steiner, T., Jin, Y., Sendhoff, B.: A cellular model for the evolutionary development of lightweight material with an inner structure. In: Proceedings of the 10th Annual Conference on Genetic and Evolutionary Computation, pp. 851–858 (2008)
14. Wang, M.Y., Wang, X., Guo, D.: A level set method for structural topology optimization. Comput. Methods Appl. Mech. Eng. **192**(1–2), 227–246 (2003)
15. Wang, N., Zhang, X.: Topology optimization of compliant mechanisms using pairs of curves. Eng. Optim. **47**(11), 1497–1522 (2015)
16. Wu, J., Dick, C., Westermann, R.: A system for high-resolution topology optimization. IEEE Trans. Visual Comput. Graphics **22**(3), 1195–1208 (2015)
17. Xie, Y.M., Steven, G.P.: A simple evolutionary procedure for structural optimization. Comput. Struct. **49**(5), 885–896 (1993)
18. Zhang, W., et al.: Explicit three dimensional topology optimization via moving morphable void (MMV) approach. Comput. Methods Appl. Mech. Eng. **322**, 590–614 (2017)
19. Zhang, W., Yuan, J., Zhang, J., Guo, X.: A new topology optimization approach based on moving morphable components (MMC) and the ersatz material model. Struct. Multidiscip. Optim. **53**, 1243–1260 (2016)
20. Zhu, J.H., Zhang, W.H., Xia, L.: Topology optimization in aircraft and aerospace structures design. Arch. Comput. Methods Eng. **23**(4), 595–622 (2016)

Optimal Truncated MobileNet-Based Image Binarization for Pose-Based Visual Servoing of Autonomous Mobile Robot

Chian C. Ho[✉] [iD] and Cian-Duo Lin

Department of Electrical Engineering, National Yunlin University of Science and Technology, Yunlin, Taiwan
futureho@yuntech.edu.tw

Abstract. Pose-based visual servoing (PBVS) can complement the frequent drift issue of light detection and ranging (LiDAR) coordinate of LiDAR-based simultaneous localization and mapping (SLAM), navigation, and servoing technology, especially when autonomous mobile robot (AMR) works on the automatic docking alignment missions for automatic pallet engaging or automatic battery charging whose alignment precision requirement is extremely stricter. But PBVS occasionally suffers from the poor detected image quality of ARTag landmark to cause the reading drift or error. This paper proposes a light-weight deep-learning image binarization method based on optimal truncated MobileNet model to preprocess the image quality of ARTag landmarks so that PBVS can evaluate the distance and pose between the ARTag landmark and the camera sensor more accurately, promptly, and steadily, for better feasibility of PBVS on the automatic docking alignment missions. Experimental results show, against conventional image-processing-based image binarization, conventional computer-vision-based image binarization, and conventional deep-learning-based image binarization, the proposed optimal truncated MobileNet-based image binarization not only raises the accuracy and reliability of ARTag's reading, but also apparently improves the effectiveness and efficiency of PBVS's operation, especially under environmental conditions of shadow occlusion, image blurring, low contrast, uneven illumination, or complex background.

Keywords: ARTag landmark · automatic docking alignment · autonomous mobile robot (AMR) · image binarization · pose-based visual servoing (PBVS)

1 Introduction

With the ever-increasing demand of automation transportation technologies in intelligent factories or intelligent warehouses, automatic mobile robot (AMR) without occupying a significant amount of fixed space to facilitate automatic material handling is the best choice [1, 2]. Consequently, research on AMRs has become more and more attractive in both academic and industrial fields, and has further extended its application to more scenes. In general, AMRs can be divided into two main categories: tracked AMRs

© The Author(s), under exclusive license to Springer Nature Singapore Pte Ltd. 2024
C.-Y. Lee et al. (Eds.): TAAI 2023, CCIS 2075, pp. 209–223, 2024.
https://doi.org/10.1007/978-981-97-1714-9_17

and trackless AMRs. Tracked AMRs require the deployment of magnetic tracks, color tapes, or QR codes, and they can only move along these tracks. Parking, acceleration, deceleration, docking and rotation totally rely on the infrastructure of laid tracks on the floor. Moreover, the track redeployment is more time-consuming and cost-expensive to redesign the hardware and software of infrastructure. Tracked AMRs has poor flexibility and adaptability to complex or specific scenes, while it also has high maintenance costs. Trackless AMRs primarily utilize light detection and ranging (LiDAR) for positioning and navigation. Trackless AMRs can detect the contours of objects in intelligent factories or intelligent warehouses, build up the depth point cloud maps of the working area, and plan navigation routes without any infrastructure deployment of laid tracks. However, the frequent drift error of LiDAR coordinate adopted by trackless AMRs for positioning and navigation is essentially 5–10 cm at minimum if no other optimization firmware or preprocessing algorithm is further applied. Besides, since LiDAR sensors use infrared light as their light source, there are certain physical limitations. For example, infrared light can penetrate glass, infrared light is extraordinarily reflected by the metal plates of machinery equipment, and infrared light is completely absorbed by some materials like fabric and paper. Therefore, in specific situations, positioning failures and navigation errors are unavoidable.

Specifically, on the automatic docking alignment missions of automatic pallet engaging or automatic battery charging whose alignment precision requirement is extremely stricter, trackless AMRs with the frequent drift error of LiDAR coordinate of 5–10 cm at minimum is not eligible to work, even not safe to work. As a result, pose-based visual servoing (PBVS) is the simplest but practical solution for trackless AMRs [3, 4]. PBVS can estimate the distance and pose between the tag landmark on the docking destination and the camera sensor on the trackless AMR, and then control the motion and rotation of trackless AMR to approach and align the docking destination precisely. With a few wallpapered and radioless tag landmarks, PBVS can offer additional simultaneous localization and mapping (SLAM) information to LiDAR-based trackless AMR for precise alignment and immediate relocalization.

This paper adopts ARTag shown in Fig. 1 as the tag landmark for PBVS functionality of trackless AMRs. Through the PBVS functionality working onto ARTag landmarks [5], trackless AMRs can obtain the location of ARTag landmarks on 3D image (camera viewing) coordinate, specifically referring to the return value of "distance" and "pose" between the ARTag landmark on the docking destination and the camera sensor on the trackless AMR. The ARTag landmark is a marker system proposed by "ARToolKit" that is an open-source computer tracking library originally for creation of augmented reality applications on the real world, and recently for facility of trackless AMR applications on the automatic docking alignment missions. The ARTag landmark makes good use of a dual-tone planar pattern, and each pattern contains a unique ID number. Apart from QR code, the graphical simplicity of the ARTag makes itself detected at a farther distance and has itself favored in the PBVS field. Since the ARTag landmark has a simple square planar pattern and a black-and-white design with black tags and a white outer frame, the distance and pose of the detected corner features are relatively stable through the intersection points of the edge lines. Therefore, the open-source project *ar_track_alvar* [6] is used to obtain the location of ARTag landmarks on 3D image (camera viewing) coordinate, as shown in Fig. 2. Under the known size of the ARTag landmark, the four corner features and four edges of the ARTag landmark can be used to estimate the distance and pose between the ARTag landmark on the docking destination and the camera sensor on the trackless AMR, through Homography (perspective) transformation.

Fig. 1. Illustration of ARTag.

Fig. 2. Detection of the distance and pose between the ARTag landmark and the camera sensor.

Figure 3 shows the overall flowchart of conventional trackless AMRs featuring with 4 operating modes of SLAM, navigation, PBVS, and dead reckoning. In general, the overall flowchart of conventional trackless AMRs, as shown in Fig. 3, can be divided 4 stages: 1) SLAM stage usually adopts Rao-Blackwellized Particle Filter (RBPF) [7] at the step of positioning estimation for SLAM and employs Occupancy Grid Mapping [8] at the step of map building. SLAM stage maps the scan of point cloud of 2D LiDAR sensor onto the real-world environment for construction of incremental map. 2) Navigation stage adopts Adaptive Monte Carlo Localization (AMCL) [9] at the step of positioning estimation for navigation, utilizes Dijkstra algorithm [10] at the step of path planning to obtain the global shortest or fastest path to the destination, and employs Timed Elastic Bands (TEB) [11] at the step of obstacle avoidance for local path planning of optimal collision avoidance trajectories. 3) Visual servoing stage involves both LiDAR-based visual servoing and pose-based visual servoing with ARTag landmarks. The 3D image (camera viewing) coordinate system built by the camera sensor (at origin) and ARTag landmark is used to estimate the distance and pose between the ARTag landmark on the docking destination and the camera sensor on the trackless AMR at the step of ARTag detection. Then, at the step of approaching ARTag, the trackless AMR is navigated by PBVS to approach the ARTag landmark on the docking destination in the 3D image (camera viewing) coordinate system. 4) Dead reckoning stage leads the trackless AMR to the final destination inertially based on the wheel odometry [12, 13], according to the return value of "distance" and "pose" from the ARTag landmark at the last moment before the ARTag landmark gets too close to the camera sensor. After the ARTag landmark gets too close to the camera sensor, the ARTag landmark will get too large to be completely detected by the camera sensor, that is, ARTag landmark is out of view field of the camera sensor.

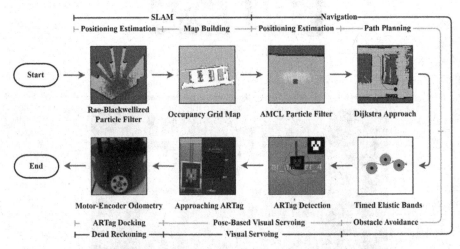

Fig. 3. Flowchart of conventional trackless AMRs.

Among 4 stages of the overall flowchart of conventional trackless AMRs in Fig. 3, the accuracy, promptness, and steadiness of automatic docking alignment missions depends heavily upon the performance of PBVS at the stage of visual servoing. Figure 4 shows the overall flowchart of conventional PBVS. It can be divided 4 stages: 1) Image pre-processing stage transforms the input image into a binary image at the step of image binarization. Then, shadow removal is performed on the image of ARTag landmarks to highlight the contours of ARTag landmarks for stable detection of the camera sensor at the step of shadow removal. 2) Image coordinate stage selects the ARTag landmark of the targeted ID of the automatic docking alignment and designates the location of the targeted ARTag landmark on 3D image (camera viewing) coordinate. 3) Visual servoing stage detects the targeted ARTag landmark, and estimates the distance and pose between the ARTag landmark on the docking destination and the camera sensor on the trackless AMR. Referring to the return value of "distance" and "pose" from the ARTag landmark, the trackless AMR is navigated by PBVS close to the location of the targeted ARTag landmark on 3D image (camera viewing) coordinate. 4) Dead reckoning stage must be activated when the ARTag landmark becomes beyond the view field of the camera sensor, because the camera sensor on the trackless AMR approaches too close to the ARTag landmark on the docking destination. Finally, the automatic docking alignment of the trackless AMR to the final destination is achieved by the wheel odometry estimation and the inertial motion control.

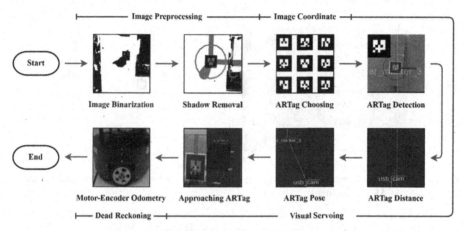

Fig. 4. Flowchart of conventional PBVS technology.

Among 4 stages of the overall flowchart of conventional PBVS technology in Fig. 4, the accuracy, promptness, and steadiness of automatic docking alignment missions depends heavily upon the detected image quality at the stage of image preprocessing. The poor detected image quality sometimes causes the drift error on the return value of "distance" and "pose" from the ARTag landmark. It not only reduces the alignment precision of automatic docking alignment, but also decreases the docking efficiency (i.e., increases the docking iteration) of automatic docking alignment, even results in the failure or accident. Therefore, the step of image binarization at the stage of image preprocessing plays a crucial role in stabilizing the reading value of "distance" and "pose" between the ARTag landmark on the docking destination and the camera sensor on the trackless AMR. It not only simplifies the background complexity but also diminishes the illumination interference, as shown in Fig. 5 (a). However, if shadow occlusion, image blurring, low contrast, uneven illumination, or complex backgrounds are happened with the ARTag landmark, plain or straightforward image binarization methods can not handle well with these poor environmental conditions. They probably fail to improve the clearness and contrast of the return value of "distance" and "pose" from the ARTag landmark, as shown in Fig. 5 (b).

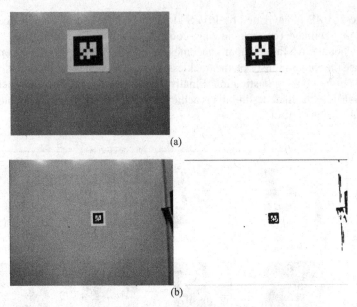

Fig. 5. Comparison between (a) high-quality image binarization and (b) poor-quality image binarization on ARTag landmark.

2 Conventional Image Binarization Methods

In general, conventional and common image binarization methods can be divided into three main categories: 1) Image-processing-based image binarization methods, including threshold from average of overall gray level [14] and dynamic threshold from maximum and minimum gray level [15]. 2) Computer-vision-based image binarization methods, including threshold from gray-level histogram and Otsu optimization [16] and adaptive threshold from local histogram [17]. 3) Deep-learning-based image binarization methods, including image binarization with selectional auto-encoder (SAE) [18] and image binarization with fully convolutional neural network [19].

However, image-processing-based image binarization methods are not effective to generate proper binary images of ARTag landmarks under environmental conditions of shadow occlusion, image blurring, low contrast, uneven illumination, or complex background. Although image-processing-based image binarization methods are efficient and straightforward in terms of computational complexity, they are not practical and feasible to real-world ARTag landmark detection issues. As for computer-vision-based image binarization methods, they have better adaptability under environmental conditions of shadow occlusion, image blurring, low contrast, uneven illumination, or complex background. They can generate better binary images of ARTag landmarks while maintaining appropriate execution speed and computational efficiency. But, in some special real-world environmental conditions, they are still not good enough to completely eliminate adverse factors, especially resulting in accompanying noise in the binary images of ARTag landmarks. Finally, deep-learning-based image binarization methods, as its name to make good use of deep learning techniques, exhibit high adaptability to various real-world environmental conditions and great capability to complex real-world environmental conditions. They can achieve the best binary images of ARTag landmarks in diverse situations. But, they require a large amount of computational time and it is contradictory for the stage of image preprocessing to consume too much computational time. In addition, deep-learning-based image binarization methods may have poorer performance in binarizing low-resolution images of ARTag landmarks.

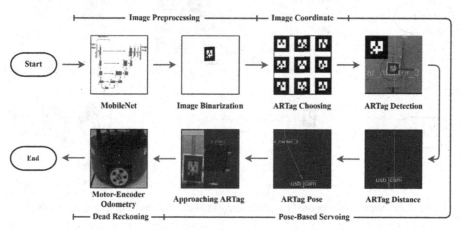

Fig. 6. Flowchart of PBVS technology with proposed optimal truncated MobileNet-based image binarization.

3 Proposed Optimal Truncated MobileNet-Based Image Binarization

This paper studies on conventional deep-learning-based image binarization methods and improves on its accuracy, promptness, and steadiness for ARTag landmark detection equivalently, against conventional image-processing-based image binarization methods, conventional computer-vision-based image binarization methods, and conventional deep-learning-based image binarization methods. This paper develops a novel and practical method of light-weight deep-learning image binarization based on optimal truncated MobileNet model at the stage of image preprocessing, as shown in Fig. 6, to enable PBVS to read the return value of "distance" and "pose" from the ARTag landmark exactly, quickly, and consistently.

In Fig. 6, at the stage of image preprocessing, a light-weight model optimized from well-known MobileNet v2 [20] is proposed to address the issues of high computational requirements and poor binarization performance on low-resolution images in conventional deep-learning-based image binarization methods.

In general, the standard fully-connected convolution of deep learning models works entirely on the spatial dimension of the input image and on total input and output channels. The computational cost of the standard fully-connected convolution of deep learning models is shown as (1).

$$C_s = W_{in} * H_{in} * Nch * k * k * Nk \tag{1}$$

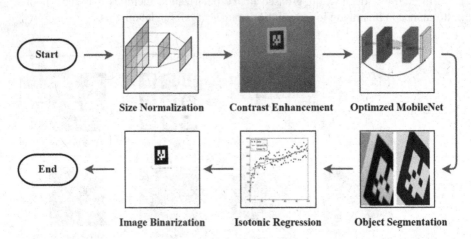

Fig. 7. Flowchart of proposed optimal truncated MobileNet-based image binarization.

Where C_s represents the computational cost of the standard fully-connected convolution. W_{in} and H_{in} are the width dimension and height dimension of the input image, respectively. Nch means the number of channel of the input image. $k * k$ implies the size of kernel map, and the width dimension and height dimension of kernel map here are assumed to be identical. Nk indicates the number of channel of kernel map. So the number of channel of the output image is also Nk.

Referring to the principle of singular value decomposition (SVD), depthwise separable convolution is adopted to decompose the standard fully-connected convolution into two operations, depthwise convolution and pointwise convolution. The output image of the standard fully-connected convolution is equivalent to that of the depthwise separable convolution, but the computational cost of the depthwise convolution and pointwise convolution are simplified as (2) and (3), respectively.

$$C_d = W_{in} * H_{in} * Nch * k * k \tag{2}$$

$$C_p = W_{in} * H_{in} * Nch * Nk \tag{3}$$

Here, C_d and C_p represent the computational cost of the depthwise convolution and pointwise convolution, respectively.

So the computational cost ratio of the depthwise separable convolution to the standard fully-connected convolution is derived as (4).

$$\frac{C_d + C_p}{C_s} = \frac{W_{in} * H_{in} * Nch * k * k + W_{in} * H_{in} * Nch * Nk}{W_{in} * H_{in} * Nch * k * k * Nk} = \frac{1}{Nk} + \frac{1}{k * k} \tag{4}$$

From (4), it is proved that the computational cost of the depthwise separable convolution has a significant computation reduction of $1/Nk + 1/(k*k)$, against that of the standard fully-connected convolution. Especially, the more increasing the channel number (Nk) or dimension size ($k*k$) of kernel map is, the more computational cost reduction the depthwise separable convolution gets. So this paper researches on how to adapt the channel number or the dimension size of kernel map, in order to optimize both segmentation accuracy and computational cost. With reference to the theorem of optimal truncation in SVD [21], the optimal channel number or the optimal dimension size of kernel map can be picked by $2.858 * y_{med}$, where y_{med} is the empirical median singular value of the output image matrix. The detailed flowchart of proposed optimal truncated MobileNet-based image binarization at the stage of image preprocessing of Fig. 6 is illustrated in Fig. 7.

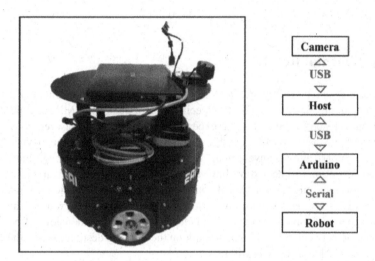

Fig. 8. Appearance and hardware architecture of trackless AMR for experiments.

In Fig. 7, the proposed optimal truncated MobileNet-based image binarization can significantly reduce the architecture complexity of well-known MobileNet v2 network and further decrease the parameter amount of well-known MobileNet v2 network, without sacrifice of segmentation accuracy. Because the optimal truncated MobileNet-based image binarization optimizes depthwise separable convolution of MobileNet v2 network with adaptive kernel map to further reduce the redundancy in the convolutional kernel representation. Optimized depthwise separable convolution with adaptive kernel map during the inference process also can further reduce both memory consumption and computation time for predictions. After the step of object segmentation, isotonic regression is also adopted to converge the training results, so higher accuracy and recall rates can be achieved. Isotonic regression algorithm minimizes the mean squared error of the training data while finding a non-decreasing approximation of the function.

Table 1. HW/SW specification of trackless AMR for experiments.

Hardware Specification	
Sensor	Logitech HD Pro Webcam C930e
Host	Intel Core i7-9750H 2.60 GHz
Controller	Arduino Mega2560
Robot	EAI Dashgo D1
Software Specification	
Operation System	Ubuntu v16.04
Computer Vision Library	OpenCV v3.1.0
ROS Framework	Kinetic
Deep Learning Framework	TensorFlow 2.5.0

4   Experimental Results

The appearance and hardware architecture of trackless AMR for experimental comparison is shown in Fig. 8, and the HW/SW specification of trackless AMR for experimental comparison is listed in Table 1.. The experimental comparison between conventional image-processing-based (IP) image binarization, conventional computer-vision-based (CV) image binarization, conventional deep-learning-based (DP) image binarization, and proposed optimal truncated MobileNet-based (OTMN) image binarization, is performed under 5 various environmental conditions: 1) shadow occlusion, 2) image blurring, 3) low contrast, 4) uneven illumination, and 5) complex background. The experimental comparison makes use of ARTag landmark with size dimensions of 5 cm. The working range between the ARTag landmark on the docking destination and the camera sensor on the trackless AMR is within 1.5 m.

Figures 9, 10, 11, 12 and 13 show the return value of "distance" and "pose" of the ARTag landmark detected by the camera sensor with 4 various aforementioned image binarization methods, under 5 various environmental conditions: 1) shadow occlusion, 2) image blurring, 3) low contrast, 4) uneven illumination, and 5) complex background, respectively. The ground truth of "distance" and "pose" between the ARTag landmark on the docking destination and the camera sensor on the trackless AMR is measured by the open-source project *ar_track_alvar* and determined by the stationary mean of the return value. From Figs. 9, 10, 11, 12 and 13, it is verified that both accuracy and reliability of the return value of "distance" and "pose" of the ARTag landmark detected by the camera sensor with proposed optimal truncated MobileNet-based (OTMN) image binarization are the best under 5 various environmental conditions.

On the other hand, Table 2. shows the average reading period of the ARTag land-mark detected by the camera sensor with 4 various aforementioned image binarization methods, under 5 various environmental conditions: 1) shadow occlusion, 2) image blurring, 3) low contrast, 4) uneven illumination, and 5) complex background, respectively. From Table 2., it is verified that the computational load of proposed optimal truncated MobileNet-based (OTMN) image binarization is the lightest under 5 various environmental conditions.

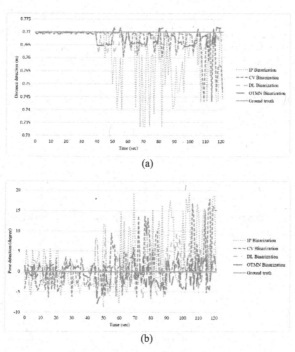

(a)

(b)

Fig. 9. (a) Distance detection and (b) pose detection comparison between 4 various image binarization methods under condition of shadow occlusion.

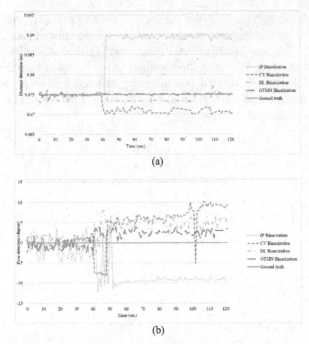

Fig. 10. (a) Distance detection and (b) pose detection comparison between 4 various image binarization methods under condition of image blurring.

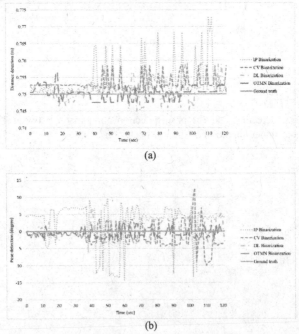

Fig. 11. (a) Distance detection and (b) pose detection comparison between 4 various image binarization methods under condition of low contrast.

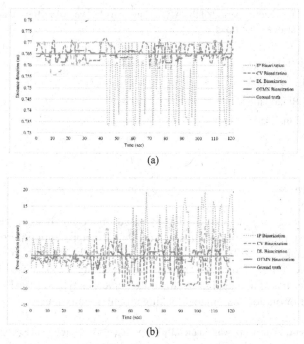

(a)

(b)

Fig. 12. (a) Distance detection and (b) pose detection comparison between 4 various image binarization methods under condition of uneven illumination.

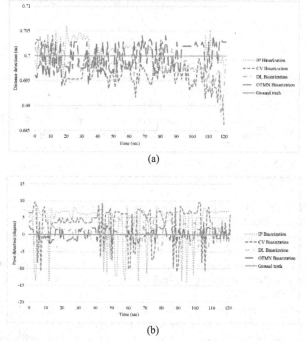

(a)

(b)

Fig. 13. (a) Distance detection and (b) pose detection comparison between 4 various image binarization methods under condition of complex background.

Table 2. The average reading period of the ARTag landmark between 4 various image binarization methods under 5 various conditions.

Method	Second per frame
IP Binarization	0.034
CV Binarization	0.034
DL Binarization	0.563
OTMN Binarization	0.192

5 Conclusions

The proposed optimal truncated MobileNet-based image binarization not only raises the accuracy and reliability of ARTag's reading, but also apparently improves the effectiveness and efficiency of PBVS's operation. Consequently, PBVS becomes more precise and reliable. Future work will involve implementing the proposed optimal truncated MobileNet-based image binarization onto numerous types of trackless AMRs for versatile indoor or outdoor automatic docking alignment missions.

Acknowledgement. This work was financially supported by the "Intelligent Recognition Industry Service Center" from The Featured Areas Research Center Program within the framework of Higher Education Sprout Project, Ministry of Education (MOE), Taiwan.

References

1. Azadeh, K., Koster, R., Roy, D.: Robotized and automated warehouse systems: review and recent developments. Transp. Sci. **53**(4), 917–945 (2019)
2. Hossain, S.G.M., Jamil, H., Ali, M.Y., Haq, M.Z.: Automated guided vehicles for industrial logistics - development of intelligent prototypes using appropriate technology. In: Proceedings of International Conference on Computer and Automation Engineering (ICCAE), pp. 237–241 (2010)
3. Zhao, L., Ding, Y.: Design of AGV low-delay visual servo system. In: Proceedings of International Conference on Audio, Language and Image Processing (ICALIP), pp. 6–10 (2018)
4. Kelly, A., Nagy, B., Stager, D., Unnikrishnan, R.: Field and service applications - an infrastructure-free automated guided vehicle based on computer vision - an effort to make an industrial robot vehicle that can operate without supporting infrastructure. IEEE Robot. Autom. Mag. **14**(3), 24–34 (2007)
5. Fiala, M.: ARTag, a fiducial marker system using digital techniques. In: Proceedings of IEEE Computer Society Conference on Computer Vision and Pattern Recognition (CVPR 2005), vol. 2, pp. 590–596 (2005)
6. Niekum, S.: ar_track_alvar. ROS Wiki [Online]. http://www.ros.org/wiki/ar_track_alvar
7. Wang, H., Wei, S., Chen, Y.: An improved Rao-Blackwellized particle filter for SLAM. In: Proceedings of International Symposium on Intelligent Information Technology Application Workshops, pp. 515–518 (2008)

8. Collins, T., Collins, J.J., Ryan, D.: Occupancy grid mapping: an empirical evaluation. In: Proceedings of Mediterranean Conference on Control and Automation, pp. 1–6 (2007)
9. Hanten, R., et al.: Vector-AMCL: vector based adaptive Monte Carlo localization for indoor maps. Intell. Auton. Syst. **14**, 403–416 (2017)
10. Deng, Y., et al.: Fuzzy Dijkstra algorithm for shortest path problem under uncertain environment. Appl. Soft Comput. **12**, 1231–1237 (2012)
11. Keller, M., et al.: Planning of optimal collision avoidance trajectories with timed elastic bands. IFAC Proc. Volumes **47**, 9822–9827 (2014)
12. Nor, R.M., et al.: Mobile robot stable-target navigation control via encoder data feedback. In: Proceedings of International Malaysia-Ireland Joint Symposium on Engineering, Science and Business (2012)
13. Wang, K., Liu, Y., Li, L.: Visual servoing trajectory tracking of nonholonomic mobile robots without direct position measurement. IEEE Trans. Robot. **30**, 1026–1035 (2014)
14. Al-amri, S.S., Kalyankar, N.V., Khamitkar, S.D.: Image segmentation by using threshold techniques. J. Comput. **2**, 83–86 (2010)
15. Eyupoglu, C.: Implementation of Bernsen's locally adaptive binarization method for gray scale images. Online J. Sci. Technol. **7**, 68–72 (2017)
16. Huang, D.-Y., Wang, C.-H.: Optimal multi-level thresholding using a two-stage Otsu optimization approach. Pattern Recogn. Lett. **30**, 275–284 (2009)
17. Zhou, S.-F., et al.: An improved adaptive document image binarization method. In: Proceedings of International Congress on Image and Signal Processing, pp. 1–5 (2009)
18. Calvo-Zaragoza, J., Gallego, A.-J.: A selectional auto-encoder approach for document image binarization. Pattern Recogn. **86**, 37–47 (2019)
19. Tensmeyer, C., Martinez, T.: Document image binarization with fully convolutional neural networks. In: Proceedings of IAPR International Conference on Document Analysis and Recognition (ICDAR), pp. 99–104 (2017)
20. Sandler, M., Howard, A., Zhu, M., Zhmoginov, A., Chen, L.-C.: MobileNetV2: inverted residuals and linear bottlenecks. In: Proceedings of IEEE Conference on Computer Vision and Pattern Recognition (CVPR), pp. 4510–4520 (2018)
21. Gavish, M., Donoho, D.L.: The optimal hard threshold for singular values is $4/\sqrt{3}$. IEEE Trans. Inf. Theory **60**(8), 5040–5053 (2014)

Analysis of Significant Cell Differences Between Cancer Patients and Healthy Individuals

Pei-Chi Sun[1], Xiaowei Yan[2], Yu-Wei Li[1], Hao-Xiang Chen[1], Hsu-Ching Li[1], Cheng-Yu li[3], and Wan-Shu Cheng[3][(✉)]

[1] Department of Electronic Engineering, National Kaohsiung University of Science and Technology, Kaohsiung, Taiwan
[2] Institute for Systems Biology, Seattle, WA, USA
[3] Department of Computer Science and Information Management, Providence University, Taichung, Taiwan
iqn.ws.cheng@gmail.com

Abstract. At the end of 2019, a global outbreak of a new coronavirus ravaged the world, and to this day, many people's bodies are still deeply affected by the virus. In order to find out if there is a correlation between different levels of cancer diagnosis and healthy samples, and to further compare the differences between healthy samples and cancer samples, we have identified a significant set of genes that highlights the differences between the two samples. Therefore, we used statistics, immunology, and artificial intelligence to analyze the blood sampling data of cancer patients diagnosed with the new coronavirus during the diagnostic period, and compared them with healthy donors. We initially found that the proportion of significant cells in the two stem cell gene sets of the cancer samples was more than about two times greater than that of the healthy samples. Therefore, in the future, we will be able to further analyze the differences between the two samples and find out the key factors that can assist in medical diagnosis.

Keywords: scRNA-seq · Artificial Intelligence · Dimension Reduction

1 Introduction

Cell-to-cell variation is a universal feature of life, and the variation affects a wide range of biological phenomena, from developmental plasticity [1, 2] to tumour heterogeneity [3]. Technological advances enable us to explore cellular heterogeneity and to describe the cell types [4, 5] and states within the human [5] using single-cell RNA sequencing (scRNA-seq) [6–8]. Obviously, cell-types identification has been one of the most effective approaches to studying various diseases, including those studies in the TCGA project [8–10] The number of immune cells and stem cells contained in the blood of cancer patients varies in different degrees of health, and there are also different characteristics, such as the level of gene expression, specific gene expression, and the number of gene responses. We conduct a series of experiments using blood sampling data from cancer patients and healthy donors [11]. The number of immune cells and stem cells in a cancer patient may vary depending on the patient's health level. There are also different characteristics, such as the level of gene expression, specific gene expression, and the number of gene signatures. In the process, we try to find out the stem cell gene set that initially identifies the difference between cancer and health when the severity of the disease is not the same.

2 Experiment

The blood sampling data came from patients with cancer, and their cancer types were categorized according to the body systems, e.g., lung cancer belongs to the respiratory system. Then we chose the reproductive system, which has the largest number of patients (four patients, namely, uterine cancer patients, endometrial cancer patients, bladder cancer patients, and ovarian cancer patients) to conduct the experiment. In the blood sampling data of the cancer patients, embryonic stem cells were identified and compared with the significant cells of healthy donors. In this experiment, the distribution and number of cells with significant embryonic stem cell genes were identified using significant genes. The significant embryonic stem cell genes of reproductive system cancer samples are compared to those of healthy samples. The comparison is to find out the differences in the genes, which can be used as a reference for future therapeutic suggestions in the field of complementary medicine.

Blood samples from cervical and bladder cancer patients and healthy donors were normalized to the stem cell gene sets ex_esp1 and prc2_targets [12] and subjected to GSEA [13] analysis. Then, PCA and t-SNE were used for the downscaling experiments. The significant cells of the samples were labeled. We found that in the es_exp1 gene dataset, the proportion of significant cells in bladder cancer was 1.8 times higher than that in healthy samples. In endometrial cancer, the proportion of significant cells was 1.8

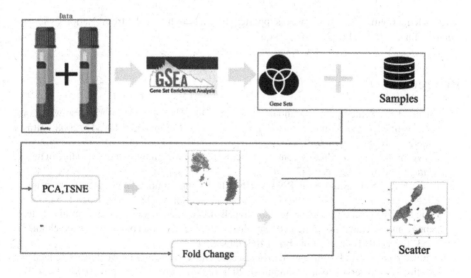

Fig. 1. System Architecture

times higher than that of healthy samples, while in endometrial cancer, the proportion was 1.6 times higher than that of healthy samples. With these results, it will be possible to further analyze the main factors that led to the increase in the number of significant cells in the patients diagnosed with these cancers (Fig. 1 and Table 1).

Table 1. Comparison of significant cell ratio between healthy and cancer samples

Gene Set	es_expl		prc2_targets	
	Significant cells[a]	HC[b]	Significant cells	HC
Healthy Donors	8.26%	1	12.17%	1
Endometrial cancer	8.02%	0.97	19.55%	1.6
Bladder cancer	14.70%	1.8	11.42%	0.9

Note:
[a] p-value <= 0.05
[b] HC is the ratio of healthy to significant cancer cells

3 Conclusion

Under the es_exp1 and pcr2_targets gene sets, we found that the proportion of significant cells in cancer samples was nearly two times higher than that in healthy samples. The preliminary experimental results show that the differences between cancer samples and healthy samples can be clearly compared with this method, and the differences and variation factors can be further explored in the future, so as to provide a supplementary reference for the medical field.

Acknowledgement. This work was supported by Research Grants from National Science Council, Taiwan (NSC 112-2221-E-126-005-).

References

1. Chang, H.H., Hemberg, M., Barahona, M., Ingber, D.E., Huang, S.: Transcriptome-wide noise controls lineage choice in mammalian progenitor cells. Nature **453**, 544–547 (2008). https://doi.org/10.1038/nature06965
2. Imayoshi, I., et al.: Oscillatory control of factors determining multipotency and fate in mouse neural progenitors. Science **342**, 1203–1208 (2013). https://doi.org/10.1126/science.1242366
3. Patel, A.P., et al.: Single-cell RNA-seq highlights intratumoral heterogeneity in primary glioblastoma. Science **344**, 1396–1401 (2014). https://doi.org/10.1126/science.1254257
4. Pollen, A.A., et al.: Low-coverage single-cell mRNA sequencing reveals cellular heterogeneity and activated signaling pathways in developing cerebral cortex. Nat. Biotechnol. **32**, 1053–1058 (2014). https://doi.org/10.1038/nbt.2967
5. Nguyen, Q.H., et al.: Profiling human breast epithelial cells using single cell RNA sequencing identifies cell diversity. Nat. Commun. **9**, 2028 (2018). https://doi.org/10.1038/s41467-018-04334-1

6. Cao, J., et al.: Comprehensive single-cell transcriptional profiling of a multicellular organism. Science **357**, 661–667 (2017). https://doi.org/10.1126/science.aam8940
7. Karaiskos, N., et al.: The Drosophila embryo at single-cell transcriptome resolution. Science **358**, 194–199 (2017). https://doi.org/10.1126/science.aan3235
8. Plass, M., et al.: Cell type atlas and lineage tree of a whole complex animal by single-cell transcriptomics. Science **360**, eaaq1723 (2018). https://doi.org/10.1126/science.aaq1723
9. Berger, A.C., et al.: A comprehensive pan-cancer molecular study of gynecologic and breast cancers. Cancer Cell **33**, 690–705.e699 (2018). https://doi.org/10.1016/j.ccell.2018.03.014
10. Liu, Y., et al.: Comparative molecular analysis of gastrointestinal adenocarcinomas. Cancer Cell **33**, 721–735.e728 (2018). https://doi.org/10.1016/j.ccell.2018.03.010
11. Su, Y., et al.: Multi-omics resolves a sharp disease-state shift between mild and moderate COVID-19. Cell **183**, 1479–1495.e1420 (2020). https://doi.org/10.1016/j.cell.2020.10.037
12. Lee, T.I., et al.: Control of developmental regulators by Polycomb in human embryonic stem cells. Cell **125**, 301–313 (2006). https://doi.org/10.1016/j.cell.2006.02.043
13. Subramanian, A., et al.: Gene set enrichment analysis: a knowledge-based approach for interpreting genome-wide expression profiles. Proc. Nat. Acad. Sci. **102**, 15545–15550 (2005). https://doi.org/10.1073/pnas.0506580102

Automated Pediatric Bone Age Assessment Using Convolutional Neural Networks

Feng-Chiao Hsu[1], Meng-Che Tsai[2,3], and Sun-Yuan Hsieh[1,4,5,6](✉)

[1] Institute of Medical Informatics, National Cheng Kung University,
No.1, University Road, Tainan 70101, Taiwan
hsiehsy@mail.ncku.edu.tw

[2] Department of Pediatrics, National Cheng Kung University Hospital, College of
Medicine, National Cheng Kung University, No.1, University Road, Tainan 70101,
Taiwan

[3] Department of Medical Humanities and Social Medicine, School of Medicine,
College of Medicine, National Cheng Kung University, No.1, University Road,
Tainan 70101, Taiwan

[4] Department of Computer Science and Information Engineering, National Cheng
Kung University, No.1, University Road, Tainan 70101, Taiwan

[5] Quanta-NCKU Joint AI Research Center, National Cheng Kung University,
No.1, University Road, Tainan 70101, Taiwan

[6] Department of Computer Science and Information Engineering, National Chi Nan
University, No.1, University Road, Puli Township, Nantou County 54561, Taiwan

Abstract. Pediatric medicine widely uses bone age determination to
assess skeletal maturity and identify developmental disorders early. However, manual assessment methods are subjective and lack consistency. To
address this, we suggest using image preprocessing to isolate vital areas
in hand X-rays and enhance features. We then enhance the Inception-
V4 model to extract features from these images, integrating gender as a
crucial reference. Our model, validated on a large dataset, demonstrates
superior bone age prediction compared to prior methods. These automated models offer precise and reliable tools for clinical assessments,
showing significant potential for practical application.

Keywords: Bone Age Assessment · Artificial Intelligence · Hand
X-ray · Convolutional Neural Networks · Deep Learning · Intelligent
Medicine

1 Introduction

Bone Age Assessment (BAA) is a crucial method pediatric endocrinologists and
orthopedists use to assess how mature a child's skeleton is while growing. It's
essential for diagnosing conditions like growth hormone deficiency and precocious
puberty. When there's a noticeable difference between a child's bone age and
their chronological age, BAA helps determine treatment timing. Hence, ensuring
the precision of BAA is incredibly vital in clinical settings.

© The Author(s), under exclusive license to Springer Nature Singapore Pte Ltd. 2024
C.-Y. Lee et al. (Eds.): TAAI 2023, CCIS 2075, pp. 228–237, 2024.
https://doi.org/10.1007/978-981-97-1714-9_19

Currently, there are two primary methods for assessing bone age, i.e., Greulich and Pyle (G&P) [4] and Tanner and Whitehouse (TW) [10] methods. Clinical professionals, such as pediatric endocrinologists or radiologists, refer to them when assessing bone age. Both methods involve evaluating X-ray images of the patient's left hand and wrist bones since this region consists of numerous chondral bones, thus making it convenient to observe changes in the bone structure as endochondral ossification takes place (c.f. Fig. 1). The G&P method is an atlas-based approach that compares the patient's left wrist radiograph with the nearest matching reference radiograph to determine bone age. On the other hand, the TW method focuses on the ossification analysis of hand bones (such as the first, third, and fifth metacarpals, radius, ulna, and short bones). It involves categorizing each bone's shape, size, and density into different stages and calculating skeletal scores of regions of interest (ROIs) as indicators for bone age assessment.

When it comes to the efficiency and accuracy of BAA, there is no consensus as of yet. The TW method is more complex than the G&P method, leading to a longer average time of 7.9 min for TW versus only 1.4 min for G&P to evaluate bone age [7]. Regarding bone age assessment errors, the G&P method yielded an error of 11.52 months ± 7.92 months, while the TW method yielded an error of 8.88 months ± 8.16 months. Despite the long-standing clinical use of manual bone age assessment methods, there still exists variation among clinical physicians regarding the BAA standards. Achieving standardized consistency has proven challenging, precisely encapsulating the challenges faced by manual bone age assessment methods.

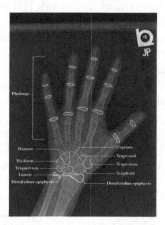

Fig. 1. X-ray image illustrating the main indicators for bone age assessment, with the bones of the left-hand wrist (outlined in green) and the metacarpals, ulna, and radius (outlined in white). (Color figure online)

In recent years, there has been an increasing trend of using artificial intelligence (AI) techniques to predict bone age, following the RSNA Pediatric Bone Age Challenge (2017) launched by the Radiological Society of North America (RSNA). The challenge champion focused on improving the model architecture [6], incorporating gender as a reference for bone age, and using data augmentation to increase model diversity and avoid overfitting. However, the second-ranked team in the challenge emphasized image pre-processing [6], using image enhancement techniques as inputs to the model and applying existing model architectures for training. Following the RSNA challenge, research on bone age can be broadly divided into two directions: (i) optimizing model performance using image pre-processing and (ii) adjusting the model architecture based on convolutional neural network (CNN) frameworks [8] to improve model performance.

In medical research, most studies in image preprocessing utilize the UNet architecture proposed by Ronneberger et al. for segmentation purposes [13]. The UNet model uses symmetrical down-sampling and up-sampling modules to achieve effective segmentation preprocessing and feature extraction for medical images. Ding et al. presented an enhanced version of the UNet architecture [3] applied to pediatric hand X-ray bone segmentation. They experimented with different numbers of down-sampling and up-sampling and utilized a multi-scale convolutional network in a lightweight UNet architecture. The results showed that their method used fewer computational resources and achieved higher accuracy in bone segmentation. Before this paper, many teams had also studied the segmentation of hand bones from X-ray images [5,11].

Xu et al. improved the CNN model structure in bone age assessment by proposing a new bone age assessment framework [17], which utilized the YOLO object detection model [12] to identify and segment 13 different bone regions in hand. Each bone region was fed into a corresponding classifier model to obtain its bone grade score. Finally, the scores from all areas were aggregated and averaged to obtain the bone age value. This paper considered the developmental status of each bone region. It used CNN as the evaluation method to calculate the bone scores of each part, proposing a comprehensive automated bone age assessment method.

This paper proposes a novel automated BAA method. The hand outline images are segmented and used as input to our modified convolutional neural network model, enabling the model to estimate bone age values more accurately. We validate the performance of our method using the publicly available RSNA Pediatric Bone Age Challenge (2017) dataset. The results demonstrate the efficacy and accuracy of our BAA model, which can effectively assist clinical practitioners in determining growth indicators in children.

2   Methods

In this Section, we introduce the methods of image preprocessing to assess bone age value. In Subsect. 2.1, we use the UNet model [13] combined with image enhancement for image preprocessing and then the preprocessed image for training in the CNN model in Subsect. 2.2. We improve the CNN model architecture and integrate patient gender for feature extraction.

2.1   Image Preprocessing

During the pre-processing stage, the regions of interest (ROIs) emphasized in the wrist joint and finger bones were identified from the TW method [10] and G&P method [4]. These ROIs serve as a basis for clinical assessment of bone age. The primary objectives of this stage are (i) to use image enhancement techniques to highlight the contours of the wrist joint and finger bones, thereby enabling the CNN model to more effectively learn the features necessary for evaluating bone age, and (ii) to use a UNet model to remove irrelevant background, unnecessary labels, and noise in the X-ray images through preprocessing, enabling the CNN model to focus on hand features only. The flowchart of our image preprocessing is shown in Fig. 2.

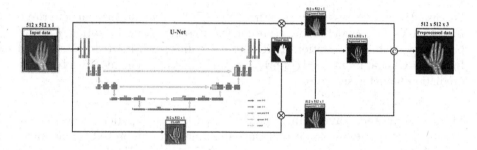

Fig. 2. The flowchart of image preprocessing.

Hand Segmentation Method. Children's hand bones mature at varying rates due to the endochondral ossification process, replacing cartilage with bone gradually. This leads to distinct shapes of hand bones like carpal, metacarpal, and digital bones at specific ages, crucial for determining bone age. Thus, we aimed to retain the complete hand outline, capturing essential details to input each bone feature comprehensively into the CNN model in Subsect. 2.2. To achieve this, we trained hand X-ray images with a pre-trained UNet model to separate the hand from the background. The UNet model [13] had been pre-trained using the Carvana dataset [2]. Finally, after threshold conversion of the images, we obtain a mask of the hand outline, as shown in Fig. 3 (B). Subsequently, we multiply the original hand X-ray image with the model-generated hand mask to obtain an X-ray image that only retains critical hand features, as shown in Fig. 3 (C).

Image Enhancement. Contrast Limited Adaptive Histogram Equalization (CLAHE) [18] is a widely used algorithm that re-balances regions with similar brightness in an image to enhance detail variations and reduce background noise. Our study used the CLAHE algorithm to enhance the original hand X-ray image. We multiply it by the hand mask generated by the UNet model to obtain an image with enhanced hand features, as shown in Fig. 3 (D). Subsequently, we apply a threshold to convert the enhanced hand image into a binary image, resulting in an image that solely captures the hand skeleton, as shown in Fig. 3 (E).

Finally, we merge three image types: (i) the initial hand X-ray image multiplied by the hand mask, creating a hand-feature focused image; (ii) an improved hand-feature image using the CLAHE algorithm, also multiplied by the hand mask; and (iii) a binary image featuring only the hand skeleton, achieved by thresholding the enhanced hand image, as depicted in Fig. 3 (F). We merge these three types of images and input them into the CNN model for training.

2.2   Feature Extraction

We use the preprocessed images from Sect. 2.1 as input for our improved Inception-V4 [14] model architecture for feature extraction. Inception-V4 comprises five modules (Inception-A, Reduction-A, Inception-B, Reduction-B, and Inception-C) containing kinds of branches and functions. The modified bone age prediction model is shown in Fig. 4.

Fully-Connected Layer. In response to the fact that patient gender has a certain degree of influence on bone age assessment, we improved the architecture of the fully connected layer in the original Inception-V4 model [14]. After applying the dropout layer, we added the feature vector to a fully connected layer, resulting in a feature vector. We combined the patient's gender information with the feature vector to create a new feature vector, which allowed for the differentiation of bone age performance between different genders of patients.

We train the neural network model using Mean Absolute Error (MAE) as the loss function:

$$MAE = \frac{1}{n} \sum_{i=1}^{n} |g_i - p_i|, \tag{1}$$

where n is the total number of patient data, g_i (ground truth) is the bone age value evaluated by the physician for patient i, and p_i is the predictive bone age value generated by the model.

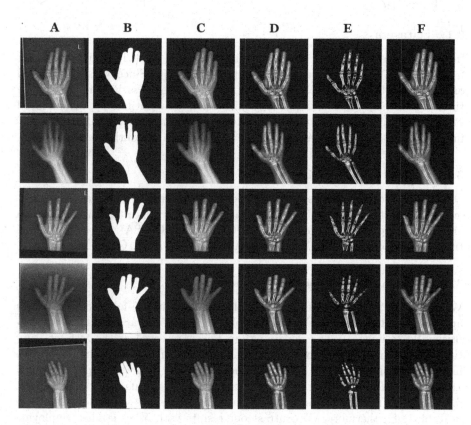

Fig. 3. The performance effect of image pre-processing (A) Original image. (B) Mask of hand outline by UNet. (C) Original image + mask. (D) CLAHE + mask. (E) CLAHE + mask + threshold. (F) Combining C, D, and E, three images as input for model training.

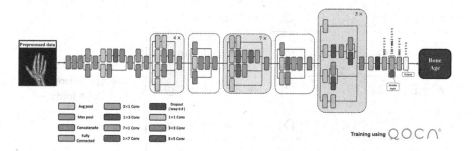

Fig. 4. The flowchart of feature extraction.

3   Results

3.1   Datasets

In the bone age prediction stage, we utilized a large publicly available dataset from the RSNA Pediatric Bone Age Challenge (2017) [6]. Since our study focused on predicting bone age in children, we excluded patients with bone age greater than 18 years and those with partially mislabeled data. Ultimately, we employed 12,405 X-ray images for our model, including 6,738 images of males and 5,667 images of females, with bone age values ranging from 4 months to 216 months.

3.2   Experimental Environment

Our automated bone age assessment model was trained on the Quanta AI medical cloud platform (QOCA®AIM), an artificial intelligence medical integration and computing platform developed by Quanta. QOCA®AIM provides model training capabilities on NVIDIA Tesla A100 GPUs with 40 GB of memory.

3.3   Bone Age Prediction Performance

We divide the RSNA dataset into five folds, conducting a 5-fold cross-validation approach as illustrated in Fig. 5. Four folds are employed as training sets (comprising 9,924 images). The remaining one-fold is reserved as the test set (containing 2,481 images). Using 5-fold cross-validation facilitates a more comprehensive assessment of our pre-processing techniques and the improved model architecture. This methodology avoids confining the evaluation to specific test data subsets. The outcomes obtained through 5-fold cross-validation are shown in Table 1. Furthermore, we contrast our results with other studies employing the RSNA dataset, as shown in Table 2. Our model's performance across the average of the five folds surpasses most of these studies. Notably, our model's performance even outperforms all others in specific folds.

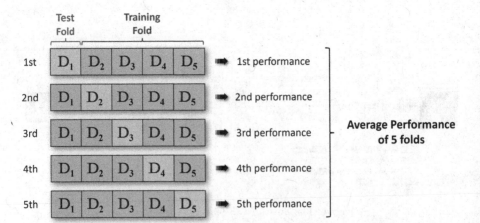

Fig. 5. 5-fold cross-validation method.

Table 1. Our approach's performance was evaluated on the RSNA dataset using 5-fold cross-validation.

D_1	D_2	D_3	D_4	D_5	Average
5.93 ± 5.31	6.08 ± 5.40	5.78 ± 5.09	4.35 ± 4.34	4.33 ± 4.33	5.29 ± 4.89

Table 2. Comparison of performance with other AI-based BAA models on the RSNA dataset.

Proposed Method	Size of Dataset	Performance in MAE (Months)
Steenkiste et al. (2018) [15]	12611	6.80
Wu et al. (2019) [16]	12500	7.38
Alblwi et al. (2021) [1]	12611	6.57
Y. Lv et al. (2022) [9]	12611	7.64
Xu et al. (2022) [17]	12600	6.53
Our Approach (5-fold CV Average)	**12405**	**5.29**

4 Discussion

This study presents a CNN-based automated bone age assessment. First, we employ a UNet architecture and image augmentation techniques to segment and enhance left-hand X-ray images. These serve as input for our refined CNN model, enabling a more accurate evaluation of bone age. We validate our models on a large-scale dataset (the RNSA public). The results demonstrate the clinical utility of our bone age assessment model in aiding pediatric growth assessment as conducted by medical professionals.

In the application within pediatric outpatient, physicians typically require the assessment of children's bone age to facilitate appropriate treatment and guidance concerning their growth status. Our automated BAA approach aids physicians in swiftly obtaining bone age values, enhancing the precision of evaluating children's growth and development. While our bone age assessment model demonstrates exceptional accuracy and efficiency, a particular disparity remains compared to conventional physician assessments. Physicians can comprehensively consider many factors when reviewing X-ray images, including the presence of congenital conditions or unique cases. These factors, beyond the scope of our model, could introduce errors in bone age prediction. Nonetheless, this underscores the necessity for further data and research to refine our model, thereby augmenting its generalizability.

We hope future research directions encompass the continuous tracking of patients and expansion of the dataset size. Additionally, a more comprehensive understanding of the factors influencing bone age, including those difficult to quantify, is essential. These efforts will contribute to further enhancing the predictive model's accuracy.

5   Conclusion

We propose an automated bone age assessment, integrating UNet architecture and the CLAHE technique for image preprocessing. Our method demonstrates exceptional performance in the 5-fold cross-validation on the RSNA dataset, with an average error of 5.29 months and even as low as 4.33 months under optimal fold. Our approach allows for real-time bone age prediction, significantly reducing clinicians' time clinically determining bone age values.

References

1. Alblwi, A., Baksh, M., Barner, K.E.: Bone age assessment based on salient object segmentation. In: 2021 IEEE International Conference on Imaging Systems and Techniques (IST), pp. 1–5. IEEE (2021)
2. Brian Shaler, DanGill, M.M.M.P.W.C.: Carvana image masking challenge (2017). https://kaggle.com/competitions/carvana-image-masking-challenge
3. Ding, L., Zhao, K., Zhang, X., Wang, X., Zhang, J.: A lightweight u-net architecture multi-scale convolutional network for pediatric hand bone segmentation in x-ray image. IEEE Access **7**, 68436–68445 (2019)
4. Garn, S.M.: Radiographic atlas of skeletal development of the hand and wrist. Am. J. Hum. Genet. **11**(3), 282 (1959)
5. Giordano, D., Leonardi, R., Maiorana, F., Scarciofalo, G., Spampinato, C.: Epiphysis and metaphysis extraction and classification by adaptive thresholding and dog filtering for automated skeletal bone age analysis. In: 2007 29th Annual International Conference of the IEEE Engineering in Medicine and Biology Society, pp. 6551–6556. IEEE (2007)
6. Halabi, S.S., et al.: The RSNA pediatric bone age machine learning challenge. Radiology **290**(2), 498–503 (2019)
7. King, D.G., et al.: Reproducibility of bone ages when performed by radiology registrars: an audit of tanner and Whitehouse ii versus greulich and pyle methods. Br. J. Radiol. **67**, 801 (1994)
8. LeCun, Y., Bottou, L., Bengio, Y., Haffner, P.: Gradient-based learning applied to document recognition. Proc. IEEE **86**(11), 2278–2324 (1998)
9. Lv, Y., Wang, J., Wu, W., Pan, Y.: Performance comparison of deep learning methods on hand bone segmentation and bone age assessment. In: 2022 International Conference on Culture-Oriented Science and Technology (CoST), pp. 375–380. IEEE (2022)
10. Malina, R.M., Beunen, G.P.: Assessment of skeletal maturity and prediction of adult height (TW3 method) (2002)
11. Pietka, E., Gertych, A., Pospiech, S., Cao, F., Huang, H., Gilsanz, V.: Computer-assisted bone age assessment: image preprocessing and epiphyseal/metaphyseal ROI extraction. IEEE Trans. Med. Imaging **20**(8), 715–729 (2001)
12. Redmon, J., Divvala, S., Girshick, R., Farhadi, A.: You only look once: unified, real-time object detection. In: Proceedings of the IEEE Conference on Computer Vision and Pattern Recognition, pp. 779–788 (2016)
13. Ronneberger, O., Fischer, P., Brox, T.: U-Net: convolutional networks for biomedical image segmentation. In: Navab, N., Hornegger, J., Wells, W.M., Frangi, A.F. (eds.) MICCAI 2015. LNCS, vol. 9351, pp. 234–241. Springer, Cham (2015). https://doi.org/10.1007/978-3-319-24574-4_28

14. Szegedy, C., Ioffe, S., Vanhoucke, V., Alemi, A.: Inception-v4, inception-resnet and the impact of residual connections on learning. In: Proceedings of the AAAI Conference on Artificial Intelligence, vol. 31 (2017)

15. Van Steenkiste, T., et al.: Automated assessment of bone age using deep learning and gaussian process regression. In: 2018 40th Annual International Conference of the IEEE Engineering in Medicine and Biology Society (EMBC), pp. 674–677. IEEE (2018)

16. Wu, E., et al.: Residual attention based network for hand bone age assessment. In: 2019 IEEE 16th International Symposium on Biomedical Imaging (ISBI 2019), pp. 1158–1161. IEEE (2019)

17. Xu, X., Xu, H., Li, Z.: Automated bone age assessment: a new three-stage assessment method from coarse to fine. In: Healthcare, vol. 10, p. 2170. MDPI (2022)

18. Zuiderveld, K.: Contrast limited adaptive histogram equalization. Graphics gems pp. 474–485 (1994)

Author Index

C.-Y. Lee et al. (Eds.): TAAI 2023, CCIS 2075, pp. 239–241, 2024.
https://doi.org/10.1007/978-981-97-1714-9

Printed in the United States
by Baker & Taylor Publisher Services